D1568815

LONDON STUDIES ON SOUTH ASIA

CRIME, JUSTICE AND SOCIETY IN COLONIAL SRI LANKA

CENTRE OF SOUTH ASIAN STUDIES
SCHOOL OF ORIENTAL AND AFRICAN STUDIES
UNIVERSITY OF LONDON

LONDON STUDIES ON SOUTH ASIA

LONDON STUDIES ON SOUTH ASIA NO. 5

CRIME, JUSTICE AND SOCIETY
IN COLONIAL SRI LANKA

JOHN D. ROGERS

CURZON PRESS
THE RIVERDALE COMPANY

First published 1987 in the United Kingdom by
Curzon Press Ltd., 42 Gray's Inn Road, London WC1
ISBN 0 7007 0192 3

First published in the United States of America by
The Riverdale Company, 5506 Kenilworth Avenue, Riverdale, MD 20737
ISBN 0 913215 24 4

© John D. Rogers, 1987

British Library Cataloguing in Publication Data
Rogers, John D.
Crime, justice and society in colonial Sri Lanka
(London Studies on South Asia, ISSN 0142-601X; no. 5)
1. Crime and criminals — Sri Lanka — History
I. Title   II. Series
364'.95493   HV7085.8
ISBN 0-7007-0192-3

Printed and bound in Great Britain by Woolnough Bookbinding
of Irthlingborough, Northants

CONTENTS

LIST OF ILLUSTRATIONS

Tables

Figure

Maps

ABBREVIATIONS

AG	Attorney-General
AGA	Assistant Government Agent
AR	*Administration Report*
CC	Crown Counsel
CH	*Ceylon Hansard*
CO	Colonial Office Records
CP	Central Province
CS	Colonial Secretary
D	Diary
DJ	District Judge
E	Enclosure
GA	Government Agent
M	*mudaliyar*
MC	Missing Cases
NWP	North-Western Province
NCP	North-Central Province
Ord	Ordinance
P	Police
PkC	Pitigal Korale Central (Chilaw District)
PkN	Pitigal Korale North (Chilaw District)
PkS	Pitigal Korale South (Chilaw District)
PM	Police Magistrate
PO	Police Officer
PR	Prisons
QA	Queen's Advocate
Sab	Sabaragamuva
SG	Solicitor-General
SLNA	Sri Lanka National Archives
SP	*Sessional Paper*
SP	Southern Province
R	*ratemahatmaya*
UCHC	*University of Ceylon History of Ceylon*
WP	Western Province

PREFACE

The main aim of this book is to explore aspects of the history of crime in Sri Lanka during British colonial rule. It follows the approach of much recent writing by attempting to place crime within its economic, political, social and cultural settings. The intention is not only to contribute to an understanding of modern South Asia through a fresh approach to social history, but to provide a case study of the history of crime in an Asian, colonial context. Enough background information is provided so that the book may be profitably read by those without any previous knowledge of Sri Lanka.

Although the entire British period (1796 – 1948) is covered, there is more detail for the years between 1865 and 1905, the era when the colonial state was established, secure and confident. If in 1905 British officials had been able to foresee the events of the coming fifty years, they would have been shocked at the suddenness of their own demise. The emphasis of this book is thus on the colonial heyday, before officials were challenged by nationalist sentiments, but after the initial period of insecurity dominated by the need to consolidate power. The research upon which the study is based was more thorough for these years. Evidence for the earlier and later periods is drawn from some of the more accessible printed and archival sources.

The geographical scope is limited to the provinces where Sinhala, the language of the majority Sinhalese ethnic group, was spoken by most people. Therefore the Northern and Eastern Provinces are excluded. Fifteen per cent of the population of the island lived in these two provinces. Their inclusion would have provided interesting comparative material, but also would have broken the overall social unity of the area under study, thus introducing another level of analysis which would have necessitated a less detailed treatment of the Sinhala regions. Few Sinhalese or other persons born in the Sinhala areas lived in the predominantly Tamil-speaking provinces, and close social links were limited to élites. Ethnic minorities within the Sinhala areas are not excluded from the study. The term 'Sinhala Sri Lanka' is used when specifically excluding the Northern and Eastern Provinces.

Sinhala place names, titles and terms are transliterated according to the system used by the Library of Congress. English forms are used for some well-known places and for some localities which had English forms of non-Sinhala origin. Diacritical marks are omitted. Personal names are given in the forms found in the sources. In accordance with the recent trend in scholarship, the newer term Sri Lanka is used in preference to the older name Ceylon.

I would like to thank the staffs of the following libraries and archives where I consulted the evidence upon which this study is based: the National Archives of Sri Lanka, the British Library, the libraries of the University of London, the Public Record Office, the Boston Public Library, the Colombo Museum Library, Dodge Library of Northeastern University, the archives of the Oblates of Mary Immaculate and the archives of the Sacred Congregation of Propaganda Fide.

This study is a substantially revised version of a thesis submitted in 1983 to the University of London. I wish to thank the Governing Body of the School of Oriental and African Studies at that university for providing me with four years of financial support for my studies. I also wish to thank the Central Research Fund of the university for supporting my research in Sri Lanka. I have benefited from discussions with too many individuals to acknowledge them all, but I would particularly like to mention the suggestions, ideas and help of T. J. Barron, P. Kulasekera, James Manor and Anna Sabasteanski. David Taylor was very helpful in his capacity as chairman of the editorial committee of the London Centre of South Asian Studies. Christopher Reynolds spent much time teaching me to read Sinhala, and helped interpret many of the Sinhala sources which are used in the book. Kenneth Ballhatchet supervised the thesis, and I am grateful for his steady encouragement as well as his intellectual criticisms.

INTRODUCTION

The organization of this book is relatively straightforward. The introduction discusses theoretical and methodological perspectives on the history of crime, and explains some of the ways they are applied in this study. It is followed by a chapter which surveys major social, economic and political developments in colonial Sri Lanka, the purpose of which is to provide information necessary for an understanding of the arguments presented later in the book.

The goal of the second chapter, which examines judicial and police arrangements, is twofold: to describe the administrative setting in which crime was committed and repressed, and to put forward an interpretation of the legal system. For most of the nineteenth century officials paid more attention to the judiciary than to the police, but in the twentieth century policy shifted and the police became central to colonial efforts at crime control. Although judicial business was conducted in English and followed procedure alien to pre-British Sri Lanka, people were able to adapt themselves to the new institutions and the courts soon handled a very heavy criminal and civil load. Colonial tribunals were popular largely because they provided Sri Lankans with opportunities to use the power of the state, not because they efficiently enforced a widely-recognized concept of justice. During the late nineteenth century some of the more manipulable aspects of the judicial system were abandoned, but even in the twentieth century the courts generated little moral authority. The importance of the police gradually increased, but as in many societies they were often regarded with suspicion, fear or contempt.

The three middle chapters each consider individual crimes: cattle stealing, homicide and riot. These offences were selected both because of their importance and because there is sufficient evidence for detailed analysis. They also serve as case studies of crimes against property, the person and the state. The incidence, geography and social setting of each offence are analysed. It is argued that although cattle stealing was affected by administrative arrangements, particularly in the twentieth century, it was more sensitive to economic influences, especially changes in land use brought on by the expansion of plantations. Cattle theft flourished in circumstances where it was profitable, and the risk

of punishment was only one factor which thieves took into
account when assessing this profitability. Homicide, on the other
hand, is interpreted as a consequence of distinctive aspects of
Sinhalese culture which changed little during the colonial period.
Most homicides were unplanned, and few brought any benefit to
the offender even if he avoided punishment. Neither government
policy nor social change had much influence on this crime. Riot
exhibited yet another pattern. Changes in types of disturbances
are traced to the formation of new social groups, and to changes in
the fortunes of older social groups, both consequences of
structural economic change. These changes in social identity set
the parameters of potential riots, but the actual incidence and
seriousness of rioting often depended on the actions of individual
officials and the presence of random catalysts which could prompt
disturbances. The three studies, taken together, are illustrative of
the variable and uneven impact of social change in colonial Sri
Lanka.

The penultimate chapter examines selected features of crime in
general, especially the social characteristics of persons thought to
be responsible for various offences. Unlike most societies, the
social profile of persons treated as criminal was not weighted
towards the poor and otherwise disadvantaged. Crime was
committed largely by Sinhalese adult men of respectable caste.
There were however differences in the types of crime persons with
certain social backgrounds were likely to commit. Emigrant
workers, regardless of ethnicity, were more often accused of
property crime, while some localities near the south-western coast
produced a large proportion of violent offenders.

The conclusion draws together themes treated in earlier
chapters, including two general issues which are discussed
extensively throughout the book: the relationship between crime
and broad forces of social and economic change, and the
effectiveness of the administration of law and order. Both topics
have attracted the attention of scholars seeking to interpret crime
in other parts of the world.

Crime and Social Change

It has been long and widely believed that urbanization and
industrialization cause large increases in crime.[1] The rise in
recorded offences in many parts of the Western world in the first
half of the nineteenth century played an important role in the

original formulation of this belief, which is still accepted by many scholars. The similarly large increase in recorded crime in many countries in the second half of the twentieth century has also been cited as support for this theory, which has strongly influenced interpretations of crime in the contemporary Third World. The standard book on crime in non-Western countries, published in 1973, asserts that social changes in developing countries in the mid-twentieth century are similar to those which 'suddenly produced extensive crime a century or more ago in Europe.' The authors explicitly link crime with progress: 'In fact, one measure of the effective development of a country probably is its rising crime rate.'[2]

Recent historical research has qualified and in many cases disputed the view that increases in crime are necessarily related to urbanization, economic growth or 'progress'. An alternative theory is that all crime rises in the initial stages of industrialization and urbanization, but that thereafter violence falls while property offences continue to increase.[3] The idea that modernization brings about a shift in criminal activity from violence to theft has also been put forward by scholars who do not necessarily accept that violence increases at the beginning of the modernization process. In Western Europe this change has been located anywhere between the sixteenth and nineteenth centuries.[4] This trend has been plausibly related to the transition from a feudal, aristocratic society which places premium on honour to a bourgeois, capitalist order which puts a higher value on property.

The most clear-cut counter-example of the link between rising crime and modernization is that of late nineteenth-century England.[5] Between 1850 and 1914 population doubled, urban population tripled and national income more than tripled. Yet recorded crime fell by one-third despite increased willingness among the police and public to institute prosecutions. Doubt has also been cast on the scale of supposed increases in crime in early nineteenth-century England, since these increases coincided with the rapid expansion of the police and changing attitudes towards lawbreaking.[6] Evidence from other European countries and the United States also points to declines in crime, including offences against property, over much of the late nineteenth and early twentieth centuries.[7] Although there has probably been a long-term decline in serious violence in Europe over the past several centuries, the relationship of this trend to patterns of theft and other property crime, or to broad forces of social change, remains obscure.

Historical research has thus proved more successful in demolishing old myths and theories about the relationship between crime and social change than it has in replacing them with sustainable generalizations. So long as criminological theory drew from ahistorical empirical data from the United States and Europe it was possible to construct theories relatively consistent with the available evidence. Historical and non-Western material has been more difficult to encompass. It is becoming increasingly evident that theories which seek to explain patterns of crime in socio-economic terms must do so in conjunction with cultural and political variables. The past practice of explaining discrepancies between theory and the empirical data as the product of 'cultural differences' is inadequate now that comparative data often show more variations than similarities.

Long-term social change, frequently defined as modernization but in studies of crime often measured by urbanization, is in this book defined by the expansion of the market economy. Although there was both urbanization and industrialization in Sri Lanka during the British period, neither of these processes were carried very far. By contrast, there was a general shift from subsistence agriculture to the production of cash crops and the provision of services. In 1796, at the beginning of British rule, the market economy was dominant only along the south-western coastal strip. In the 1840s, when coffee plantations were established on a large scale, it expanded into the central highlands. From this time on the position of subsistence agriculture declined in other regions, though the pace of this change was uneven. The process provides a good opportunity for correlating economic change with patterns of crime. The relevance of more specific indices of social change, including urbanization and rates of literacy, are discussed as sub-themes where appropriate.

My findings emphasize the importance of distinguishing among different types of offences, and point to the futility of seeking to interpret all crime within a single framework. The three crimes examined in detail, cattle stealing, homicide and riot, all exhibit different relationships with the expansion of the market economy, and even these three crimes are not representative of crime in general. Moreover, it is not clear that the changes which took place were related so much to any general process of social change as to the specific economic and social changes which occurred in Sri Lanka. In other words it is possible that local social and ecological facts may be of more importance when interpreting crime than broad processes such as modernization. For instance, it may be that the rise and fall of certain forms of property crime is more closely related to their profitability than to changes in economic and social structures.

Little of scholarly value has been written on crime in colonial South Asia, but the work which is available has shown a strong positive relationship between property crime, including robbery, and depressed economic conditions.[8] It is probable that the importance of what has been sometimes termed in India as 'famine crime' preceded British rule. Research on crime in Europe before around 1850 has also shown a direct relationship between economic conditions, especially the price of grain, and crime, especially theft.[9] Sri Lanka, like India, was subject to periodic increases in the price of grain, but the link between crime and economic hardship was not as strong as one would expect from the Indian evidence. It is argued that this difference may be partially accounted for by the higher standard of living in Sri Lanka, but also that the motives and social composition of offenders in normal times were such that depressed economic conditions did not necessarily lead to substantial increases in criminal activities.

Criminological theory, supported by evidence from North America and Europe, assumes that the poor commit a disproportionate amount of crime.[10] As a corollary, it is generally accepted that many marginal social groups, especially economically-depressed ethnic minorities, also have high rates of crime. Historians of North America and Europe have generally confirmed the propensity of the poor to appear in criminal records. Scholars accept that prison statistics and other official data often discriminate against the poor and marginal, but the frequently overwhelming preponderance of these groups among those treated as criminal is thought partially to reflect social reality. On this point the Sri Lankan case proves to be striking. When considering a whole range of variables it is found that those social characteristics indicative of a low position of wealth or status do not appear among persons treated as criminal more often than one would expect from their proportion among the general population. In some instances better-off persons are disproportionately numerous.

Three possible explanations come to mind. It may be that the Sri Lankan system of crime control was more fair than most others, that it did not discriminate against those least able to defend themselves, and that the 'real' profile of Sri Lankan law-breakers was not much different from those of other societies. It could even be argued that in the special circumstances of colonialism the judicial system was biased against mainstream groups in order to increase the state's control over them, and that in fact the poor and marginal, as in all societies, committed most crime. These suppositions are rejected because there is little evidence to support them. Instead it is argued that the unusual social profile of lawbreakers did reflect social reality.

Crime and the State

A second major theme is the effectiveness of the state in preventing and punishing crime. The importance of studying government activity is on one hand methodological. Since much of the information available about crime comes from officially-generated sources, it is essential to understand the workings of the administration even when interpreting crime within a social and economic framework. Attempts to analyse the increase in reported crime in early nineteenth-century England illustrate the point. Reported crime increased several times between 1800 and 1840, but so did the efficiency of government in recording offences. Those who seek to interpret this increase as a reflection of rapid social change which led to increased lawlessness must still consider the changes in administrative arrangements and popular attitudes which may have distorted the relationship between the reported and 'real' rates of crime. Similar problems arise in this study.

The failure to find broad patterns relating crime with social and economic change has led some scholars to examine in detail the possibility that government policy may have exercised an independent influence on patterns of crime. Research has shown clearly that a 'modern' pattern of crime control developed in Western Europe and North America in the nineteenth century.[11] The eighteenth-century practice of harsh but selective punishment was condemned as barbaric, and was replaced with an attempt to impose lighter but more certain penalties. To this end police forces on the contemporary model were created, and imprisonment became a standard punishment. Retribution was replaced with discipline. Traditionally this change has been seen as an aspect of progress, fuelled by humanitarian ideals. Some historians now view it as an attempt by the state to exercise more effective though subtle control over the lower classes.

In many ways changes in government policy in nineteenth-century Sri Lanka were similar to those in Britain. In some instances reforms in Sri Lanka even preceded those of the colonial power. Treason and murder were the only capital crimes after the assumption of British control in 1796, but the death sentence continued to be imposed in Britain for less serious offences until around 1830. Moreover, the simplification of the structure of the courts along utilitarian lines proceeded more thoroughly in Sri Lanka than in Britain itself. But in other ways the colony lagged behind, especially when government expenditure was at stake. Consequently policing had a low priority, and regular police were established in rural areas only in the twentieth century. The gradual extension of the state's role in crime control certainly affected some sorts of crime, particularly property crime, but government institutions rarely worked in the ways intended by higher officials.

Besides these changes in government policy familiar to students of European history, the fact that Sri Lanka was a colonial polity had important consequences. This can be seen most clearly in the operation of the judicial system. The failure of the courts to operate according to the legal norms under which they were established is a familiar theme in South Asian studies. Charges of litigiousness and widespread perjury have gained widespread acceptance in both India and Sri Lanka.[12] The British established legal institutions in both countries around the same time and in similar political and cultural contexts. Although the rate of litigation in India was not as high as in Sri Lanka, interpretations by modern scholars of the Indian legal system provide some starting points for an analysis of Sri Lankan justice, and are worth pursuing here in some detail. Interpretations fall into two broad categories: those which emphasize conflict between Indian and British cultural values, and those which attribute the difficulties of the courts to the nature of disputes in South Asian society.

The most well-known exponent of the 'culture conflict' view is Bernard Cohn.[13] He has argued that differences between British and Indian legal norms inevitably led to a divorce in Indian minds between justice and the colonial courts. He identifies four specific value conflicts. First the courts treated persons as equals, but Indians viewed people as having widely different inherent worths. Second, legal decisions based on ideas of contract did not fit the value system of Indian villagers. Third, the courts desired a clear-cut outcome. According to Cohn, Indians preferred a compromise solution, or at least the fiction of a compromise. Finally, the colonial courts settled only disputes brought before them. According to Indian values the courts should have looked further and settled the real dispute which lay behind the ostensible complaint. As a result of these value conflicts litigants had no respect for the courts and manipulated them.

There have been two important responses to Cohn's argument, both of which emphasize the nature of social conflict in Indian society. Robert Kidder has argued that there was no clash of values, but that on the contrary the attraction of the courts was that they were in theory able to pass down clear-cut and decisive decisions.[14] Litigants went to court because they had adopted 'Western' legal values. The difficulty was that the courts were unable to function effectively. Kidder's fieldwork, carried out after independence, shows that litigants who approached the courts honestly were unlikely to gain any benefit. Emphasizing the failure of the courts to resolve civil disputes within a reasonable period of time, Kidder argues that the fault lay with the structure of typical disputes in India. The personalized nature of disputes caused litigants to pursue all possible legal strategies even when it would have been more rational to compromise. Litigants were likely to be neighbours who had long been on hostile terms. Oliver Mendelsohn has carried Kidder's argument one step further.[15] He attributes the failure of the courts to the intractable nature of land disputes, rather than the structure of conflicts in general or faults in the system of justice. He believes that any judicial system would be overwhelmed by what he sees as contradictions in Indian rural society.

Although Cohn, Kidder and Mendelsohn all used some historical sources, their explanations of the deficiencies of South Asian courts were mainly inspired by fieldwork. This perspective is inadequate for an understanding of the colonial legal system because the post-independence practices evolved over a long period of time. Cohn does not show why Indians responded to alien courts with enthusiasm rather than indifference. It is after all unlikely that any culture conflict present when British courts were first established would continue unresolved and unchanged for over a century. The distinctions which he makes between South Asian and British values also seem exaggerated. Law in British India was not strictly locked into enforcing equality and contract.[16] Kidder and Mendelsohn, on the other hand, attribute litigiousness and perjury to an exceptional amount of hostility and conflict in South Asian society, but they fail to explain why this aggression was channelled into formal litigation. In addition, the stress which they place on the feasibility of indefinite delay as a cause, rather than a consequence, of the misuse of the courts seems misplaced. Although there were delays in the criminal courts, they seldom lasted more than a few months. Yet the same problems which plagued the civil courts prevailed.

The interpretation of the courts advanced in the second chapter of this book accepts many of the arguments put forth by these scholars, but provides a fuller model of judicial behaviour which is historical as well as functional. It is argued that specific policies implemented at the outset of British rule led to the development of a judicial system which did not coincide with either British or indigenous notions of justice but which was none the less compatible with local culture. Aided by court officials, lawyers and unofficial legal advisers, Sri Lankans used the courts as they used the spirits and demons of popular Buddhism. Both were perceived as amoral sources of power which responded more or less predictably to specific modes of address. That the new system generated little moral authority was less important than the fact that it gave many Sri Lankans access to the power of the state.

Crime and History

My contention that the functioning of the courts was a consequence of the implementation of specific judicial policies in a unique cultural and social setting points to the historical approach of the book. Both the expansion of the market economy and the imposition of colonial institutions took place in the context of long-established and complex cultures which shaped the form of the new social arrangements that appeared during the colonial period. This study is not constructed to test general theories about the relationship between crime and social change or the state. These themes are dealt with time and time again, but the possibility that they may be irrelevant, or that unique cultural, social or ecological facts are more important, is left open.

Some of the other issues discussed in this book have been central to historical writing on South Asia which treats more traditional subjects. One of these is the importance of colonialism. Did British rule transform South Asian society, or was state penetration weak in most rural areas? The study of crime and justice is one of the few fields where there is evidence about relations between the state and the people at the lowest level. It is argued in this study that although the courts did matter, they often failed to operate in the ways intended by British policy-makers. A resilient indigenous legal culture grew up around the courts, and attempts by government to change this culture were unsuccessful. The state was of course sometimes perceived as an alien entity by peasants living in remote rural areas, but this was not because it was Western. Such alienation from official institutions is common to many societies with isolated peasant populations; it was not necessarily an outgrowth of colonialism. The colonial courts, despite their formal structure which was modelled on British lines, were far less alien to the average Sri Lankan than they would have been to the ordinary Englishman.

Another important theme in the modern history of South Asia is the rise of nationalism. If, as is argued here, the representatives of the state at the local level were widely viewed as indigenous, what prompted nationalist agitation? The cynical answer is the spoils of patronage. Some historians have argued that nationalism was the outgrowth of the desire by élites to gain economic and political power, and that they manipulated indigenous symbols to this end. Few would deny that there are elements of truth in this explanation, but it has been criticized as incomplete because of its bias towards élites and its failure to explain why nationalist symbols had such wide appeal. In Sri Lanka Sinhalese-Buddhist cultural nationalism was linked with other grievances and was sometimes expressed through rioting, but in the absence of élite leadership it was not channelled into demands for constitutional concessions from the British. Events in India made this distasteful task unnecessary. There were few explicit and illegal anti-British protests during the last century of colonial rule.

There remains the possibility that much social protest was expressed indirectly through crime. In historical studies generally the interest in 'social crime' has declined because detailed research has found common thieves and bullies, not social bandits and grain rioters. Sri Lanka was not an exception in this regard. Some crimes were acts of protest, but within the overall context of illegal activity they were marginal. What is striking about crime in Sri Lanka is the relatively high economic and social status of criminals. Though certain crimes served to even out the distribution of power and income, other crimes had the opposite effect. Illegal activities often helped high-status groups maintain their positions.

Another current trend in historical writing in South Asia is to move away from analysis at the local, regional or national levels and instead attempt to trace the linkages between various localities and the wider society, economy and culture.[17] The study of crime offers some opportunities for this type of analysis.

Geographical comparison of patterns of lawbreaking sometimes throws light on more general differences in social and economic conditions. Criminal behaviour is important evidence for the reconstruction of all social relations.

Methodology and Sources

Crime has been studied from a great variety of perspectives. In part this diversity is the result of wide variations among legal systems, popular definitions of crime and patterns of illegal activity. It is also a reflection of differing disciplinary and ideological inclinations among scholars.

As a starting point, crime is defined as actions which are contrary to criminal law. Its content changes according to time and place. The main advantage of this definition is its precision. In societies such as colonial Sri Lanka, in which criminal law was made up of a set of rules, under this definition it is not normally difficult to determine whether or not an action was criminal. No claim is made for the universal usefulness of this definition; others would have to be found for societies in which law is not defined by a relatively clear, usually written, set of rules, or in which no distinction is made between civil and criminal law.

Under the legal definition of crime, it is in theory possible to determine the number of crimes committed in any one place over a period of time.[18] In practice neither scholars nor officials ever have sufficient evidence to put forth an accurate, exact figure. The 'dark figure' of crime, that is the difference between 'real' and reported rates of crime, may be substantial even for serious offences in twentieth-century developed nations.[19] Perhaps more importantly, the total number of crimes committed would be of little interest because there is great variation in the meaning and significance of individual criminal acts. To be useful, crime rates must be broken down into specific categories of offences.

A second advantage of the legal definition is that it reflects a political reality. Though not all laws are enforced with equal vigour, criminal law defines crime as it is officially recognized. Even when this definition differs from widely-accepted popular definitions, those who transgress the legal definition may well be punished. The administration of law and order may enforce another definition of crime which is different from the legal definition. This practical definition is equally a political reality, but it is constantly changing, lacks precision and may be arbitrary:

therefore it is not a useful definition to adopt. This is not to say that differences between the legal and practical definitions should not be an important theme for analysis.

Another view is that crime is those actions which are punished by the state.[20] This definition is partially motivated by the recognition that factors such as the race or social class of the offender and victim, rather than the nature or actual commission of an offence, may determine whether or not there is a conviction. It has the advantages of being very precise and of reflecting the social reality of the operation of the administration of law and order. Its weakness lies in its very narrow scope. Crime is equated with punishment, but most offences are unpunished.

Some scholars define crime as deviance from a social consensus of permitted behaviour.[21] This view takes into account the general view that crime is or ought to be those actions which are considered so immoral or damaging that they should be subject to punishment. Proponents of this definition often assume that criminal law is closely related to the consensus, although they accept that law may be tardy in reacting to changing attitudes. The main disadvantage of this definition is its vagueness. Since it is accepted that the consensus varies according to time and place, it is not clear how one distinguishes between a legitimate consensus and a deviant subculture. The scholar may assume that the consensus is the same as his or her own idea of crime. Alternatively, the moral values of a particular group within the society under study may be adopted. Another option, accepting criminal law as an accurate reflection of the social consensus, is less helpful than the legal definition because it precludes the study of differences between criminal law and popular conceptions of morality.

The legal definition of crime adopted here should be seen only as a starting point. The two alternative definitions discussed above point to its limitations. Whether one believes that ideas of morality determine the content of criminal law or that they instead serve as justification for the state or a social class to exert economic and political control, the relationship between law and morals is important. In either case, the actual functioning of official institutions may differ greatly from their declared purposes. The study of crime includes how and why the boundaries of crime change, the extent to which the legal definition is accepted, and the reasons why the authorities are more likely to punish certain legally-defined crimes than others.

This approach is consistent with much historical writing on crime, the quantity of which has increased greatly in recent years, especially in relation to Europe and North America.[22] Previously many historians perceived crime as abnormal and peripheral, fit only for study by specialists in deviance. Current research assumes that crime and justice do not exist in a social vacuum, that they are at least partially political creations, and that they are inextricably involved in society. This view is not new; in fact it was put forward by Durkheim and other nineteenth-century writers, but it was often disregarded after the study of crime was taken over by the new discipline of criminology in the early twentieth century.[23]

The decision to organize the book around the analysis of specific crimes rather than district studies or thematic issues reflects my conviction that crime is best understood as an 'umbrella concept' which encompasses many different modes of human behaviour.[24] The diversity of crime accounts for the unconvincing nature of attempts to explain it by all-encompassing theories. Murder, petty theft and tax evasion, for instance, all have different motives and consequences. The fact that in many societies all three are illegal does not mean that they have a similar social or historical significance.

The use of quantification in studies of crime tends to obscure this diversity. Crime rates often distort more than they clarify. This point may be illustrated by the different ways of measuring the following set of crimes: (a) a gang robbery with six offenders and two victims, (b) five cattle thefts, involving sixteen offenders and eight head of cattle, and (c) a murder with a single assailant. According to one crime rate, for which the number of offences is counted, seven crimes were committed. Each case of cattle theft has the same value as the murder and the gang robbery. Under another widely-used method, for which the number of persons accused is used, there were twenty-three offenders. Here the value of the robbery is not equal to that of the murder, but is instead six times greater. The cattle thefts are five times more significant than the murder when offences are counted, but sixteen times as important when the number of offenders make up the crime rate. Some scholars and officials have sought to avoid distortions by counting only crimes defined as 'serious'; this adjustment would not affect the example given above, for all of the crimes mentioned would normally fall into this category. Another alternative is to create an index whereby a number of factors, including the 'seriousness' of the offence, and perhaps the value of any property involved, are taken into account. Such efforts may eliminate some common inaccuracies, but no set of criteria can avoid distortion caused by the quantification of unlike incidents.

The approach of this book, with its emphasis on the study of specific crimes, reduces but does not eliminate the problem. As the case studies make clear, there was much variation in the circumstances of even the relatively narrowly-defined categories of cattle theft and homicide. Some distortion through the quantification of similar but not identical events is inevitable. None the less, crime rates for cattle theft and homicide prove very useful when analysed in conjunction with detailed information from other sources about the social settings of these crimes. In some instances it is possible to break down these rates further by motive or other circumstances.

The other methodological problem in determining crime rates is that of accuracy. It is well known that the authorities are aware of only a small proportion of crimes, and that administrative processing of those crimes further distorts official statistics. These difficulties are discussed in detail at those places in the book where crime rates are presented and analysed. At this point it is sufficient to mention that it is accepted that there were differences between the real and reported rates, but that for some crimes over certain periods of time the difference was fairly constant. A thorough understanding of the way official statistics were collected and of the workings of the administration is shown to be essential for the proper interpretation of these data.

Quantitative material is also used as evidence for the criminal proclivities of persons with certain social characteristics. Some data on convicted prisoners are available. More useful is my enumeration of persons who were listed in the *Hue and Cry*, a bi-weekly bulletin published by the police. This publication contained detailed descriptions of persons who failed to appear at court to answer a criminal charge. Their social characteristics, the type of crime of which they were accused and the district in which the crime took place were recorded for the period 1896 – 1905 (Appendix A). These 4,505 persons are treated as representative of persons considered responsible for crime during the mature colonial period.

Finally, the study of homicide is largely based on a quantitative analysis of details of 1,482 cases committed during the years 1883 – 9 and 1900 – 4 (Appendix B). Each case was examined and classified according to sixteen variables which describe some of the circumstances of the incident and the social characteristics of the persons involved. Again, this data base is not used to determine the overall frequency of homicide, but to provide information about the types of people who were involved and the proximate causes of the crimes.

The above discussion may give the impression that this is a predominantly quantitative study. This is true only in the sense that the significance of crime is directly related to its frequency; the bulk of the evidence is found in narrative form. There are a few works by scholars which deal directly with aspects of my subject.[25] Official documents account for a large proportion of the primary sources. Several categories are used, including semi-official diaries, annual reports, the proceedings of special commissions and correspondence both within Sri Lanka and between Sri Lanka and London. Non-official sources are also important. The press, polemics and literature all provide perspectives and information not otherwise available.

NOTES TO INTRODUCTION

1   Jones, *Crime, Protest, Community and Police in Nineteenth-Century Britain*, 9; Monkkonen, *The Dangerous Class*, 8 – 9; O'Brien, 'Crime and Punishment as Historical Problem', 509; Tilly & Lodhi, 'Urbanization, Crime, and Collective Violence in 19th Century France', 296; Gatrell, 'The Decline of Theft and Violence in Victorian and Edwardian England', 238.
2   Clinard & Abbott, *Crime in Developing Countries*, v. Also see Shelley, *Crime and Modernization*, 41 – 2.
3   Shelley, 35 – 7; Clinard & Abbott, 18 – 19, 35; Zehr, *Crime and the Development of Modern Society*, 135.
4   Cameron, *Crime and Repression in the Auvergne and the Guyenne 1720 – 1790*, 191 – 3; Sharpe, *Crime in Seventeenth-Century England*, 191, 214; Stone, 'Interpersonal Violence in English Society, 1300 – 1980'; Zehr, 125 – 6.
5   Gatrell, 240.
6   Ibid., 239 – 40.
7   Shelley, 33 – 4; Tilly & Lodhi, 304; Gurr, *Rogues, Rebels, and Reformers*, 35 – 66; Brantingham & Brantingham, *Patterns in Crime*, 185 – 91.
8   Kitts, *Serious Crime in an Indian Province*, 16 – 17, 44, 64 – 5; Arnold, 'Dacoity and Rural Violence in Madras, 1860 – 1940'; Arnold, 'Looting, Grain Riots and Government Policy in South India 1918', 132; Bayly, *Rulers, Townsmen, and Bazaars*, 90 – 1, 198, 295 – 6; Yang, 'The Agrarian Origins of Crime', 292 – 3; Haikerwal, *Economic and Social Aspects of Crime in India*, 50 – 65; Trivedi, 'Law and Order in Oudh 1856 – 77'.
9   Zehr, 43 – 55, 84 – 5; Sharpe, 198 – 200; Rudé, *The Crowd in History*, 22.
10 Radzinowicz & King, *The Growth of Crime*, 13.
11 Wright, *Between the Guillotine and Liberty*; Emsley, *Policing and its Context, 1750 – 1870*; Gurr, 117 – 62.

12   For some historical references to India, see Carstairs, *Human Nature in Rural India*, 276 – 83; Carstairs, *The Little World of an Indian District Officer*, 14 – 15; Walsh, *Indian Village Crimes*; Walsh, *Crime in India*, esp. 9 – 57.

13   Cohn, 'Some Notes on Law and Social Change in North India'; Cohn, 'Anthropological Notes on Disputes and Law in India'. Also see Rudolph & Rudolph, *The Modernity of Tradition*, 255 – 61.

14   Kidder, 'Courts and Conflict in an Indian City'.

15   Mendelsohn, 'The Pathology of the Indian Legal System'.

16   Washbrook, 'Law, State and Agrarian Society in Colonial India'.

17   Robb, (ed.), *Rural India*; Bayly; Meyer, 'Depression et malaria à Sri Lanka'.

18   Gatrell, 245 – 7.

19   Radzinowicz & King, 21 – 4.

20   Taylor, Walton & Young, *The New Criminology*, 91 – 138.

21   Ibid., 139 – 71; Gatrell, 245 – 6.

22   Useful reviews of this body of research include Jones, 1 – 32; O'Brien. The periodical *Criminal Justice History: An International Annual* is a product of this trend.

23   Taylor, Walton & Young, 67 – 90; O'Brien, 509.

24   Sharpe, 189 – 91.

25   Two books mainly concerned with the administrative history of the police contain much information about crime: Pippet, *A History of the Ceylon Police 1795 – 1870*, I & Dep, *A History of the Ceylon Police (1866 – 1913)*, II. The history of the judicial system is covered in Nadaraja, *The Legal System of Ceylon in its Historical Setting*; Samaraweera, 'The Judicial Administration of the Kandyan Provinces of Ceylon, 1815 – 1833'; Samaraweera, 'The Ceylon Charter of Justice of 1833'. A more ambitious interpretation of the colonial legal system, discussed in Chapter Two, is Samaraweera, 'British Justice and the "Oriental Peasantry" '.

CHAPTER 1

POLITICS, ECONOMY AND SOCIETY

The aim of this chapter is to provide the background information necessary to understand the arguments of this book. The first section treats the colonial administrative and political structures. It is followed by accounts covering the main economic and social developments of the British period.

Administration and Politics

European penetration of Sri Lanka began in the sixteenth century, when the Portuguese established control over some coastal areas.[1] Their rule was rarely peaceful, for they competed for power with Sinhalese and Tamil states. The Dutch replaced the Portuguese in the seventeenth century and established a relatively stable colony in the coastal regions of the island. The main concern of their administration was to profit from the monopoly over cinnamon, the principal export commodity. Only the Kandyan Kingdom maintained its independence in the interior. After 1739 it was ruled by members of the southern Indian Nayakkar dynasty, who adopted the roles of Sinhalese kings. The British ousted the Dutch in 1796, and two decades later, in 1815, assumed control over the entire island. The Kandyan Kingdom fell quietly to the British as a result of its internal weaknesses and divisions, but part of the aristocracy led a major rebellion in 1817–18. After it was crushed, the British took direct administrative control over the Kandyan districts.

In the early years of British rule the avowed principle of government policy was the continuation of policies of the previous regimes, the Dutch in the coastal areas or Low Country, and the Kandyans in the interior.[2] In practice there were innovations, partially because of the perceived need to reduce the influence of headmen, and partially because British officials naturally governed on the basis of their own training and inclinations. In 1829 a Royal Commission of Enquiry, appointed because of recurrent annual deficits, began an investigation of the colony's affairs.

Four years later a wide-ranging set of reforms, named after the
two commissioners, William Colebrooke and Charles Hay
Cameron, was implemented.[3] Many of the institutions and
practices established at this time remained intact until the
twentieth century.

The island's administration was unified under a government
structure shaped like a pyramid. At its apex was the Governor. He
made policy with the aid of an Executive Council which was
composed entirely of senior officials. He also presided over a
Legislative Council which included a non-official minority.
Governors generally appointed one representative for each of
three Sri Lankan ethnic groups, the Sinhalese, Tamils and
Burghers (Eurasians). The other three non-official positions were
filled by local British residents. After the Legislative Council was
expanded in 1889 a Ceylon Moor and an extra Sinhalese
representative were also included.

All legislation had to be approved by the Legislative Council,
but the Governor could control this body by ordering the official
majority to vote in a certain way. Normally such action was
unnecessary. In the 1860s there was open conflict between the
Governor and the non-official members over the size of the
colony's military contribution to the imperial budget and other
financial matters, but this fracas was the exception rather than the
rule.[4] The proceedings of the Legislative Council were sent to
London for the perusal of the Colonial Office and were reported
in detail by the local press. Legislation had to be confirmed by the
Colonial Office, which took note of any opposition. Governors
generally tried to get as much support as possible from the
Legislative Council, and they usually succeeded.

Although the legislative branch was clearly subservient to the
executive, the Supreme Court exercised power independently.
Initially vacancies were filled from Britain, but by the late
nineteenth century at least one of the three judges was Sri Lankan.
Judicial officials at lower levels were normally members of the
civil service. They were subject to transfer, but the executive
branch was unable to interfere with specific decisions. Appeals
were heard by the Supreme Court.

The Governor administered the colony through the highest
ranking civil servant, the Colonial Secretary. All heads of
department carried on a voluminous correspondence with this
official. Outside of Colombo, the capital, the main representatives
of colonial power were the government agents and assistant
government agents. These officials were responsible for the

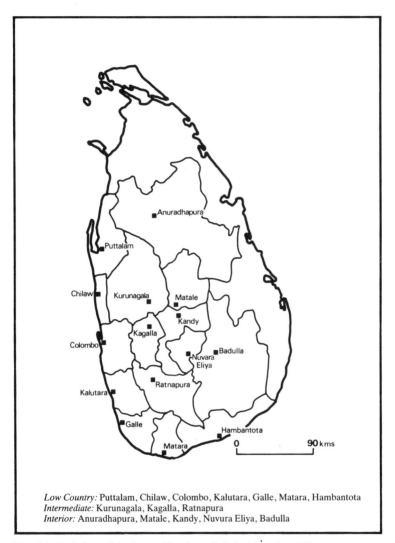

Low Country: Puttalam, Chilaw, Colombo, Kalutara, Galle, Matara, Hambantota
Intermediate: Kurunagala, Kagalla, Ratnapura
Interior: Anuradhapura, Matale, Kandy, Nuvura Eliya, Badulla

Map 1.1: *Kachcheris,* Districts and Regions, Sinhala Sri Lanka, 1900.

collection of revenue and the general administration of the
districts where they were stationed. Each worked from a
permanent district headquarters called the *kachcheri* (Map 1.1.).

In the years immediately following the Colebrooke-Cameron
Reforms civil servants were ill-paid and allowed to participate
actively in outside economic ventures. Many owned coffee
plantations, and not unnaturally were more concerned with the
success of their investments than with carrying out government
policy.[5] In 1845 salaries were raised, provision was made for
pensions, and restrictions were placed on economic activities. As a
result, civil servants gradually developed a stronger bureaucratic
ethos. This trend was strengthened in the late nineteenth and early
twentieth centuries by the establishment of more stringent
educational requirements and by the expansion of technical and
specialist administrative departments.

Revenue officials ruled their districts through several levels of
headmen. The lowest officials on the administrative tier were the
village headmen, who were normally men of substance. The chief
headmen, who were called *mudaliyars* in the Low Country and
ratemahatmayas in Kandyan districts were persons of high status
and much wealth. They exercised territorial jurisdiction over areas
often inhabited by tens of thousands of people. The extent to
which British administrators depended on them for information
varied greatly according to the social composition of the district
and the competence of the civil servant in charge. Another
important Sri Lankan official was the *kachcheri mudaliyar*, who
was in charge of the *kachcheri* staff and who often acted as an
interpreter. These officials should not be confused with the many
honorary and titular *mudaliyars* created by the British. Unless
otherwise specified the term *mudaliyar* refers to officials with
territorial jurisdiction.

In most districts only a few high-ranking headmen were paid a
salary. Many lower-level headmen received a legitimate income by
retaining a proportion of the fees paid to them for issuing various
licences and for other duties. The reliance of the government on
untrained and largely unsupervised headmen undermined government policies which were formulated as if headmen would act as
local bureaucrats.

The provincial boundaries established by the Colebrooke-
Cameron Reforms were deliberately designed to cut across
traditional political and ethnic lines. This policy was motivated by
a utilitarian-inspired belief that the island should be administered
in a unified way. In the second half of the nineteenth century

government policy shifted, partially as a result of agrarian unrest in parts of the interior in 1848. Many officials believed that these disturbances were prompted by needless interference with traditional society. It was felt that the more conservative backward-looking elements no longer represented a serious threat to British authority, but could on the contrary be placated and transformed into loyal allies. The 'native aristocracy' of Kandyan districts were all members of the Goyigama caste, and most were members of the Radala subcaste which had been influential in the Kandyan Kingdom. The authority of these headmen was increasingly supported by officials, and three new Kandyan provinces were created (Map 1.2). In the Low Country the link between social status and government appointments was less rigid, but nevertheless important. A group of predominantly Protestant families known as 'first-class Goyigamas' dominated the ranks of the *mudaliyars*.[6] Some governors saw the 'native aristocracy' as a counterweight to upwardly-mobile Low Country families, many of them non-Goyigama, who had taken advantage of the commercial and educational opportunities of British rule.

In the second half of the nineteenth century urban local government provided the small but growing English-educated élite with a limited opportunity to exercise political power. Municipal councils were first established in Colombo and two other towns, Galle and Kandy. Local boards, with less power than municipalities, held sway over smaller towns. Officials acted as chairmen of both these bodies, but some councillors were elected by Sri Lankans who met certain property requirements. In many rural areas village committees were established. The name was misleading, for the jurisdiction of each committee included many settlements. Though the president of each committee was appointed, councillors were elected by universal manhood suffrage. The proceedings of the village committees, unlike those of all other official bodies, were in Sinhala, not English.

Government revenue was much less dependent on the surplus from subsistence agriculture than in neighbouring India. The grain tax usually amounted to about one-tenth the value of the rice crop, considerably less than the burden imposed on the Indian peasantry.[7] In the nineteenth century it provided little more than ten per cent of government revenue. It was abolished in 1892, amidst justified concern that its harsh enforcement had contributed to rural destitution in some districts.[8] Customs duties and related levies were more important, accounting for about one-third of government proceeds. The revenue from arrack and toddy

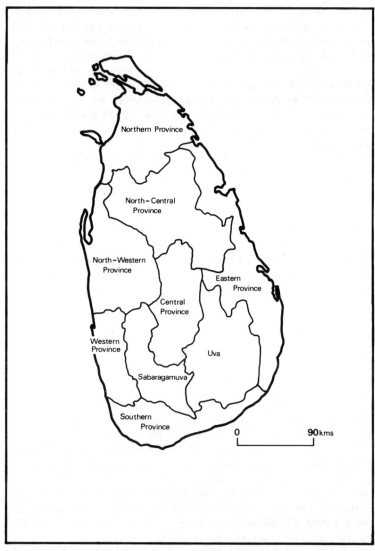

Map 1.2: Provinces, Sri Lanka, 1900. Uva was formed from the Central Province in 1886 and Sabaragamuva from the Western Province in 1889.

provided a significant portion of official income, as did the salt monopoly, railway receipts and income from the commutation of an annual labour levy on adult men.

The administrative structures set up by the Colebrooke-Cameron Reforms, though subject to some change in the nineteenth century, remained largely intact until the early twentieth century. In 1912 official control over the Legislative Council was reduced when an election was held for an 'Educated Ceylonese' seat. More significant concessions were made in the 1920s, when a majority of the Legislative Council was elected by a franchise limited by ethnicity, education and wealth. This arrangement proved unsatisfactory because there was no corresponding transfer of executive power. The non-official majority was able to reduce the power of civil servants but powerless to fill the ensuing void.

Under the Donoughmore Constitution of 1931 the Legislative Council was transformed into the State Council, the members of which were elected by universal suffrage. Executive power in many fields was turned over to seven committees of the State Council. The chairmen of these committees made up a Board of Ministers. Although the Governor retained direct control over defence, finance and justice, Sri Lankan politicians wielded an increasing degree of executive power. The influence of government agents and chief headmen, on the wane since 1920, declined still further. In 1936 the post of District Revenue Officer was created to supersede the *mudaliyars* and *ratemahatmayas*. Full independence was granted in 1948.

The Economy

Sri Lanka bore many traits of a classical colonial economy. The island exported raw materials and imported food, textiles and other goods. Although this pattern was well established as early as the sixteenth century, the expansion of the market economy during British rule was unprecedented. More and more land was needed to grow crops for export and in some cases for the domestic market. The extent, timing and nature of this trend varied geographically, but by the early twentieth century virtually all districts were affected.

Coffee was introduced into the central highlands in the 1840s, and quickly became the most important cash crop. It was produced not only on large British-owned estates, but also in small gardens owned by the indigenous inhabitants, the Kandyan Sinhalese. The Sinhalese were however generally unwilling to work as labourers on large estates. Impoverished Tamil peasants from southern India were used instead. Since much of the work on coffee plantations was seasonal, most of these workers returned to India once the harvest was over. The 'Indian Tamils', as they came to be called, were of low status and had a reputation among British planters for being docile. The Sinhalese were thought lazy because of their reluctance to work for planters, but the poor living conditions of estate labourers are ample explanation of the failure to recruit Sinhalese workers.

Disaster, in the shape of a leaf disease, struck the coffee industry in the 1870s.[9] By 1878 productivity had fallen and Sri Lanka's economy faltered. The depression was not limited to the coffee-growing area; there was also a decline in employment in the packing industry in Colombo, and many temporary emigrants from maritime areas who had earned their livelihood providing services in the previously-expanding economy of the central highlands were forced to return home. Around 1883 the economic outlook began to improve. With great rapidity tea replaced coffee as the major plantation crop, and soon its acreage surpassed that of coffee at its height, for tea could be grown at more varied elevations than coffee. The change of crop was not without important social consequences. Unlike coffee, tea could not easily be grown profitably on smallholdings. Thus the Kandyan Sinhalese were denied a full share of the renewed prosperity. Moreover, because tea required a more stable labour supply than coffee the plantation Tamils became more settled, though many continued to retain some ties with India.

Tea and coffee were not the only important export crops. A coconut belt had grown up along the south-western coastal fringe during the late eighteenth century. Elsewhere, the tree had grown randomly at lower elevations, and the nut was used for local consumption. In the nineteenth century the amount of land devoted to coconut cultivation expanded sharply, especially in Chilaw and Kurunagala districts. The value of coconut products consumed within the island was larger than the value of exports, but substantial amounts of coconut oil and copra were sent overseas.[10] Unlike tea estates, coconut plantations were generally owned by Sri Lankans, especially by the urban élite which had become wealthy by taking advantage of entrepreneurial opportunities. Many had made their fortunes by buying the arrack and grain tax rents from the government, through providing services and transportation for plantations, and by the production and sale of coconut products.

Graphite mining was another industry which became important in the second half of the nineteenth century. Most mines were owned by Sri Lankans. Mining activity was very sensitive to the price of graphite on the international market. A sharp rise in 1898 – 9 resulted in increases in the wages offered miners, and led to a general, if temporary, wave of prosperity for Sinhalese labourers, for other employers were obliged to follow suit.[11] The sensitivity of the graphite industry to international demand may be illustrated by the sharp fluctuations in the value of graphite exports as a proportion of the value of rice imports: in 1890 this proportion was eighteen per cent, by 1895 it had fallen to seven per cent, but in the boom year of 1899 it soared to sixty per cent.[12] The importance of graphite mining declined late in the colonial period.

Rubber was first grown commercially in the 1890s. Its acreage expanded quickly as a response to demand fuelled by the emergence of the automobile industry. Rubber passed coconuts in importance as an export crop in the first decade of the twentieth century. Although more than half of rubber production was controlled by British interests, there was also significant invest-ment in the industry by Sri Lankans. Most rubber was grown in Kalutara, Kagalla and Ratnapura districts. Although many Sinhalese were employed on rubber estates, there were local influxes of Indian Tamils into districts where rubber was established. The rubber industry was badly affected by the depression of the 1930s, but its position as the second most important export was not threatened.

Other cash crops, such as tobacco, cinnamon, arecanuts and citronella, were grown in gardens and on small plantations. In some instances these products were grown by peasants who sold their produce to local traders who in turn supplied urban merchants and exporters. Like coconut and rubber, many of these crops were also grown on estates owned by the urban élite. The steady expansion of land given over to the production of cash crops and the growth in population inevitably resulted in a decline in the proportion of villagers able to make a living from subsistence agriculture. The market economy provided other employment opportunities for poorer villagers.

Fluctuations in the world economy had a strong effect on the economic health of the island in the first half of the twentieth century. Conditions were depressed in 1918 – 21 because the high price of rice, a major import, was coupled with low prices for

many of the colony's exports.[13] The increased demand for rubber
in the early 1920s resulted in general prosperity, but in 1926 the
terms of trade again turned against Sri Lanka.[14] In the years after
1930 the world depression caused severe hardship. Unemployment soared, and many small producers of cash crops went
bankrupt. There was some recovery in the late 1930s, but the
Second World War led to further disruption. Some Sri Lankans
were able to take advantage of employment opportunities brought
about by increased government expenditure, but the high
inflation rate of the war years cut the standard of living of many
Sri Lankans.[15]

Food production, though largely neglected by the government
in the early nineteenth century, remained very important.[16] Rice
was the staple crop which was grown in most villages where its
cultivation was ecologically possible. Most rice fields were owned
in unequal shares, and the produce was distributed accordingly
when the crop was harvested. Alternatively, the tract could be
subdivided, or the responsibility for cultivation could be rotated
from year to year. In principle all children, regardless of sex or
parentage, were entitled to equal shares of property when a land-
holder died intestate. In practice a married daughter did not claim
her share unless she continued to live in her natal village after
marriage. Under Roman-Dutch law, which gradually came to be
enforced in the Low Country, all children were allowed a share in
the inheritance. The ensuing tension between popular and legal
norms concerning a married daughter's rights was an important
cause of land disputes, and also contributed towards the increased
fragmentation of shares. Population growth and restrictions on
settling forest land were other causes of this fragmentation.
Shares were often bought and sold, but the cultivators were not
necessarily displaced as a result. The share system of land
ownership did not meet the approval of the British, and
legislation was passed which made it possible for any shareholder
to force the division of a tract. When this happened owners of
small shares were left with tiny, uneconomical holdings, which
they were forced to sell.

Sri Lanka did not grow enough rice to feed its people. This
shortfall was not a new development, but the scale of rice imports
rose sharply, increasing ninefold between 1840 and 1900. Most
people who lived on the south-western littoral consumed imported
rice, while the plantation workers and those who provided
services for the plantations were almost entirely dependent on it.
In the villages of the interior little imported rice was used because

local production was adequate. When crops failed, people could not afford to buy imported rice anyway, though in some districts a number of villagers received income from seasonal work on plantations. Rice grown in Sri Lanka did not in general enter the market economy, although there were local transfers by barter and gift.

Rice was supplemented by other foods grown in the villages. Gardens normally surrounded village dwellings. Like rice fields this land was often owned in shares. Fruits and vegetables grown in these gardens formed an important supplement to the rural diet. Most produce was consumed locally, but the cash market gradually expanded, especially in the Low Country and around towns.

Grains were also grown on *chenas*, forest land which was cleared, burnt and cultivated once every five or ten years. In pre-British times *chena* cultivation formed an integral part of the economy of many villages. The government saw *chena* cultivation as a threat to the state's right to forest land, a matter of some importance because the sale of Crown land provided a significant proportion of official revenue in the nineteenth century. Moreover, many officials believed that *chenas* caused soil erosion and that the grains produced on them were unhealthy. Under Ordinance 12 of 1840 forest land was declared the property of the Crown, and in some districts a large proportion of it was sold for plantation development. In the 1840s most of those who acquired this land were British, including some civil servants. Later in the century many Sri Lankans purchased forest land from the Crown, and villagers also sold much *chena* land to speculators and capitalists. As a result, *chena* cultivation disappeared in many districts. Even when there was suitable Crown land available, *chena* licences were often refused. This policy caused great hardship in villages where it was not possible to grow enough rice for the needs of the residents.

The expansion of commerce required a revolution in transportation.[17] At the beginning of the nineteenth century there were only tracks and canals in the Low Country, and paths in Kandyan districts. The British soon constructed roads, mainly for military reasons. By the mid-century economic considerations were more important, and although roads continued to be built, more attention was paid to the construction of railway lines. The initial impetus for the development of the railway came from British planters who wanted a cheaper and quicker way to transport goods to and from their plantations. The Colombo-to-Kandy line

was completed in 1868, and fifty years later there was an extensive
network which included a coastal line from Puttalam to Matara
and which linked Colombo with Anuradhapura, Kurunagala,
Matale, Badulla and Ratnapura. The advent of motorized
transportation further improved communications. By 1930 over
two thousand buses and a similar number of lorries plied the
island's roads.

Although Sri Lanka was a small island, there were marked
differences in local economic structures even within the Sinhala-
speaking areas. Ecological patterns accounted for some of these
variations. Specific cash crops were profitable only in certain
districts. Most early plantation development was at the higher
elevations, especially in the central highlands, which covered parts
of Kandy, Nuvara Eliya and Badulla districts. Subsistence
agriculture was also influenced by patterns of rainfall and other
geographical conditions. The northern part of Sinhala Sri Lanka,
including large parts of Puttalam, Anuradhapura, Kurunagala and
Matale districts, was in the dry zone which received less rainfall
than the wet zone of the south-western and central portions of the
island. Rice cultivation was more difficult in the dry zone, which
also included parts of Hambantota and Badulla districts.

No general geographical division of Sinhala Sri Lanka into
regions can serve all purposes of analysis, but identifying districts
which shared some attributes is a useful tool if not used
indiscriminately. Three regions have been identified: Low
Country, Intermediate, and Interior. The Intermediate and
Interior areas together made up the Kandyan districts, the
geographical area under the sway of the former Kandyan
Kingdom. The boundaries of these regions are shown on Map 1.1.

The Low Country, which contained about half of Sinhala Sri
Lanka's population, corresponded roughly to the area which was
subject to direct Dutch and Portuguese political influence. There
were perhaps 500,000 inhabitants in the early years of British rule.
Its population grew steadily, reaching about one million in 1870,
two million in 1915 and three million in 1946.[18] The population of
Colombo, by far the largest city, grew from around 20,000 early in
the century to 160,000 in 1901 and 360,000 in 1946. The term
'Rural Low Country' is used to mean the Low Country with the
exception of Colombo. The next largest town, Galle, had a
population of 37,000 in 1901 and 49,000 in 1946. The entire
coastal fringe from Chilaw south to a few kilometres into Hambantota district was the most densely populated part of the island.
The littoral was well integrated into the market economy even

before the beginning of British rule, and it was families from this area who were able to gain wealth through trade and other capitalist ventures when the cash economy expanded inland in the nineteenth century. Many Low Countrymen of more modest means emigrated for much of the year to work in expanding sectors of the economy. Coconuts and other garden produce were grown everywhere and fishing was an important industry in seaside villages. Arrack and toddy production generated a great deal of wealth in Kalutara district. Further inland within the Low Country, the economy was based largely on rice cultivation, although tea and rubber were introduced into Kalutara in the 1890s, and there were coffee plantations in Matara before the spread of the leaf disease. The interior of the Low Country was not divorced from the market economy even during the nineteenth century. Cash was raised to pay taxes, to buy salt and cloth, and to purchase Indian bone-dust fertilizer. In the twentieth century population growth and increased use of land for cash crops led to a relative decline in the importance of subsistence agriculture.

The Intermediate region was transformed in the late nineteenth century by the establishment of plantations. The area had been on the periphery of the Kandyan Kingdom, and in the early years of British rule it remained an impoverished backwater. Even at the end of the nineteenth century it was overwhelmingly rural; the largest town, Kurunagala, had a population of less than 6,500. The first plantation crop to be introduced on a large scale was coconut, and the pace of its expansion increased rapidly in the late 1880s and 1890s, mainly in Kurunagala district. Much of this land was purchased from the Crown; other tracts were bought after a shareholder of a garden forced its division and sale. The plantation owners were mainly Low Country Sinhalese from the littoral who were seeking to invest capital which they had made as entrepreneurs, and they usually hired Low Countrymen to manage their estates. After around 1890, tea and rubber made similarly quick and extensive inroads into Kagalla and Ratnapura districts. Graphite mining also expanded in Kurunagala and Kagalla. One social consequence was a large influx of Indian Tamil and Low Country Sinhalese immigrants into all three districts. The population of the region increased from around 425,000 in 1870 to over 1,200,000 in 1945.

The Interior area included the heart of the former Kandyan Kingdom, the central highlands where coffee was first established in the 1840s. The fortunes of the coffee and tea industries have already been discussed above, and it uncertain whether Kandyans in coffee districts had by 1900 recovered the standard of living which they had attained in the early 1870s. Although Indian Tamils lived mostly on estates, their sheer numbers had a significant social effect. More Tamils than Sinhalese lived in Nuvara Eliya district, which during the Kandyan Kingdom was inhabited almost entirely by Sinhalese. The Interior region also included large parts of the dry zone which were sparsely populated, where famine was not uncommon. Late in the nineteenth century some efforts were made to improve irrigation facilities in these areas, where people often had to depend on *chenas* for their livelihood. Like other areas of Sri Lanka, the region's population grew under British rule. The number of inhabitants increased from around 600,000 in 1870 to 1,600,000 in 1945.

Social Divisions

The inhabitants of Sinhala Sri Lanka were divided by ethnicity, religion, language, caste, wealth and other characteristics. Many of these categories were related to each other. For instance, if one knew a person's ethnic identity one could predict his or her religion with some confidence. Yet none of these social features overlapped entirely, and none were 'fundamental'. Their relative importance varied according to context.

The most obvious social division, at least to the British, was that of ethnicity. The three major groups were the Sinhalese, Tamils and Moors. Although nineteenth-century immigration decreased the Sinhalese proportion of the population, their dominance was never in doubt. In the early twentieth century two-thirds of Sri Lankan residents were Sinhalese, as were between three-quarters and four-fifths of residents of Sinhala Sri Lanka. Their language, of Indo-Aryan origin, was probably brought to Sri Lanka by immigrants from northern India over two thousand years earlier. A large proportion of the ancestors of the Sinhalese were more recent immigrants from southern India who adopted Sinhalese language and culture. In the late nineteenth century Sinhalese élites invented a racial consciousness which was based on the assumption that all who spoke Sinhala were of Aryan origin.[19] This belief gained wide currency among Sinhalese of all social strata in the twentieth century.

Tamils were divided into two discrete groups, Ceylon Tamils and Indian Tamils. Ceylon Tamils, many of whose ancestors had lived in Sri Lanka for perhaps one thousand years, lived mostly in the Northern and Eastern Provinces, outside the purview of this book. A small number, some of them wealthy, settled in Colombo, and others were employed throughout the island as government functionaries. Indian Tamils, recent emigrants from southern India, had a very low social and economic position.[20] As well as providing the bulk of labour for large plantations, they carried out menial tasks in Colombo and other urban centres. By the end of the nineteenth century Tamils accounted for about one-third of the population in the Interior area. In the Intermediate and Low Country regions less than one-tenth of residents were Tamil.

Moors accounted for about five per cent of the population of Sinhala Sri Lanka. Most knew no home other than Sri Lanka, though there was a small community of Coast Moors which retained strong ties with Muslims in southern India. Moors were geographically scattered but had concentrations in the Eastern Province and Puttalam district. Although there were many Moor villages where rice cultivation was the principal economic activity, Moors were often pictured as traders and shopkeepers, and they had a strong presence in towns.

Other ethnic groups were very small but important. The Malays were an urban community many of whom lived in Colombo and Hambantota. Indian Chettiars controlled most rice imports and served as bankers for the emerging class of Sri Lankan capitalists. Burghers were persons of mixed European and Asian ancestry. Those who claimed descent from Dutchmen had a high social status, and English was the language of the home in many Burgher families. A large number were employed in government service. The British, who were considered part of a European racial group, were the ruling race. They dominated the upper levels of government, controlled much commerce, and owned the great coffee and tea plantations.

Ethnic minorities were concentrated in urban areas. Although the Sinhalese were the largest ethnic group in the city of Colombo, in 1911 they accounted for only forty-four per cent of the municipality's population. Tamils made up twenty-two per cent of Colombo residents, Moors nineteen per cent, and Burghers eight per cent. Other towns also had fewer Sinhalese residents than their rural hinterlands.

Language broadly followed ethnic lines. The most widely spoken was Sinhala, the language of the majority community. Tamils and Moors spoke Tamil, though many Moors were bilingual. Some élite families, both Tamil and Sinhalese, spoke English better than any other tongue. English was the official language, and was used in courts and government departments. In 1901 about four per cent of males and one per cent of females were literate in English. Literacy in Sinhala and Tamil was more widespread; about forty-five per cent of men but only ten per cent of women living in Sinhala Sri Lanka were literate in any one language. The extent of literacy gradually increased in the first half of the twentieth century.

Religion was also associated with ethnicity. This link was strongest among Moors and Malays, who were without exception Muslim. The dominant religious beliefs among Sinhalese and Tamils were respectively Buddhism and Hinduism, but Christianity had made inroads into both ethnic groups. About nine per cent of the Sinhalese were Christians. Most were Roman Catholics and lived near the coast in Chilaw, Colombo and Kalutara districts. They were descendents of persons who had adopted Christianity during Portuguese rule. A somewhat smaller proportion of Tamils living in Sinhala Sri Lanka were also Christians. Most Burghers were Protestants, as were some wealthy Low Country Sinhalese families who had a tradition of government service.

The second half of the nineteenth century was a time of religious revival and controversy, especially in the Low Country.[21] Three traditions took part: Buddhism, Roman Catholicism, and Protestantism. Priests and laymen of all three religions organized educational institutions and missionary propaganda. Beginning in the 1860s, Catholics and Buddhists established newspapers to rival long-standing Protestant organs. These newspapers devoted much space to religious dogma and disputes. The Catholic and especially Buddhist revivals were partially reactions to earlier activities of Protestant missionaries, who as part of their strategy to gain converts had produced polemical literature and established schools, including those which provided the best available English-language instruction.

The Buddhist revival gained momentum in the 1870s after a series of public debates between Buddhist and Protestant preachers increased Buddhist self-confidence. Among its financial supporters were wealthy traders and entrepreneurs, including many non-Goyigamas. After 1880 Buddhists received aid from European Theosophists, a development which partially offset the presence of Christian missionaries from Europe. The Buddhist revival provided opportunities for upwardly-mobile social groups to gain status denied them by the largely Protestant *mudaliyar* familes of the Low Country, but it was also a way for Sinhalese to challenge indirectly apparent British scientific, economic and political superiority. The discovery of impressive ruins which illustrated the past existence of a great Sinhalese-Buddhist civilization in the dry zone provided Buddhists with proof that their religion was not the cause of their colonial status.

As in India, caste was an important social institution. In Sinhala areas most Ceylon Tamils were of high caste while a majority of Indian Tamils were of low caste. The Sinhalese were also divided into castes, although unlike Hinduism, neither Buddhism nor Christianity provided caste with religious sanction.[22] Caste among the Sinhalese differed in that concepts of purity and pollution were not widespread. There was no Brahman or priestly caste, though admission to the Buddhist monkhood was generally limited to members of four 'respectable' castes. Although there was an unclean caste, the Rodi, whose members were regarded not unlike Indian 'untouchables', it was very small, accounting for well under one per cent of the population.

There was no unified Sinhalese caste 'system'. In Kandyan districts, where multi-caste villages were common, there were ritual and service ties between castes. These links were weak or non-existent in the Low Country, where most villages were identified with only one caste. The structure of Sinhalese caste was unusual in that a majority of Sinhalese belonged to a single caste, the Goyigama, which was also traditionally the highest caste. A further twenty per cent of Sinhalese were members of one of three 'respectable' castes which were not openly subservient to any other caste. Although hierarchy was not expressed by ritual along the coastal strip, inequality remained fundamental to perceptions of caste. A family's status, of which caste was part, was defined by the search for marriage partners. The refusal to accept a marriage proposal was often interpreted as a statement of superiority.

Goyigamas probably accounted for somewhere between fifty and sixty per cent of Sinhalese. The traditional occupation of this caste was cultivation. In communities which were economically and socially based on growing rice, Goyigama dominance was clear throughout the nineteenth century and beyond. Although along the coast and in towns their numbers and wealth were less secure, substantial numbers of Goyigamas entered the new urban élite. Elsewhere the chief headmen and large rice-field landowners were invariably Goyigama. Nevertheless, a majority of Goyigamas, in common with the rest of the population, lived in relative poverty.

Three other castes of high status, the Karava, Salagama and Durava, were concentrated near the south-western coast. None had ritual or service ties with Goyigamas. The Karavas, whose traditional occupation was fishing, numbered around ten per cent of the Sinhalese population. Many were also engaged in carpentry and other artisan trades. Although a large proportion of Karavas were poor, some members of this caste successfully took advantage of entrepreneurial opportunities within the expanding market economy.[23] Karavas were as a result disproportionately represented in the wealthy and English-educated élite. In particular, many families from the village of Moratuva, about fifteen kilometres south of Colombo, were among the wealthiest of the island.[24] The Karava élite resented the tendency of élite Goyigamas to regard them as inferior, and claimed equal or greater status. In the late nineteenth century Karava and Goyigama spokesmen carried out periodic verbal battles through pamphlets and in the press. This controversy was known as the Kara-Goyi contest.

The traditional occupation of Salagamas, who made up about seven per cent of the Sinhalese population, was cinnamon peeling. Under Dutch and early British rule their fortunes had varied according to colonial policy towards the cinnamon industry, which at that time provided most of the country's export earnings. The Colebrooke-Cameron Reforms freed Salagamas from their traditional obligations. Some of them, like some Karavas, seized available economic opportunities and joined the new élite. Less fortunate caste members provided much of the labour for graphite mines. Most Salagamas were casual labourers, cinnamon peelers and agriculturalists.

The Durava was a considerably smaller caste than the Salagama, and its social status was probably slightly lower. The traditional occupation of Duravas was toddy tapping, or climbing trees in order to extract sap with which to make toddy, a mild alcoholic drink. A few Durava families entered the new élite, but many continued in their tradiitional occupation.

Twenty or so low castes accounted for between one-fifth and one-quarter of the Sinhalese population (Appendix C). Many were very small or were found only in certain districts. The largest of the lower castes was the Vahumpura, which numbered perhaps six per cent of the Sinhalese population. Traditionally Vahumpuras were associated with the making of jaggery, a sweet substance derived from the jaggery palm tree. Most lived in rural areas, where they eked out meagre livings as cultivators. The economic position of those who lived near the coast was higher, and there were wealthy Vahumpura traders in Colombo.[25] They were, however, unable to evade their low social status.

Work was highly differentiated according to sex.[26] Women had many tasks to perform in the fields and in the home. When they participated in the market economy, they were usually confined to menial positions, many of which did not bring them into much contact with men. In some coastal areas basket making was a major female occupation. Even in towns women did not normally act as traders. Indian Tamil women lived and worked on the plantations with their families.

Members of certain ethnic and caste groups clustered into specific occupations. Many traditional caste occupations, such as cinnamon peeler, washerman, toddy tapper, fisherman and blacksmith, were still largely performed by their respective castes. Nevertheless, cultivators and labourers were drawn from all castes, and there were few caste monopolies. In any case, correlations between birth-determined groups and occupation did not need to have any historical or ritual justification, as the number of Karava carpenters, Moor masons, and Indian Tamil plantation labourers demonstrated.

The relationship between wealth, occupation and birth-determined social characteristics such as caste is a problem common to much research on South Asia. There is no widely-accepted model for the task of identifying for analysis categories which reflect divisions of occupation and wealth. There was little class consciousness in the European sense among the peasantry or urban workers in the nineteenth century, though occupational groups such as washermen, carters or fishermen could unite at the local level to protect their economic interests. Only in the twentieth century did skilled workers in Colombo begin to organize along working-class lines. There is little evidence that social class was a conscious force among other groups during British rule, with the possible exception of the new élite, or 'middle class'.[27]

One approach is to oppose the peasantry to the rest of the population, most of whom can be loosely described as labourers, and then to identify élites which stood above the mass of the people.[28] In Sri Lanka there was a national élite which was prominent in Colombo and Moratuva. Its economic base lay not in manufacturing but in commerce, contracting and land. Many élite families made fortunes in the first half of the nineteenth century and then invested their wealth in agriculture, usually in plantations. They rarely lived in the countryside, but their investments brought them prestige as well as profits. A good English-language education was considered a necessity for their male children, some of whom entered government service or one of the professions. In the twentieth century it was the growth in the power and influence of this élite, along with the example of the Indian movement for independence, which led directly to the end of colonial rule. Only English-educated politicians participated in the legislative institutions through which the British devolved political power in the 1920s and 1930s. The granting of universal suffrage in 1931 did not immediately undermine their position. Below this top crust was a growing group which included teachers, notaries, minor government functionaries and moderately successful traders. These persons were not necessarily well off, but they were literate in Sinhala if not in English and had a relatively high standard of living; they may be termed local élites. They gained direct political influence only after the 1956 election, eight years after independence. In rural areas the economic base of some wealthy families, including those which dominated the office of *ratemahatmaya* in Kandyan districts, remained their ownership of large tracts of rice fields. These families may be described as a traditional élite; in the twentieth century they either found new sources of wealth and influence or became local notables. None of these élites had sharply defined boundaries, and there was much overlap among them.

A complementary approach to social classification is to group persons by a series of social characteristics. In this study the bi-weekly bulletin *Hue and Cry*, which listed descriptions of persons for whom magistrates had issued warrants, provides the necessary data. It includes information about age, sex, caste, religion, occupation and birthplace. Quantification of most of this material presents few methodological difficulties; the exception is the variable 'occupation'. The first task is to separate out cultivators, who are defined as landowners or tenants whose livelihood was in agriculture, usually the production of rice. Excluded from this group are persons who worked in fields, gardens and plantations for a cash wage, but who had no stake in land. These latter are classified in a residual category called labourers, which included coolies, carters and service workers, such as blacksmiths and washermen, who usually worked for a fee or wage. Some of these 'labourers' were thus in fact small businessmen, albeit usually on a petty or part-time basis. Domestic servants and white-collar workers, though they worked for a wage, are classifed separately because they are easily distinguishable in the colonial sources. Other categories are traders, fishermen, 'loafers' and 'others'.

There are two main limitations to the use of these categories. First, it was common for persons to follow more than one occupation. Many Kandyan peasants worked on plantations for three or four months each year. Low Countrymen emigrated to the interior, often temporarily, to take advantage of employment opportunities. Moreover, a large proportion of traders and persons who followed service professions also owned land and sometimes cultivated it themselves. The official descriptions presumably reflected the most recent activity of the person concerned; when interpreting data drawn from the *Hue and Cry* the flexibility of occupational boundaries should be kept in mind.

Secondly, membership in these occupational categories tells us little about the wealth of the person concerned. Cultivators included both well-off landlords and their much poorer tenants. Some merchants were very rich, and even village storekeepers were often among the wealthier inhabitants of a locality. But there were also many petty traders who barely eked out a living. The disparities were perhaps less great among labourers, but skilled workers, such as carpenters, railway employees and miners, often commanded wages three times those of a common labourer. Even the pay of domestic servants varied widely depending on the status of the employer and the sex and duties of the employee. These categories are thus unsatisfactory for use in ways similar to class analysis in European history. Fortunately there is no need to rely on occupation alone to assess social and economic status. Although the other social characteristics available are not directly related to wealth, they are amenable to ranking in a general social and economic sense. When a social profile of a certain group is constructed using these variables, its place in the social hierarchy is usually evident.

NOTES TO CHAPTER 1

1   For a survey of the history of Sri Lanka before the establishment of British rule, see K. M. de Silva, *A History of Sri Lanka*, 1 – 235.
2   C. R. de Silva, *Ceylon under the British Occupation 1795 – 1833*; P. D. Kannangara, *The History of the Ceylon Civil Service 1802 – 1833*.
3   Samaraweera, *UCHC*, III, 77 – 88; Mendis, (ed.), *The Colebrooke-Cameron Papers*.
4   Digby, *Forty Years of Official and Unofficial Life in an Oriental Crown Colony*, I, 263 – 87, 322 – 4 & II, 40 – 9.
5   K. M. de Silva, *UCHC*, III, 213 – 17.
6   Peebles, 'The Transformation of a Colonial Elite'.
7   Roberts, *UCHC*, III, 133 – 9.

8   Wesumperuma, 'The Evictions under the Paddy Tax'.
9   Sharpe, *AR Kurunagala 1880*, 66; Saunders, *AR Colombo 1881*, 6A; F. Templer, *AR Kandy 1878*, 25; Moysey, *AR Matale 1878*, 45; King, *AR Badulla 1878*, 38 & *AR Badulla 1879*, 57.
10   Ferguson, *Ceylon in 1903*, 49–52.
11   Vigors, *AR Kalutara 1898*, B28; Fowler, *AR Colombo 1899*, B5; Hill, *AR Kagalla 1899*, J11; Wace, *AR Galle 1899*, E15; Fox, *AR Kalutara 1900*, B35.
12   Calculated from Peebles, *Sri Lanka: A Handbook of Historical Statistics*, 152, 217.
13   *SP 4 1922*, 3; Hellings, *AR Galle 1919*, C2; Fraser, *AR Colombo 1921*, A2; De Glanville, *AR Kalutara 1921*, A18; Harrison-Jones, *AR Matale 1921*, B16; Jayawardena, *The Rise of the Labor Movement in Ceylon*, 220–1.
14   Meyer, 'L'impact social de la depression en milieu rural', 674.
15   Indraratna, *The Ceylon Economy*, 33–45.
16   For peasant agriculture see Roberts, *UCHC*, 119–64; Obeyesekere, *Land Tenure in Village Ceylon*; Meyer, 'The Plantation System and Village Structure in British Ceylon'. The relationship between the plantation and subsistence agricultural sectors has been much studied, but remains controversial. In addition to the above references, see Peebles, 'Land Use and Population Growth in Colonial Ceylon'; Roberts, 'The Impact of the Waste Lands Legislation and the Growth of Plantations in British Ceylon'; Bandarage, *Colonialism in Sri Lanka*.
17   Wickremeratne, *UCHC*, III, 303–16.
18   The first modern census was carried out in 1871, and others followed at ten-year intervals. There were also several censuses taken in the early years of British rule, but their reliability is uncertain. When using the 1871 census I have increased the published figures five per cent in order to account for under-enumeration.
19   Gunawardana, 'The People of the Lion'.
20   Jayawardena, 5, 16–22; Samaraweera, 'Masters and Servants in Sri Lankan Plantations'; *SP 49 1906*.
21   Malalgoda, *Buddhism in Sinhalese Society 1750–1900*, 191–262; Wickremeratne, 'Religion, Nationalism and Social Change in Ceylon, 1865–1885'; Obeyesekere, 'Personal Identity and Cultural Crisis'; Boudens, *Catholic Missionaries in a British Colony*, 99–110, 131–54. There was also a revival of Hinduism in areas dominated by Ceylon Tamils, especially Jaffna.
22   The standard work on Sinhalese caste is Ryan, *Caste in Modern Ceylon*. Also see Roberts, *Caste Conflict and Elite Formation*; Stirrat, 'Caste Conundrums'.
23   Roberts, *Caste Conflict*, esp. 98–130.
24   Ibid., 269–78; Peebles, 'The Transformation', 164–215.
25   Roberts, *Caste Conflict*, 154, 175, 318–19; *Times*, 28 Sept 1875; Dep, 7; Jayasekera, 'Social and Political Change in Ceylon, 1900–1919', 30. Further evidence is a list, analysed by Roberts, of the 'principal Sinhalese rich' in five Colombo wards in 1915. Of the 72 persons whose caste he identified, 6% were Vahumpura. (35% were Goyigama, 31% Karava, 11% Salagama, 10% Durava and 8% others.) Of the 17 unidentified persons, 7 bear the name Fernando, which was common among Vahumpuras as well as Karavas. I would argue that Roberts's informants would be less likely

to identify Vahumpuras, and that the real proportion was higher than 6%. Roberts, 'Elite Formation and Elites, 1832 – 1931', 213.

26 MacDougall & MacDougall, *Sinhalese Domestic Life in Space and Time*, 153 – 60; Denham, *Ceylon at the Census of 1911*, 310, 457 – 9; Alexander, PO, *AR Galle 1906*, D11.

27 Meyer, 'Bourgeoisie et société rurale à Sri Lanka (1880 – 1940)'.

28 Roberts, 'Elite Formation'.

CHAPTER 2

THE ADMINISTRATION OF LAW AND ORDER

The most prominent feature of the administration of law and order in colonial Sri Lanka was the popularity of the courts. In the nineteenth century the number of persons who were each year involved in civil and criminal cases often exceeded the adult male population of the island.[1] One official noted that 'most English people die without having been inside a court, and regard it as a misfortune to be entangled in a lawsuit. . . . [but] To the Ceylonese the judicial aspect of government is more prominent than the administrative.'[2] This assessment appears valid, but the authorities did not take satisfaction from it. They did not believe that the high rate of litigation was primarily the result of an excessive amount of crime or an unusually large number of valid civil disputes. Nor did they think that Sri Lankans prosecuted a larger than normal proportion of true criminal cases because of their faith in the effectiveness of British justice. Instead, from the very beginning of British rule it was the nearly unanimous opinion of officials and literate Sri Lankans that there was an inordinate number of false accusations. It was widely believed that the courts were used to further disputes which were not necessarily related to the ostensible complaint. An explanation of the contradiction between these two themes, the seeming failure of the courts as shown by the consistent and convincing allegations of widespread perjury, and their seeming success as demonstrated by their immense popularity, lies at the heart of this chapter.

My contention is that although the colonial legal system was influenced by culture conflict at the beginning of British rule, it was soon adapted and accepted as an integral social institution by the mass of the people. The major point of conflict was the means of determining whether or not a defendant was guilty, not the definition of criminal offences or the failure of the British to take into account status differentials. Also important was the decision to hold all proceedings in the English language. Although the assumptions behind British judicial procedure were not popularly accepted, the courts soon ceased to be alien because they were used by Sri Lankans in ways which fit indigenous norms.

Unfortunately, from the British viewpoint at any rate, the dispute-solving model adopted by the Sinhalese had little to do with British conceptions of justice. Instead the courts were treated as an amoral source of power which could be used by those skilful enough to manipulate them.

The first three sections of this chapter survey the development of government policy towards crime. The first section examines the institutions established during the first half-century of British rule. Little attention was paid to policing during this period. Official energies were instead directed to the establishment of a judicial system similar in many ways to that of Britain. Policy towards policing is examined in the second section. A modern police force was established in the 1860s, but until 1906 it remained largely confined to urban areas. Headmen were relied upon to perform police duties in the countryside. In the 1890s a serious effort was made to transform them into a rural police force. It was the failure of this attempt which led to the gradual expansion of the regular police into rural areas in the first half of the twentieth century. Judicial policy in the late nineteenth and early twentieth centuries is examined in the third section. Government during this period sought to clarify the law and simplify judicial procedure. Although delays were mitigated and judicial efficiency improved, the courts continued to exercise little moral authority.

The fourth section looks beyond government policy to the actual workings of the police and judicial institutions, as far as possible from the perspective of the inhabitants. It is shown that there was very often little to be gained from approaching government institutions with attitudes which would have been considered proper by British administrators. The final section shows how Sri Lankans were none the less able to use the courts as a legitimate and acceptable, if sometimes disreputable, way to solve disputes.

The Establishment of the Colonial Judicial System

During the first few years after the British first gained control over the Low Country there was much administrative confusion.[3] Under the Dutch there were formal courts which tried serious criminal cases, but both European officials and headmen were empowered to judge summarily petty cases and to punish offenders with a fine or whipping.[4] The British were suspicious of the loyalty of headmen, and soon stripped them of their judicial powers. They established a three-tier court system which had exclusive authority to punish crime.[5] All proceedings were held in English, a language with which very few inhabitants had familiarity. The courts were dependent on interpreters from the very beginning of British rule.

The Supreme Court was composed of two judges who were the only officials other than the Governor appointed directly by the Crown. It had original jurisdiction over serious offences. Provincial courts, staffed by civil servants who had other duties, tried some criminal cases. At the bottom of the judicial system, magistrate's courts handled petty crime and committed more serious offenders for trial in one of the higher tribunals. They were mostly staffed by Burghers, many of whom had served the Dutch colonial government. Policing was left largely in the hands of headmen, who were in theory supervised by magistrates. Under the Dutch, revenue headmen were responsible for apprehending lawbreakers, but in 1806 the British created a new class of local headman, called *vidanes*, to carry out police duties. In the early years of British rule *vidanes* were allowed ten per cent of the value of any recovered stolen property when they were instrumental in gaining a conviction.[6]

When the Kandyan Kingdom was annexed in 1815 the administrative structures of the Low Country were not applied there. The Kandyan judicial system, which included tests by oath and ordeal as well as trials conducted by various grades of headmen, was initially left largely intact.[7] After the rebellion of 1817 – 18 the judicial powers of headmen were limited to trying petty cases. British agents of government, whose primary responsibility was the collection of revenue, were given judicial duties, and the Board of Kandyan Commissioners functioned much as the Supreme Court in the Low Country, with the power to hear appeals and with original jurisdiction over serious criminal offences.[8]

The court system was unified under the judicial charter of 1833. The result was a set of institutions based on English principles, especially the ideas of the utilitarian Jeremy Bentham.[9] The lower-level courts were abolished and the remaining judicial powers of Kandyan headmen were eliminated. A reconstituted Supreme Court was given authority over the entire island, with original criminal jurisdiction for serious crime. District courts, with exclusive geographical jurisdictions, were established to try all lesser offences. The Queen's Advocate, a civil servant, had overall responsibility for the legal branch of administration, but the Supreme Court was entirely independent. The district judges of Colombo and Kandy later came to have a similar independent status. Other judicial officials were transferred at will by the Governor, from station to station and department to department, but the Colombo secretariat could not interfere with specific judgments.

The Dutch courts applied Roman-Dutch criminal law in the Low Country, though it is unlikely that it was adhered to by headmen or officials trying minor offences.[10] It was British policy to enforce Roman-Dutch law, as amended by British proclamations. In practice, Roman-Dutch criminal law was gradually replaced by English law because British judges were influenced by English precedents and modes of reasoning.[11] A similar process took place in Kandyan districts. There the indigenous law was unwritten, and although the Board of Kandyan Commissioners, relying on assessors, at first attempted to enforce Kandyan criminal law, within fifteen years of annexation the same mixture of Roman-Dutch and English law which prevailed in the Low Country was generally applied.[12] The reforms of 1833 affected only the structure of the courts, not the law which they administered. Utilitarian ideas such as codification and the setting of fixed punishments for specific offences were not implemented. In 1852 the demise of Kandyan law was made formal by legislation which extended all Low Country criminal law to Kandyan districts.[13]

In the decade after 1833 it became apparent that the district courts, which had original jurisdiction in all civil cases and most criminal ones, were unable to handle the litigation brought before them without long delays. They were clogged with cases because there was no procedure for summarily trying minor offences. As a result a third, lower tier to the court system, the police courts, was added in 1843.[14] In an effort to avoid delays brought about by the technical procedures of the district courts, police court decisions were not subject to appeal and lawyers were barred from appearing in trials. Verdicts were, however, subject to 'review' by the Supreme Court on six rather ill-defined grounds, a procedure which led to much confusion. In 1854, appeals were introduced on matters of law and lawyers were allowed to practise in these courts. These reforms were partially aimed at reducing the influence of court officials and other persons who served as unofficial lawyers.[15]

The legal profession served as a means of upward social mobility for Burghers, Sinhalese and Tamils. Before 1833 only British and Burgher lawyers were allowed to practise in Colombo courts, but this restriction was lifted by the reforms of that year, and by the mid-century few British lawyers practised in Sri Lanka.[16] Although much litigation was carried out without professional legal advice, the bar grew quickly, and the more competent lawyers were able to command high fees. There were two official categories of legal advisers: advocates and proctors.[17] Both were certified by the Supreme Court. Higher standards were set for advocates, who dominated Supreme Court business. They had to satisfy the judges that they had had the education of an English gentleman.

In the nineteenth century the judicial system did not depend on either the headmen or the police for the initiation of criminal prosecutions, but on private individuals. A man who felt he had been victimized by a crime and who wished to have the perpetrators punished could accuse the person or persons whom he suspected before either a justice of the peace or a police magistrate.[18] If he did not suspect any particular person, he had no redress.

In most districts the same person held the posts of justice of the peace and police magistrate, but it was necessary for the complainant to determine in which capacity he wanted this official to act. The distinction was based on the seriousness of the offence. The magistrate summarily tried cases in the police court, where the maximum punishment was three months imprisonment, twenty lashes, a fine of five pounds, or any two of the above.[19] The justice of the peace, on the other hand, did not himself try cases. If, after examining witnesses, he was satisfied that there was sufficient evidence for a trial in one of the superior courts, he sent details of the case to the Queen's Advocate, who made the decision on whether or not it would go forward. District courts had the power to inflict punishment of up to one year in prison, fifty lashes, a fine of one hundred pounds, or any two of the above. There was no formal limit to the punishment which the Supreme Court could impose, though in practice the death sentence was passed only in cases of murder.

The law did not specify which court should try most specific offences. The criterion for the complainant, and then the judicial officials, was the amount of punishment which the crime warranted. The initial decision of the complainant was not without importance, for if, after hearing the evidence of witnesses, the justice of the peace decided that the case was not serious enough to be sent to a superior court, he could not then and there try it as a police court case. Instead the complainant, defendant, and witnesses had to come back and testify all over again, usually on a different day, when the official was acting in his capacity as a magistrate. Similarly, a serious case brought before the magistrate had to be presented a second time before the justice of the peace. The distinction between these two offices, usually held by the same person, was an important cause of delay.[20]

To add to the confusion, in many smaller localities one official held not only the two posts just discussed, but was the district judge as well.[21] Some officials objected to this arrangement in principle, but the government felt that the cost of additional personnel was too great to warrant changing it. The justice of the peace did, however, have to justify any decision to commit a case to a superior court. He sent a transcript of the testimony to Colombo, where it was perused by a secretariat official who might ask for more evidence before accepting or changing the local recommendation.[22] All Supreme Court cases and selected district court cases were prosecuted by a government official.[23]

Most reported crimes were brought before police courts, many of which were located in the plantation areas of the Central Province (Map 2.1). In 1868 there were thirteen police court sites in the Central Province, or one for every 40,000 inhabitants. In contrast, there was only one police court in Kurunagala district, which had a population of over 200,000 but very few Europeans. Although regular use of itinerating magistrates was made in some areas later in the century, many villages remained thirty or forty kilometres from the nearest police court, and some were much further distant.

Although all testimony was recorded on paper in English, the procedure of police court trials was relatively simple. Both the complainant and defendant could summon witnesses who were subject to both cross-examination and re-examination. The magistrate could then decide the case on the spot, though postponements were often granted on the grounds that witnesses were missing. After 1854 appeals to the Supreme Court on matters of law were allowed. The right of appeal on questions of fact was introduced in 1874, but restricted after 1885.[24] Although the formal rules of police courts were almost entirely of British origin, in practice the atmosphere was influenced by climatic and other considerations. John Capper, a journalist, contrasted the ambience of Colombo Police Court with the minor courts he had known in Britain: 'How different from the vicinity of the law courts at home! There, everything is cool, solemn, silent, orderly; here, it is all glaring sunshine, dirt, noise, dust and effluvia.'[25]

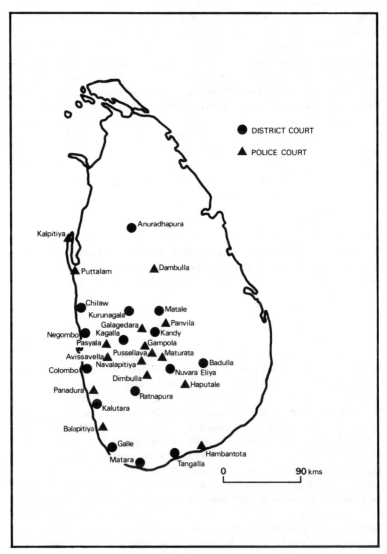

Map 2.1: Police Court and District Court sites, 1870.

There were thirteen district courts in Sinhala Sri Lanka (Map 2.1). District judges, unlike many magistrates, were experienced officials. Cases could be tried with the aid of assessors, or local men of respectable income or property, but this option was rarely exercised in criminal cases. The judge determined the guilt of the accused, and passed sentence, but the opinions of any assessors were recorded for the benefit of the Supreme Court in case an appeal was made. Witnesses were examined according to the same procedure as at police court trials. Also like police court trials, witnesses had to pay their own expenses, even though they sometimes had to travel long distances, especially when a trial was postponed several times. Although some officials recommended that the expenses of the district court witnesses be paid by government, nothing was done, apparently for financial reasons.[26]

Supreme Court cases were decided differently. The British introduced trial by jury to the Low Country in 1811, and this institution was retained after 1833.[27] Though cases were presided over by one of the three judges of the court, questions of fact were decided by a jury of thirteen men. The judge instructed the jury about legal points. Four criminal sessions, each of which usually lasted from one to three weeks, were held annually at Colombo, and at least two sessions were held each year at Kandy and Galle. Cases were tried at other localities according to the geographical distribution of serious crime.

At first potential jurors were classified by ethnic group and caste, but after the 1840s they were assigned to one of three lists which were drawn up on the basis of language capability.[28] Jurors had only to be 'of sufficient intelligence and respectability', but in 1868 a financial test was instituted in order to exclude low-status white-collar workers.[29] When a Sinhala or Tamil jury heard a case, all proceedings not in the language of the jury were translated for its benefit. Since the official language of the court was English, all testimony in other languages was translated regardless of the composition of the jury. In practice most cases were tried with an English jury. Except in the Central Province, Europeans were almost always in a minority.[30]

The judicial changes implemented in the first half of the nineteenth century represented a break with many eighteenth-century practices. New distinctions were established between executive and judicial power, and between civil and criminal law. More importantly, the British courts were founded on the acceptance of abstract and impersonal principles which had no firm base in Sri Lanka. In pre-British times judges had made decisions on

the basis of all known information. Some officials recognized that
the new system was alien, but expected that the judicial system
would act as a progressive force which would promote the
adoption of British norms about justice. Despite some improvements in judicial efficiency, this hope was little realized.

Government Policy towards Policing

Though the judicial system itself was symmetric in structure, the
administration of law and order was unwieldy and uncoordinated.
The police, headmen and courts did not work together. In the
early years of British rule the government paid far more attention
to the judicial system than to either the police duties of headmen
or the establishment of a regular police force. This bias was no
doubt at least partially a reflection of the haphazard organization
of policing in Britain itself at the beginning of the nineteenth
century. The high level of criminal litigation which ensued was
taken as a sign that this policy had failed. In the late nineteenth
century efforts were made to build an organized system of
policing, but rural districts remained largely unpoliced until the
twentieth century.

Headmen were relied on in rural areas. They had wide powers to
arrest persons suspected of committing such crimes as theft,
burglary, and serious assault.[31] In theory all arrested persons were
supposed to be brought before a judicial official within twenty-
four hours, but in practice more time often elapsed.[32] At the
village level the same person generally handled police and revenue
matters in Kandyan districts, while different officials performed
these duties in the Low Country. Police headmen in Sri Lanka
were not equivalent to the village watchmen of India, who were of
low social status. In Sri Lanka the police role of the headman was
not a profession, but an additional source of authority for a
village notable.[33]

Since the headmen were neither recruited, trained nor even
supervised in a consistent manner, it is not surprising that they
were generally inactive when it came to dealing with crime. Their
main duty was to arrest wanted persons; they rarely reported or
investigated crime during the early years of colonial rule. There
was little incentive for them to be active in this regard, for only a
few high-level headmen received a salary. Headmen were inclined
to use police powers in their own interests rather than act as
bureaucratic tools.

There was also a regular police force, but during the first half of the nineteenth century it was small, poorly paid, and limited largely to Colombo, Galle, and areas where there were coffee plantations.[34] Its main task was not to detect or prevent crime, but to maintain order on public occasions, perform guard duties and apprehend well-known criminals. In 1852 an official report stated that the 'uselessness of the force, as at present constituted, is too notorious to need much remark.'[35] It was not until the 1860s that a determined effort was made to expand the police and to use it as an instrument to suppress crime. This move stemmed largely from the perceived success of the police in Britain and India.[36] George W. R. Campbell was recruited from India to reorganize the force.[37] He remained in Sri Lanka as Inspector-General for twenty-five years.

Under Campbell's leadership the sanctioned strength of the force rose from around 700 in 1866 to over 1,600 in 1879.[38] Its duties were largely urban; over half the force was stationed in Colombo and there were also large contingents in Kandy and Galle. The police normally went to villages only to investigate specific serious crimes, usually homicides, but even then they were not always involved. They could also be temporarily stationed in villages at the expense of the inhabitants as punishment for unsolved crimes. The police had no organizational link with the courts, despite the designation of the lowest tier of the judicial system as 'police courts'.

The duties of the ordinary policeman, who was known as a constable, were arduous, at least in Colombo. He was supposed to be on his beat twelve hours out of every twenty-four, one week by day, the next by night. Men were sometimes on the beat twenty-one out of twenty-four hours during the transition between day and night duty. Campbell pointed out that London policemen worked only eight hours each day and were given one day off each week. He wanted to hire more men and reduce the number of hours each constable spent on duty. But the necessary funds were not forthcoming and the beat system established by Campbell soon after he took charge remained unchanged for over twenty-five years. Men were often punished or dismissed for failing to remain alert while on duty. About one-fifth of the force had to be replaced each year, partially because many recruits were found unsuitable.

The career of Ibrahim Nanno represents a not untypical career pattern among constables in the second half of the nineteenth century.[39] He joined the force as a third-class constable in 1870 at the age of nineteen. At first promotion came regularly. He reached the second class in 1873 and became a first-class constable in 1876, when twenty-four years old. As a result of these promotions, his salary rose from 15 to 22.50 rupees a month. But in April 1878 he was cautioned for being intoxicated while on duty, and when discovered drunk in 1882 was reduced to the second class. Six years later, having 'consorted with a person of bad character' while stationed in a low-caste Sinhalese village, he was transferred to Colombo at his own expense. There, in 1892, he was found asleep and drunk on his beat, and was reduced to third-class constable and the fifteen rupees salary upon which he had started over twenty years earlier. In 1895 he was promoted back to the second class, but two years later, at the age of forty-five, a medical board found him unfit for duty 'due to chronic rheumatism and cracked feet'. All in all, he had been departmentally punished on twenty-seven occasions, an average of once for each year he had spent in the force.

Nanno received a pension, as did all policemen who joined when under thirty years of age and who served for twenty or more years.[40] The prospect of a pension must have attracted many men into a profession in which prestige was low, the pay not particularly good, and discipline strict. Another inducement was income from tips and bribes, the importance of which will be discussed later in this chapter.

Campbell's force was not ethnically representative of the island's population. Though the Sinhalese accounted for over two-thirds of Sri Lanka's inhabitants, they made up less than one-third of the force. This disparity was not as striking as it first appears, for the Sinhalese were proportionately less prominent in urban areas, where most policemen were stationed. Nevertheless, the paucity of Sinhalese undermined the force's authority among the majority ethnic group. Not only were the Sinhalese under-represented, but only about half the Sinhalese in the police professed Buddhism. Equally important in setting the force apart was the strong representation of Malays, who accounted for only 0.3 per cent of the population, but for nearly one-third of policemen. Many Malays were descendants of men first brought to Sri Lanka as soldiers in the earlier days of colonial rule. After the disbandment of their regiment, the police became a customary occupation for Malays.

The ethnic and religious composition of the force varied greatly according to rank. A majority of the small number of officers, those whose rank was superintendent, assistant superintendent or inspector, were British or Burgher. Malays made up between forty and fifty per cent of sergeants. The group least represented in proportion to its population, Sinhalese Buddhists, accounted for an even smaller proportion of sergeants than they did of the force as a whole.

Campbell was aware of the disadvantages of having so few Sinhalese in the police, especially in higher posts. Soon after arriving in Sri Lanka he pointed out that 'one of the great wants in the Ceylon Police is the want of officers in the rank of Inspectors who have family or personal influence among the native community.'[41] In order to fill this lacuna he hired three Sinhalese 'of good family'. They were not required to wear normal police uniform, or to cut their hair short, both of which were considered demeaning. The experiment was not a great success, though all three stayed in the force for some time.[42]

Despite Campbell's efforts, there remained a general dissatisfaction with the 'criminal state' of the island. Judicial statistics, which were compiled more systematically as time went by, continued to show a high number of offences. In the late 1880s there was a spate of burglaries in Colombo. A. H. Giles, an officer in the Bengal police, was called to Sri Lanka in 1888 to investigate policing in the island. Though his subsequent report did not directly criticize Campbell, it did attack the overall structure of the police and judiciary.[43] Giles wanted to see the judicial and revenue branches of government drawn more closely together on the Indian model. Above all, he sought to bring the headmen, or 'village police', fully into a police structure which would cover the entire island. Although Giles's suggestions concerning the judiciary were not adopted, his report served as the basis for police reform.

Campbell and his higher-ranking colleagues were forced to retire.[44] All were over fifty-five years old. Giles was critical of the stagnation in the upper ranks of the force; of four provincial superintendents, two had held their position since 1871 and the other two since 1873. He wanted talented members of the civil service to take temporary appointments in the police, but though agreeing in principle, the government could not spare officers from revenue and judicial work.[45] In any case, the police did not offer a high enough salary for any but the most inexperienced official. Instead, young gentlemen were hired from England. Unfortunately their quality did not prove to be high.[46]

The organization of policing was fundamentally changed.[47] The new system, which was implemented in 1892, took away from the

Inspector-General direct control over the force. Henceforth, he commanded only the police in the city of Colombo. Elsewhere government agents took charge, with the Inspector-General retaining responsibility for promotions and discipline. As headmen were also under the authority of government agents, it was hoped that the two groups would begin to work together.

Magistrates were given a more active role. Giles's proposal to make them subservient to government agents was rejected, but they were given some responsibility for supervising the work of both the regular police and the headmen, who were now designated the 'rural police'. For the first time headmen were supposed to report all crime directly to the magistrate, who was in turn required to record the case even if there was no specific person accused. Magistrates also had to state their reasons for dismissing a case. Previously no distinction had been made between acquittals, cases which were dismissed because there was no evidence that the accused had committed the crime, and cases dismissed because no crime had been committed.

The precise organization of the rural police varied from province to province. In some districts revenue officials made energetic efforts to turn headmen into active policemen. In the Western Province forty-four village sergeants were hired and each was paid fifteen rupees a month.[48] Though this salary was the same as that of a third-class constable, the lowest police rank, village sergeants were much better off because they served in their own localities, were not subject to discipline, and had other income. It was their duty to report all crime in their areas, and to investigate serious cases. After a few years this scheme was pronounced a failure. A. R. Dawson, the Government Agent, noted in his diary that 'the work of the village sergeants is simply ludicrous. They do nothing but draw their monthly salaries.'[49] So the position was abolished, and official efforts were concentrated on unpaid police *vidanes*, whose jurisdictions covered several hamlets or a village.[50] Each *vidane* was given forms in triplicate on which to record information about crimes. A fund was established to reward headmen for good police work, but it proved difficult to manage properly. If rewards were given for keeping a village free of crime, then cases were suppressed by headmen. If it was known that a bad record led to the dismissal of a headman, then his enemies reported false cases.[51]

In many districts headmen could not or would not undertake their new duties. In Kandyan districts there had not previously been a specific class of headman assigned police duties. The headmen now made responsible thought police work beneath their dignity.[52] Another obstacle to the smooth functioning of the system was the geographical restrictions on each headman's authority; investigations often stopped on the border of an administrative division. Perhaps more serious was the failure to understand, or accept, bureaucratic mores which were at the centre of the system. The government tried to implement a 'scientific' approach to crime, but despite the exhortations of officials, headmen did not report crimes promptly. A decade after the reforms were implemented, officials, especially in Kandyan districts, still complained that the new system was confusing and not understood by those who were supposed to work it.[53]

There were few changes in the duties and conduct of the regular police in the years after Campbell's departure. Outside Colombo the force was theoretically under the control of government agents who had many other duties and usually spared little time for the police. Any *esprit de corps* the police had possessed disappeared.[54] One consequence was a significant increase in violence within the force.[55]

Attempts were made to improve the public image of the police. More Sinhalese Buddhists were hired; by 1900 they made up more than one-quarter of the force. Recruitment was also restricted to certain castes. Campbell had allowed low-caste Sinhalese to join, but L. F. Knollys, the new Inspector-General, accepted only Goyigamas, Karavas, Duravas and Salagamas.[56] After 1898 the latter two of these castes were also excluded, a fact which led to protests from élite Salagamas when it became generally known.[57] These changes did not lead to any change in popular perceptions of the police, partially because there were still few Sinhalese officers. In 1905 E. B. Alexander, the Superintendent for the Southern Province, admitted that the police were not good at detection. He noted that 'officers of other nationalities, no matter how capable, have little chance at getting at secrets of a Sinhalese village.'[58] The problem was identical to that identified by Campbell forty years earlier.

There is little evidence that the new system led to increased co-operation between the regular police and headmen. No effective mechanism was established to link the two groups. Putting both the police and headmen under the control of government agents did not ensure that they worked together. Headmen continued to feel socially superior to the regular police.[59] In 1904 Henry Blake, the Governor, decided that the system was inadequate. He wrote to the Secretary of State for the Colonies that 'the police system is unsatisfactory and the regular police inefficient, if not corrupt, while for police purposes the unpaid headmen are equally untrustworthy.'[60]

In 1906 the system of policing was again reorganized.[61] Overall control was returned to the Inspector-General, and for the first time the jurisdiction of the regular police was extended to cover entire districts. Many new rural police stations were opened in the Western, Southern and North-Western Provinces. In these 'policed provinces' crime was to be reported in the first instance to headmen who would in turn notify the police of serious offences. The system was not intended to supersede the police role of headmen, but to complement and support it. Minor crimes, including petty assault and the simple theft of articles worth less than twenty rupees, remained the responsibility of complainants.

Many headmen regarded the establishment of police stations with jurisdiction over their localities as a challenge to their own authority. For at least a decade after 1906 relations between the police and headmen were often poor.[62] Many of those first placed in charge of rural posts proved unsuitable, and were dismissed for abuse of power. Despite these difficulties, by around 1920 most headmen co-operated to some extent with the police.[63]

Official attempts in the late nineteenth and early twentieth centuries to reform and strengthen the police duties of headmen were carried out at a time when the overall influence of headmen was on the wane. New social groups, clerks, carters, traders, teachers and notaries, challenged their authority. In Kandyan districts headmen had difficulty dealing with immigrants from the Low Country.[64] In coastal areas social mobility led some lower castes and classes to assert themselves against headmen.[65] In most districts there were factions opposed to local headmen. The introduction of the police into rural areas further hastened the decline of headmen as a class. Police constables and sergeants tended to address headmen in disrespectful terms, and the possibility of such humiliations dissuaded many of the more wealthy villagers from accepting the post of headman.

Under the energetic leadership of H. L. Dowbiggin, Inspector-General from 1913 to 1937, the police gained sophistication which may have given them a relative advantage over some law-breakers.[66] The force expanded, working conditions improved, and for the first time a limited capacity for detection was developed. Use was made of modern inventions, including fingerprinting, photography, automobiles and telephones. By systematically analysing crime reports, the police were able to 'map' outbreaks of crime and gain clues to the identity of the perpetrators. Fowl thieves, burglars, and gang robbers were detected by this method. Night patrols were started in some rural areas, and they sometimes caught burglars or cattle thieves red-handed.

The force also became more ethnically representative of the population. The proportion of Sinhalese policemen passed the fifty per cent mark in the 1920s, and continued to rise thereafter. The numbers of Malays and Burghers in the force remained greater than their strength in the population as a whole, but to a much lesser extent than earlier. For political reasons British officers continued to hold about one-half of the senior posts.

Government Policy towards the Courts

There was a widespread feeling as early as the 1840s that the judicial system suffered from too much technicality and formality. This view dominated government policy towards the courts in the later nineteenth century. Officials sought to simplify the judicial process and clarify the criminal law. The ensuing reforms were implemented piecemeal and did not fundamentally change the system, but procedure was considerably more summary by 1900 than it had been fifty years earlier.

An important innovation in judicial policy was set in motion in 1871 by the passing of legislation which authorized the Governor to establish village tribunals in designated districts.[67] The name of the new institution was misleading, for each tribunal covered many settlements. The new courts were designed to relieve police courts of petty offences.[68] They normally tried cases to which only 'natives' were parties. Sinhalese, of status equivalent to that of a *mudaliyar* or *ratemahatmaya*, were appointed as presidents of the tribunals. The jurisdiction of the new courts was limited to petty theft and assault, malicious damage to property, cattle trespass and the violation of rules made by local government in matters such as irrigation. The president and councillors were supposed to encourage an amicable settlement, but if they failed the president could convict wrongdoers and fine them up to twenty rupees. Convictions could be appealed, not to any judicial authority, but to the government agent and then the Governor. The tribunals were intended to provide a way for rural residents to settle disputes without legal formalities. Unlike all other courts, proceedings were in Sinhala, not English.

The idea of village tribunals was attractive to many British officials who thought that they were resurrecting ancient village institutions.[69] Other officials, especially those who observed the operation of the tribunals in the Low Country, were more sceptical.[70] The Assistant Government Agent at Matara agreed that the establishment of village tribunals had led to a decrease in the number of police court cases, but asked 'what good end is obtained by merely removing the scene of litigation from one set of courts to another, and doubling the amount of litigation in the process, and how it is supposed that by increasing litigation two-fold the peace and harmony of the district is secured, and litigation robbed of all the rancour and bad feelings it engenders in the ordinary courts?'[71] In 1904 another official described the tribunals as 'mere schools for litigators'.[72] Despite such criticisms, the British found these courts useful and by the end of the century they had jurisdiction over most rural areas. It was certainly cheaper for government to try cases in village tribunals than in police courts.

When village tribunals were first established it was felt by some officials that they would reduce the power of headmen. It was argued that many disputes which were previously resolved by headmen would be taken to the new courts.[73] In fact village tribunal presidents were often relatives or allies of chief headmen, who usually controlled appointments of other headmen. Over twenty years after the introduction of village tribunals the Government Agent at Kurunagala discovered that presidents refused to accept any criminal plaints not endorsed by the village headman.[74] Thus the headman had a veto over criminal prosecutions for the petty offences over which village tribunals had exclusive jurisdiction. Foreseeing this enhancement of the authority of the traditional élite, parts of the upwardly-mobile Low Country population, including many Karavas from Moratuva, opposed the establishment of tribunals.[75]

The 1880s saw a major effort to clarify the law and simplify court procedure, both of which were seen as essential prerequisites for improving the efficiency of the judicial system. The law of criminal procedure was reformulated and brought together in one ordinance, and a penal code partly based on Indian law was adopted.[76] The intention of this legislation, which was implemented in 1885, was to reduce technicality and speed up justice.

The office of justice of the peace was abolished. Its functions and those of the police magistrate were consolidated in the office of police magistrate. The complainant no longer needed to make a distinction between petty and serious crime; all criminal charges were now brought before the same official. The magistrate decided whether to try a case summarily or to set in motion the process of committing it to a superior court. He was also given the power to convict on any charge within his jurisdiction, even if another offence was originally specified on the charge sheet.

The penal code listed all criminal offences, thereby eliminating the position of Roman-Dutch criminal law as the residuary criminal law of the island. Judicial officials were given more guidance as to punishment than had been available previously, but a great deal of discretion remained. The maximum penalty for an offence was set higher than the maximum punishment that the court which usually tried the crime was empowered to inflict. For instance, the maximum period of imprisonment for simple theft was three years, much longer than the six months term which a police court could now impose. If the magistrate before whom an accusation of theft was initially brought felt that three years imprisonment was appropriate, he had to commit the case to the Supreme Court.

Humanitarianism also influenced the reforms. Hangings were henceforth carried out behind prison walls; the public spectacle which executions had provided came to an end. The frequency and severity of corporal punishment was also reduced. James Longden, who was Governor from 1878 to 1883, thought that 'the number of lashes allowed is positively inhuman', and that 'the physical condition of most natives makes this a more serious punishment than in England.'[77] The power to inflict this punishment was taken away from police courts, and district courts were limited to ordering a total of twenty-five lashes. These reforms were the culmination of a gradual movement throughout the nineteenth century towards a decrease in the use and severity of corporal punishment.[78] This trend was partially reversed in the years after 1885 because many officials felt that the prison regime was too lenient and that flogging was the only effective deterrent to crime. In the 1890s magistrates were given the power to order corporal punishment as punishment for specific offences.[79]

Though flogging was restricted, the length of sentences which lower courts were empowered to impose was doubled. Police courts could impose sentences of up to six months, and district courts of up to two years. These changes were aimed at speeding up trials and saving government expenditure by allowing some cases which would have previously been tried in the Supreme Court moved to district courts, and by having other cases tried by police courts instead of district courts. The increased use of lower courts met with the general approval of officials. It was felt that prompt punishment 'has a better deterrent effect than a sentence of longer imprisonment.'[80]

In the 1890s there was periodic tinkering with judicial policy. Officials felt that the procedure for trying criminal cases was still too complicated. In 1892 magistrates were given the power not to record testimony when the sentence was not to exceed imprisonment for one month or a fine of twenty-five rupees.[81] Another ordinance allowed a magistrate to try summarily cases which he would normally commit to the district court, if he himself was also the district judge.[82]

A more ambitious change sought to require complainants to present their cases orally to the magistrate, instead of through a written statement composed by an intermediary. Since the establishment of British rule certain persons, called outdoor proctors and petition-drawers, had made a living by helping people in their dealings with the administration, including the courts.[83] The outdoor proctor or tout sought business and acted as an agent for petition-drawers and proctors. The petition-drawer acted as an unofficial lawyer. A potential litigant sometimes went through three persons: the tout, petition-drawer and proctor. Proctors had to give up to twenty to fifty per cent of their fees for custom received through petition-drawers.[84] Not that an official proctor was necessarily called upon to take up the case; often clients received only the less expensive advice of petition-drawers, who drew up as many as ninety per cent of all criminal plaints.[85]

Petition-drawers and outdoor proctors were often regarded with distaste by officials, some of whom blamed them for fostering perjury and false cases.[86] One official described outdoor proctors as men who 'hover about the streets leading to the courts, like so many ill-omened birds of prey, from early morning till late at night, and who have no trade or legitimate calling but who subsist by swindling.'[87] Many officials believed that 'as a rule, men of inferior or no education and of low morals resort to petition-drawing as a means of livelihood.'[88] Part of this negative image may be attributed to the general British dislike of South Asians who had acquired some knowledge of English and who followed some Western customs, but who had not fully assimilated the values of an English gentleman. Nevertheless, petition-drawers did not have a particularly good reputation among Sinhalese. The Buddhist-managed *Lakrivikirana* divided them into two categories.[89] The smaller group was literate in English, Sinhala and Tamil, and performed its duties well. The members of the larger group charged lower fees but had a poor knowledge of English. The relationship between these men and their clients was likened to that between a cobra and its prey.

When the government, with the intention of circumventing petition-drawers, proposed legislation to require all criminal plaints to be presented personally, some judicial officials argued that not all petition-drawers were dishonest, and that they served a function in the judicial system because there were too many complaints for magistrates to settle without help.[90] The fees charged by lawyers were said to be too high for ordinary people to afford. One senior official believed that the legislation would in any case fail in its object of circumventing intermediaries: 'Witnesses will still be tutored. The Magistrate will record the complaint in the words of the party — as he has been instructed by the outdoor proctor — and the case will then go on, subject to the same conditions as at present.'[91] As an alternative a licensing system was proposed. Despite this opposition, the government went ahead and enacted legislation which required magistrates to hear all complaints orally.[92] A Sinhalese member of the Legislative Council thought that magistrates would have difficulties carrying out the spirit of the legislation: 'A crowd appears in the Police Court in the morning and unless plaints are presented and the names called out it will be somewhat difficult for the Magistrate to ascertain who are the people who have come to offer plaints and it will depend on some minor Court official or the peons as to who are admitted to the precincts of the Court.'[93] The Attorney-General replied that the magistrate could stand before the crowd and shout for the complainants to come forward and then interview the men who had done so.[94]

Other changes in judicial policy at the end of the nineteenth century were the result of a shift in European legal thought which placed more emphasis on the identity of the convicted person, as opposed to the actual offence, when determining punishment. Legislation was passed in 1891 which sought to differentiate between first-time and repeating offenders. Magistrates and judges were given the power to release upon probation for good conduct first offenders who had committed an offence not punishable by more than three years imprisonment.[95] The legislation was felt to be a success, for in 1898 the types of crimes covered by it were expanded.[96] Around the turn of the century about twelve per cent of persons sentenced to imprisonment were released under this law.[97]

While provision was made to treat first offenders leniently, other legislation was passed to ensure that 'habitual criminals' received harsher punishment. This category was first defined officially in 1894. Legislation was passed which required that persons who had been sentenced to an aggregate of more than three months imprisonment during the past seven years be committed to a superior court when charged with another offence. The definition of an habitual criminal was altered in 1897 and again in 1899, when the time limit was dropped and two or more convictions with an aggregate of imprisonment of over six months became the standard.[98] Habitual criminals were also required to report once a month to a police station after they were released. In addition, district courts were given the power to imprison these men for up to four years. Thus the maximum term of imprisonment which could be inflicted without a jury quadrupled between 1884 and 1899.

In the twentieth century the focus of government policy shifted from the judiciary to the police, and few changes were made in the structure or procedure of the courts. The main innovation was the gradual increase in the number of Sri Lankan magistrates and judges.[99] After around 1910 the proportion of Sri Lankans in the civil service, which had long hovered around ten per cent, began to increase. Most were routed into judicial rather than revenue appointments. The proportion of Sri Lankan judges received a further boost in 1923 when it was decided to fill most posts from the local bar, and by 1930 eighteen of forty-two appointments were held by lawyers. These men were thoroughly anglicized, and did not necessarily run their courts differently from their British counterparts.

The Colonial Administration in Practice

Despite the widespread impression that many court cases were either false or trivial, the judicial system was not regarded as illegitimate. Far from shunning the courts, Sri Lankans made what very often seemed to the British excessive use of them. During the early years of British rule many officials observed that there was a high level of both civil and criminal litigation.[100] The earliest comprehensive statistics, which were compiled in the 1860s, indicated that about seven or eight per cent of the population were accused of some criminal offence each year.[101] Not all of these charges may be taken as evidence of 'litigiousness', for one-quarter to one-third of prosecutions were for regulatory offences, such as gambling and tax evasion, which were normally prosecuted by the police or other government agencies.

The overall level of criminal litigation dropped in the late nineteenth century. This trend was largely the result of changes in government policy. In 1872, when a fifteen cent stamp fee for criminal plaints was instituted, the number of police court cases immediately fell by one-third.[102] The simplification of criminal procedure also may have discouraged false cases because defendants were put to less inconvenience when the charge had little or no evidence to substantiate it. In the 1880s and 1890s around five to six per cent of the population were accused annually, about one-third of them in village tribunals.[103] There was a large increase in the total number of criminal charges in the early twentieth century, but most of these offences were minor regulatory infractions, such as traffic and safety violations. A large proportion of this increase was also accounted for by the new offence of failing to send children to school, which in 1920 accounted for nearly one-quarter of all criminal cases.

When one considers that relatively few women were accused, and that a large proportion of the population were children, it is clear that a remarkably high number of adult males, around one in five, were brought before the courts each year. If one assumes that there was an average of one complainant and four witnesses for each two persons accused, over one-half of all men appeared in a criminal court as a defendant, complainant or witness every year. Many others were involved in civil suits or attended court as spectators.

Officials compared the judicial statistics with those of India and found that there were proportionately several times more cases in Sri Lanka.[104] This difference cannot be explained by a higher level of prosecutions for regulatory offences. Sri Lankans instituted charges of crimes against the person and property many times more frequently than did Indians. There was no consensus about whether or not this high rate reflected a higher amount of crime, or if the difference could be attributed to false cases in Sri Lanka or the failure to report crime in India. Some of the difference may be accounted for by the greater number of court sites and judicial officials in proportion to population and area in Sri Lanka than in India.

Both the official and non-official élites believed that many charges were not true, but there was no agreement about the proportion of false cases, or about the number of crimes which were never reported. There were also differences of opinion about the degree of malice involved. A minority believed that a large number of cases were based on minor grievances, and that complainants rushed to court in the passion of the moment.[105] According to this view, these cases were dropped when tempers died down. The courts served as a safety-valve, acting as an alternative to violence when emotions ran high.

The more general view was less charitable, placing more emphasis on the belief that Sri Lankans habitually lied in court. Many officials believed that a large number of false cases were prosecuted, and that many were successful. H. W. Gillman, a district judge, believed that 'natives find both profit and amusement in bringing false cases, and that they have a natural talent for lying.'[106] J. H. Eaton, a magistrate, declared: 'It almost goes without saying that there is hardly a case that comes before our courts, to which the natives are parties, in which this crime [perjury] is not more or less freely indulged.'[107] Henry Blake, who was Governor from 1903 to 1907, believed that 'in the majority of cases tried in Ceylon the evidence is unsatisfactory, as there is not alone an utter disregard for truth, but an extraordinary ingenuity of invention.'[108] Another official thought that less than ten per cent of the criminal plaints filed at Negombo were true.[109]

The available statistics offer some support for the allegations that there was much perjury. Not only was the number of court cases higher in Sri Lanka than in India, but the proportion of convictions to cases was much lower.[110] In the 1860s, less than ten per cent of accused persons were convicted. Thereafter the conviction rate steadily increased, reaching twenty-five per cent or more early in the twentieth century. This trend was partially because of increased efficiency on the part of police and judicial officials, but also because an increasing proportion of accused persons were charged with regulatory offences, for which the conviction rate was higher than for offences against the person or property, which were usually prosecuted privately. The conviction rate for these latter offences rose from around five per cent in the 1860s to fifteen per cent in the twentieth century.

One reason for the low conviction rate was that a large number of cases were dismissed without trial, sometimes because the complainant did not follow through with the prosecution. In the first half of the ninteenth century only one-fifth to one-quarter of all criminal cases were decided on the merits of the evidence.[111] Around the turn of the century, when the rate of litigation was lower and officials were less willing to allow complainants to drop charges, about one-half of all cases came to trial. Those which were dropped were not necessarily false. Many were settled out of court. It is also possible that magistrates gave defendants the benefit of the doubt when in the preliminary inquiry both sides produced witnesses who appeared unreliable.

Colonial officials put forth two related explanations for the prevalence of perjury. One blamed the inherent 'litigious' nature of Sri Lankans, and in particular the Sinhalese. The other pointed to 'inappropriate' institutions of government, arguing that the judicial system was too advanced for a backward people. The first view was expressed in its extreme form by a frustrated magistrate: 'Love of litigation is hereditary with the people, and is the very breath of their nostrils. Wealth is only desirable in so far as it enables them to indulge in litigation, and the height of their ambition is to succeed in a case, especially if thereby their enemy is punished.'[112] In its more moderate form 'litigiousness' was linked with government policy. British officials admitted that their institutions were not working, and attributed this failure to social conditions. Some hoped that education would in time solve the problem.[113] Others proposed bringing the executive and judicial branches of government closer together, as in India, in the hope that a more authoritarian system would generate more respect.[114] This course was rejected partially out of inertia, and partially because it would have been strongly opposed by the English-educated Sri Lankan élite, who held judicial posts and dominated the legal profession, but who were excluded from the executive branch of government. They rightly feared that they would not be appointed to judicial posts which carried executive responsibilities.

That Sri Lankans were involved in much litigation and that the judicial system was based on alien principles cannot be denied, but contemporaries did not successfully explain the link between these two facts. If Sri Lankans were inherently 'litigious', the system of administration would not matter. If the institutions were inappropriate, why were they not ignored? To assert that both litigiousness and inappropriate institutions were the causes of perjury was tautological, for the tendency towards litigation was explained by the inappropriate institutions, and the inappropriateness of the institutions by the fact of too much litigation.

Late nineteenth-century judicial reforms did streamline court procedure, but they had little effect on the way in which the administration of law and order was popularly perceived. The widespread perjury, especially on the part of accusers, demonstrated that government institutions enjoyed little moral authority. Some British officials hoped that the judicial system would gradually gain acceptance and function as intended, but there was little opportunity for Sri Lankans to observe the principles which lay behind the rule of law. Officials did not articulate these values in a way understandable to the people.

It was widely believed that middle and low-level government employees accepted gifts in return for favours. There is much evidence that constables and sergeants of the regular police unofficially augmented their incomes.[115] In Colombo policemen often took advantage of municipal health, safety and traffic regulations in order to 'tax' carters, rickshaw drivers and others who made their living on the streets of the capital, and in the twentieth century bus drivers regularly bribed the police. Many officials and others believed that police evidence before the courts was unreliable.[116] Accusations were also made against the police for active complicity in crime, but proof was difficult to come by. In 1879 Campbell, the Inspector-General, became convinced that the Navalapitiya police were regularly involved in burglaries.[117] Neither were the higher ranks immune. Inspectors, some of them Englishmen, were dismissed from time to time for accepting bribes or for other dubious practices.[118]

Headmen did not consistently function as exponents of the rule of law when carrying out their duties. Their positions were often used for their own benefit. Few headmen willingly enforced the law against kinfolk or other allies. Although many officials and newspapers proposed that they be paid a modest salary, only the chief headmen received official remuneration.[119] When headmen's posts became vacant, many were sold by the chief headmen to the highest bidder.[120] Village headmen used their control over minor administrative matters, especially the threat of reporting the illicit cultivation of *chenas* or the cutting of timber on Crown land, to receive a steady unofficial income.[121] Despite the exhortations of the British, they were very often reluctant to carry out police duties which brought them no profit.

Another obstacle to headmen serving as representatives of the principles behind the legal administration was their own participation in crime. Occasionally a chief headman was discovered to be involved in organized extortion, requiring services and gifts from the headmen and people under his jurisdiction beyond those which were customarily expected.[122] Lower-level headmen were frequently involved in various offences, especially cattle stealing.[123] A particularly serious problem was the protection of criminal relations by headmen.[124] When headmen were put in the position of choosing between protecting relations and carrying out their duties they chose the former.

Neither were judicial and court officials free from the taint of corruption. Although there is no direct evidence that officials at the judicial secretariat in Colombo accepted bribes for dismissing or weakening criminal cases prosecuted in the superior courts, there were persons who claimed to act as agents for such transactions.[125] The taking of bribes by petty officials was more prevalent. The Queen's Advocate, Richard Morgan, noted in his diary upon the death of the interpreter at the Kalutara courts that 'he was a very worthy man, and, though an interpreter of a court, perfectly honest.'[126] In some courts a payment was needed to see the magistrate, or to ensure that one's case was heard promptly.[127] S. M. Burrows, when Government Agent at Kurunagala, described the Police Court clerks there as 'utterly corrupt'.[128] Even physical access to a court hearing was not guaranteed. One magistrate asserted that weak complainants sometimes had their cases dismissed because they were unable to push through the crowd which blocked the doorway into the court.[129]

Corruption was not normally a problem among judges and magistrates, but in the early and mid-nineteenth century many of these officials were incompetent or excessively eccentric.[130] Even in the late nineteenth century few were talented and hardworking men. Sir John Phear, who was Chief Justice for a short time in the late 1870s, felt that many magistrates 'manifest as a rule want of knowledge of the practice of the Courts, of the business of their office, and of the law which they have to conform and carry out.'[131] In 1884 the Governor, Arthur Gordon, wrote that 'District Judges are those who are too stupid or incapable to hold Revenue Offices.'[132] Ten years later the Attorney-General noted that judicial officers were chosen 'because considered unfit for the revenue branch of the service'.[133] It was clearly the desire of young, ambitious civil servants to receive revenue as opposed to judicial appointments, for career prospects were much better in the revenue department. The higher administrative posts in the colony were usually held by members of the civil service, but the top judicial positions were normally filled from the professional bar.[134]

Leaving aside the question of the relative competence of revenue and judicial officials, many magistrates, especially those in small towns, were young, inexperienced, and had very little knowledge of the island and its peoples. It was widely believed that inexperienced magistrates were taken in by false evidence and relied too heavily on interpreters and clerks.[135] In theory civil service recruits were supposed to pass an examination in law and a first language test and then be attached to a senior police magistrate for six months. In practice the demands of the administration made the latter appointment impractical. Sometimes a young civil servant would be appointed to a subordinate revenue position immediately after passing the first law examination. Two or three years later he might suddenly be appointed a full-time magistrate, even though by that time he had probably forgotten all of the law which he had learnt.[136]

More subtle than corruption, but just as damaging to the judicial process, were variations in court procedure which must have seemed arbitrary to many Sri Lankans. Magistrates were frequently transferred, and since they had little common training and virtually no supervision, they ran their courts differently. Some spoke the local languages; others relied exclusively on court interpreters. There were magistrates who appear to have relished ordering corporal punishment, but a minority thought it inappropriate and seldom included flogging as part of a sentence. Some officials relied on the evidence of headmen; others believed that the intrigues of headmen were a major cause of crime.[137] The reputation of the individual magistrate was an important part of the popular image of a court, and this personal factor obscured the theoretical, legal consistency. One indication of the differences of approach was provided in 1899 by F. R. Ellis, the Government Agent of the Western Province.[138] He compared the judicial returns of two magistrates who had jurisdiction over adjacent districts which were similar in their police arrangements and social composition. One magistrate had declared fifty-one per cent of all cases false. The other had classified only sixteen per cent of charges in this manner. The proportions of convictions varied by nearly the same degree.

In the Supreme Court the guilt or innocence of the accused was decided not by the judge but the jury. Again, there was much variation in attitudes. L. B. Clarence, a Supreme Court judge, felt that juries often reached the wrong verdict and that they were inappropriate for Sri Lanka. He argued that issues of fact were more difficult than in Britain because there was much false testimony and also because 'precision of observation with regard to time and distance is quite unknown to a large proportion of witnesses.'[139] In addition, it was difficult to find impartial jurors. Among the Sinhalese and Tamils, Clarence argued, convictions were difficult when the accused had a position of influence. Burghers presented another problem: 'With regard to the Eurasians, it is notoriously difficult, even upon the strongest evidence to induce a jury, in which the Eurasians are in a majority, to convict a Eurasian.'[140] Clarence also asserted that cultural and language differences could produce misunderstandings. European jurors know little about Sri Lankans, while Sinhalese and Tamil jurors did not always know English well enough to understand the judge.

Some of these reservations about juries were shared by other officials, but the local bar would have objected strenuously to attempts to abolish or restrict the jury system.[141] Supreme Court judges often had little experience in Sri Lanka, and were unfamiliar with local customs and culture. Juries served as a safeguard against this ignorance. Though jury service was regarded as an important right by many members of the Sri Lankan élite, it was considered an irksome duty by the British planting community, and in order to reduce the burden of service the size of juries was twice reduced during the late nineteenth century.[142]

The occasional release of prisoners due to technical errors or on points of law was another practice which reinforced a sense of unpredictability about judicial decisions. Sri Lankans did not view some of the reasons behind the overturning of convictions as just. An 1853 Supreme Court decision which set aside a conviction on the charge of 'taking forcible and unlawful possession of the product of the Complainant's garden' may serve as an example.[143] The proclamation under which the conviction had been obtained specified that in order to constitute an offence such an action had to be carried out 'without the authority of a competent Magistrate'. The conviction was reversed because the magistrate had failed to mention on the charge sheet that the alleged offence had taken place without such lawful authority. On another occasion, Gordon was outraged when a Supreme Court judge released some prisoners because the magistrate had incorrectly described 'theft of cattle' as 'cattle stealing' on the charge sheet.[144] These decisions may well have encouraged people to view criminal litigation as a game of skill.

Senior British officials did not always fully accept the rule of law. A riot case in 1902 provides an example.[145] Several men were convicted by a jury even though the evidence which was laid before the court to support the charge was inconsistent. The judge publicly rebuked the jury, and wrote to the Governor, J. West Ridgeway, asking him to pardon the convicted men. Supported by

the Government Agent, Ridgeway refused to do so on the ground
that it was commonly believed in the district that the men were
guilty. Over a year after the trial the mother of one of the
convicted men sent a petition to Edward VII, quoting the remarks
of the judge. The Colonial Office asked Ridgeway for more
details, including a transcript of the trial testimony. Ridgeway
strongly resisted freeing the men, though he admitted that the
evidence placed before the court had not demonstrated their
guilt. His successor, Blake, was also convinced that the men were
guilty, but agreed to release them.

Popular Ideas of Justice

Vijaya Samaraweera has pointed out that the ideal viewpoint for
understanding the colonial legal system is that of the 'typical
litigant'.[146] He argues that the judicial system was established on
principles alien to Sri Lanka, and that the use of English
prevented people from speaking directly to magistrates. He
further asserts that during the nineteenth century litigants did not
understand the way courts worked and were in awe of their
proceedings, and that the intermediaries between litigants and
justice, lawyers, court officials and petition-drawers, had little
sympathy with or understanding for the average Sri Lankan.
     This interpretation, which broadly parallels Bernard Cohn's
argument that the Indian judicial system was manipulated
because of culture conflict between British and Indian legal
norms, does not explain why Sri Lankans used the courts so
often. It also fails to take into account the fact that a large
number of men were familiar with court proceedings. Although
some of the more sophisticated lawyers may well have been
culturally alienated from the mass of the people, these practi-
tioners charged high fees and served only the élite. Less successful
proctors, petition-drawers and to a lesser extent court officials
were dependent for their livelihoods on establishing a reputation
for effectiveness. Those who did not fulfil their clients' wishes
lost income. Samaraweera cites Leonard Woolf's novel *The
Village in the Jungle* to support his characterization of the
average litigant as ignorant of court procedure, but Woolf's
novel was set in an impoverished, dying and atypical village in the
dry zone. In fact, the complainant in the case Samaraweera cites
was knowledgeable about court procedure. It was the defendant,
an unusually ignorant peasant, who was in awe of the courtroom.

J. Vijayatunga's novel *Grass For My Feet*, set in a Low Country village fifteen kilometres from Galle, portrays more typical villagers who were familiar with the proceedings and personalities of the Galle courts.

It is not my intention to dispute Samaraweera's assertion that the newly-imposed colonial judicial system was alien to Sri Lankan values, but to explain how, in spite of this, the system proved popular. It is necessary to show more precisely the link between 'culture conflict' and the operation of the legal system; otherwise the scholar in effect falls back on more subtle restatements of the litigiousness-inappropriate institutions tautology put forth by colonial officials.

It has already been noted that Kandyan and Roman-Dutch criminal law were only briefly valid in British courts. No drastic changes resulted from their fall into disuse, for there was broad agreement between British and Sri Lankan norms as to what constituted crime. Theft, robbery, assault, homicide and cheating were condemned by all. In the words of an official who examined British records dating from soon after the conquest of the Kandyan Kingdom: 'The most noticeable fact which strikes a reader of the minutes of the Board of Kandyan Commissioners, is the remarkable similarity between English ideas respecting various offences . . . and those of the Kandyans.'[147]

As in all societies, there were some disparities between the official definition of crime and the views held by a large number of people. Not all of these differences were primarily due to cultural confrontations between British and Sri Lankan values. Coffee stealing from large plantations provides an example. A police officer reported that 'in some villages the young men are brought up from their childhood with the idea that according to ancient Kandyan custom the highland on which the [coffee] estate has been opened belongs by right of inheritance to the village below and in helping themselves they are only taking the rent of the ground.'[148] In contrast, the British regarded coffee stealing as a serious crime which threatened the prosperity of the colony. This difference of opinion was not caused by cultural misunderstanding but by social conflict. At issue was the right of the state to sell forest land to British planters. The villagers and the British agreed in principle that 'theft' was wrong, but differing conceptions of property rights resulted in differing opinions about whether or not the taking of plantation produce was really theft. Disputes between the state and the peasantry over the use of common land are not confined to colonial societies.

Other crimes which were not accepted as wrong by large numbers of people included tax evasion, gambling, the illicit sale and consumption of alcohol, and the use of Crown land for felling timber, *chena* cultivation and graphite mining.[149] None of these offences reflected any general clash between East and West. Examples of clashes between the state and large social groups over similar economic and social issues may be found in many periods of European history. Culture conflict over alcohol and gambling was probably stronger between those influenced by Buddhist revivalist ideas and the common people than between Sri Lankans and the British.

There were however some differences between British and Sri Lankan definitions of crime. Some of these had to do with the importance of status distinctions. Verbal abuse was traditionally a crime among the Sinhalese, but the courts stopped trying this offence in the 1820s in the Low Country and a decade later in Kandyan districts. It is possible that many cases of petty assault were instituted as retaliation for verbal abuse. More generally, colonial criminal law made little allowance for variations in caste status. Under Kandyan law it was not an offence to kill a high-caste woman who had had sexual relations with a low-caste man.[150] In 1873, after a case of murder in which the victim was a Rodi, the Assistant Government Agent at Nuvara Eliya commented that 'the victim was of the lowest caste, to which they [the Sinhalese] clearly believe that the principles of natural justice and law are not applicable.'[151] In the Kandyan Kingdom status was also a consideration when determining punishment.[152] Many Sinhalese viewed flogging as suitable for low-caste persons; it was considered much more demeaning if administered to a man of high caste. Although the failure of the courts to take into account Sri Lankan ideas about status may have led some people to experience injustice, it scarcely explains the extensive perjury and high level of litigation.

Punishments administered by the colonial courts were more inflexible than those available through indigenous judicial procedures, but the change was neither sudden nor drastic. Not only were the standard nineteenth-century British sanctions of fine, imprisonment and whipping commonly used during the eighteenth century, but the early British courts also punished offenders with branding, the pillory, banishment and the confiscation of property, all familiar punishments in Dutch and Kandyan times. The main difference was that restitution, often viewed as appropriate by the Sinhalese, was not possible through the colonial court system. Conciliation and compromise were other important indigenous principles that carried official sanction in pre-British times but which were not accommodated by the formal institutions set up by the British. In many parts of the Kandyan Kingdom both civil and criminal disputes could be taken to a *gamsabhava*, or village council which attempted to bring about an amicable settlement. In the Low Country headmen often played a similar role. Restitution could be required as a part of a punishment. Alternatively it could be the result of negotiation between the complainant and defendant. In the Kandyan Kingdom a man convicted for assault could be handed over to the complainant to be beaten, and thefts were often resolved by the return of the stolen property, plus further compensation. In 1829 a convicted prisoner petitioned that he should have been allowed to free himself from a charge of robbery by rendering compensation.[153] Instead, he complained, he had been brought to court, fined, whipped and sentenced to two months imprisonment.

The structure of the British court system, combined with the lack of effective policing, ensured that compromise and restitution remained possible during the nineteenth century for all but the most serious crimes. The institution and prosecution of criminal cases was the responsibility of the complainant. The large number of court cases in which the complainant dropped the prosecution is an indication that many cases were settled informally. Although *gamsabhavas* died out after the imposition of British rule, headmen and other intermediaries often negotiated compromises. This state of affairs was not radically different from that preceding British rule, when adherence to the decisions of *gamsabhavas* and petty headmen was voluntary, dependent on social pressures. In the Kandyan Kingdom dissatisfied persons could take cases to more formal courts. Although it may be argued that the effectiveness of local social pressures not to take the crime to court declined as a consequence of colonial rule, this change was gradual, and therefore does not explain why the rate of criminal litigation was highest in the first half of the nineteenth century.

Trials by ordeal and by oath also continued to be available. In 1899, when on tour in the interior of the Low Country, a British official discovered that trial by ordeal had been frequently practised in a village. Supervised by a headman, people thrust their hands into boiling oil. The official believed that it 'was quite clear that there was a very general belief in the efficacy of the trial.'[154] The use of oaths in informal judicial procedures was

probably much more prevalent. The president of a village tribunal
in another Low Country district reported that peasants often
made use of ritual to solve minor disputes.[155] In one such ritual the
defendant touched his head three times in the presence of his child
or mother. This was taken as proof of his innocence, especially
when the case had been brought on suspicion.

The gods could be publicly called upon to mete out justice. On
the night of 30 May 1871 burglars broke into a Buddhist temple in
Kagalla district.[156] Not only were various articles stolen, but a clay
statue was smashed, presumably as part of a search for valuables.
The next day the monk organized a procession with drummers and
with the aid of a temple priest (*kapurala*) appealed to the god of a
nearby shrine to take revenge on the robbers by killing them.

Culture conflict between the British and Sri Lankans over the
boundaries of crime, concepts of status and appropriate punishments was real, but it did not account for the general approach to
the courts discussed earlier in this chapter. These changes were no
more disruptive than those which occur from time to time in non-
colonial societies.

A more important difference between British and indigenous
judicial norms lay in the means of determining guilt or innocence.
In colonial courts evidence had to be presented according to set
procedures; otherwise it was declared invalid. In contrast, the
Sinhalese did not separate crime from either the social setting
within which the action had taken place or from the social setting
of the court itself. Decisions by judges in the Kandyan Kingdom
took into account all the available evidence, including the personal
knowledge of the judge and others in attendance, which was likely
to be extensive. Sinhalese law was unwritten, and there was great
flexibility both in its application and in judicial procedure. When
the evidence was inconclusive trials by oath or ordeal were
legitimate options. Though the refusal of one of the parties to a
dispute to make an oath was admissible as evidence in British
courts, these other ways of trying cases were generally ignored or
disapproved of by the colonial authorities.[157]

The technical way in which judicial decisions were made in the
colonial courts was alien to indigenous tribunals but not to
Sinhalese culture in general. The most convincing way to interpret
Sinhalese perceptions of the colonial courts lies not in the judicial
proceedings of Dutch or Kandyan times, but in the cultural
precedent set by perceptions of the gods and spirits of popular
Buddhism. There, power was exercised without any clear moral
authority, sometimes in a quasi-judicial manner, as when cases

were decided by oath. The supernatural beings of the Sinhalese could be manipulated by humans so as to influence events, but their ethical position was ambiguous.[158] Gods on the upper end of the divine hierarchy mostly granted favours, and punished humans only with good cause. Demons and spirits had no such moral qualities. Many of these beings could be manipulated through ritual, and illness or other bad fortune was often attributed to sorcery. Although in theory sorcery could result in the target's immediate death, this variety was believed to be difficult and dangerous to carry out. On the other hand, there was a general belief that less serious forms of sorcery resulting in illness, injury or other bad fortune, were commonly practised.

The different purposes of payments to influence the outcome of court decisions in Kandyan and British times illustrates the divergent approaches to these tribunals. Bribes in the Kandyan Kingdom were paid to the judge, and it was accepted that both sides would contribute. The gifts to the judge were one aspect of his knowledge of the case which would influence his decision. In the colonial courts payments were not made to the judge, but to witnesses, court officials and lawyers whose task it was to manipulate the evidence placed before the judge in order to produce an outcome favourable to the client. These payments were equivalent to those made to specialists who were skilled in influencing demons and spirits.

Important for an understanding of the way in which the colonial judicial system was used is an analysis of the ritualistic approach to demons and spirits. What one said was neither true nor false. Instead, it was either effective or ineffective. A specific combination of sounds was 'sacred to a certain demon, for whom it has an unaccountable, mysterious, and irresistible fascination, from which he cannot free himself.'[159] These sounds were incomprehensible to those without a specialist knowledge. Similarly, court proceedings were in a strange tongue: English.

Seen in this light, the rampant perjury is explicable. Witnesses often delivered their testimony according to a set speech. For example, many cases of burglary followed the same pattern. The thieves were said to enter the house at night, tie up the persons inside, threaten to murder them if they made any noise, dig up the floor to search for money, and so on.[160] Litigants, lawyers and petition-drawers told witnesses what to say in court. In cases where there was no true evidence testimony tended to follow a set pattern. When there was evidence, the prosecution had no compunction about strengthening it with lies. Thomas Skinner, an able government employee, wrote in 1849 that witnesses could 'be obtained for evidence of any character. Perjury is made so complete a business that cases are as regularly rehearsed in all their various scenes by the professional perjurer as a dramatic piece is at a theatre.'[161] Fifteen years later another official described the way an experienced litigant tutored witnesses: 'He examines, cross-examines, corrects, and directs those in their parts who are to appear in the real court and give their testimony regarding what they know, or are to pretend to know, on the day of the trial.'[162]

Cattle stealing, a crime which was often carried out at night and for which in many cases there was no true evidence, was particularly noted for testimony delivered in a set manner. Sri Lankans did not believe that it was morally wrong to convict a known cattle thief on false evidence, and officials often complained that true cases were spoilt by complainants who added additional false evidence. One experienced judicial official commented that evidence in cattle stealing cases might be recorded on a stereotyped printed form to be used by judges and magistrates.[163] Frederick Campbell, when District Judge at Tangalla, also noted that cattle stealing prosecutions were identical: 'For example, no two parties ever happen to be together, and witness the removal of a stolen animal, one sees the removal at one, and another at another place, whilst a third sees the removal of the flesh.'[164] T. B. Panabokke, when Police Magistrate at Matale, was also suspicious: 'The usual evidence was that so-and-so lost his animal and that two or three people at different places, when they went to turn water to their fields, met the accused driving the animals away. The witness speaks to the accused, whereby the witness has an opportunity of recognizing the thieves and the animal with its brandmarks.'[165] E. M. Byrde, the Police Magistrate at Anuradhapura in 1896, noted that 'cattle stealers do not go about, as witnesses would wish one to believe, removing stolen cattle in broad daylight or along frequented high roads by moonlight.'[166] The testimony of a witness in a case tried at Matara early in the nineteenth century illustrates the lack of plausibility of much court testimony: 'I saw the two prisoners drive a head of cattle — It was in the high road — It was about two hours before dark — We asked them where are you going with the animal — Is this not the animal of the schoolmaster?'[167] The prosecution case quickly broke down under cross-examination.

Such testimony was not necessarily regarded as morally wrong. Richard Gombrich has pointed out that the idea of truth as an autonomous secular value has no firm base in Sinhalese village society.[168] Telling the truth was recognized as desirable, but when truth came into conflict with a more important value, such as justice, it could easily be discarded. Court testimony was seen as a formula to manipulate power and was evaluated on the strength of its effectiveness. The morality of court testimony depended not on its truthfulness, but on the intention of the testimony. False testimony in support of a just cause was moral; for an unjust cause it was immoral. It many cases, especially those which were related to long-standing feuds, both sides no doubt viewed themselves as in the right. In such instances court cases were like contests.

Persons who wished to manipulate the spirits and demons operated with the advice and help of specialists such as temple priests, exorcists, and mediums. At the courts the same function was performed by touts, petition-drawers and proctors. Both groups were somewhat disreputable. There were also judicial parallels to the pitfalls to which a sorcerer was vulnerable. A mistake in ritual rendered it ineffective and could be dangerous. Similarly, a mistake in the testimony of the complainant or one of his witnesses caused the prosecution to fail, and a serious mistake could result in imprisonment for perjury. The parallel also held on the side of the defence. The intended victim of sorcery could take counter-measures by appealing to a supernatural being, and these counter-measures could in some cases transfer the intended harm to the person who had initiated it. Similarly, the defendant could render the case ineffective by giving or arranging for skilful testimony in his defence, or he could file a counter-case which, if successful, would result in the punishment of the original complainant.

Just as the requirements of different spirits varied, so different results were obtained depending on the magistrate, judge or jury. Villagers were well aware of the reputations of different officials. In 1830 a monk living in Bentota, a village on the south-western coast, singled out George Turnour, an Englishman whose career had been in Kandyan districts, as an unusual arbitrator in that he understood Sinhala.[169] J. Vijayatunga, writing of the second decade of the twentieth century, noted that men in a Southern Province village gossiped about the various Supreme Court judges.[170]

There were, of course, differences between taking a grievance to a supernatural being and instituting a case before a magistrate. It is not my intention to argue that villagers confused the two institutions, or that they thought magistrates and demons to be similar types of beings. But sorcery provided the precedent which showed the Sinhalese the most effective way to approach the courts. The most important difference between the two approaches ensued from the public setting of the court case. The bringing of a criminal accusation was an open act, and its results were much more clear-cut because the punishment, if any, was publicly proclaimed. In contrast, any misfortune which might happen to a person accused before a spirit might be attributed to sorcery. It is likely that the courts, being more of a known quantity, were held in less awe than the spirits and demons.

The operation of the judicial system was subject to social change, and the various judicial and police reforms of the later nineteenth century did improve the efficiency of the courts and lessen technical aspects of court procedure. Among the results of the changes were an increase in the conviction rate and a decrease in the rate of litigation. Nevertheless, the fundamental perceptions by the people of the headmen, police and courts seem to have altered little. The number of English-educated Sri Lankans who fully understood and even accepted the principles behind English justice was quickly growing, but this class did not propagate Western ideas to the masses. Though many English-educated Sri Lankans were lawyers, in this role they fit in neatly with the role of the temple priest. The lawyer was a technician, a man who manipulated the judicial system, and he took any case as long as the client could pay the appropriate fee. Besides, a shift in the values of the people towards a desire for British-style justice would not automatically have brought about change, for the vested interests in and out of the administration would have continued to operate as before. This is perhaps the situation found by observers of the legal process in post-independence South Asia.[171] The operation of the village tribunals, established in order to circumvent the formal proceedings of the other courts, shows the tenacity of the legal system once established. The proceedings of these courts were in Sinhala, the judges were Sri Lankan, and lawyers were barred from appearing before them. Yet it appears that litigators and judges behaved little differently than in police courts.

The wealthy, upwardly mobile, aggressive and sophisticated certainly benefited from the colonial administration of law and order, but they did not always have everything their own way. In 1897 a petition from the North-Central Province noted that the local *ratemahatmaya* could influence the Government Agent through his control of the information supplied to that official, but that he could not determine the outcome of court cases.[172] Judicial judgments were often dependent on the personality of the magistrate, or the composition of the jury. The demons and spirits too could be arbitrary and unpredictable.

NOTES TO CHAPTER 2

1 Ramanathan, *AR SG 1892*, A1, A8; Campbell, *AR P 1867*, 189 – 93; Cayley, *AR QA 1877*, 5B; King, *AR DJ Badulla 1869*, 192.
2 Smythe, *A Ceylon Commentary*, 45.
3 C. R. de Silva, 310 – 15.
4 Nadaraja, 5 – 9.
5 Ibid., 59 – 63; C. R. de Silva, 315 – 18; P. D. Kannangara, 66 – 77.
6 C. R. de Silva 266 – 7; P. D. Kannangara, 85 – 6; Regulation 6 1806, CO54/ 25.
7 C. R. de Silva, 298 – 9; Samaraweera, 'The Judicial Administration', 126 – 33. For descriptions of the Kandyan judicial system, see Hayley, *A Treatise on the Laws and Customs of the Sinhalese*, 58 – 103 and d'Oyly, *A Sketch of the Constitution of the Kandyan Kingdom*, esp. 33 – 58.
8 Samaraweera, 'The Judicial Administration', 134 – 50; C. R. de Silva, 305 – 8.
9 Samaraweera, 'The Ceylon Charter of Justice of 1833'; *Law Reform in Ceylon*.
10 Nadaraja, 13.
11 Ibid., 232 – 3; Clarence, 'The Administration of Justice in Ceylon', 43 – 4; Sitting Magistrate Colombo, 10 Sept 1829, CO416/14.
12 Nadaraja, 184; Samaraweera, 'The Judicial Administration', 141 – 5; C. R. de Silva, 308.
13 Nadaraja, 185.
14 Ibid., 99; *Law Reform in Ceylon*, 34 – 6; Anderson to Grey, 7 Oct 1854, CO54/309(49).
15 *Law Reform in Ceylon*, 90 – 1; Anderson to Grey, 7 Oct 1854, CO54/309(49); Pippet, 82 – 3; Digby, *Forty Years*, II, 305 – 16.
16 Petitions 103 & 104, 10 May 1829 & 2 June 1829, CO416/29; d'Alwis, *Memoirs and Desultory Writings*; Peebles, 'The Transformation', 270 – 5; Samaraweera, 'British Justice', 128; Fernando, 'The Legal Profession of Ceylon in the Early Twentieth Century', 1 – 2.
17 Grenier, *Leaves from my Life*, 89 – 95; Thomson, *Institutes of the Laws of Ceylon*, 540 – 57; Ord 11 1868; *SP 17 1889*, 74.
18 Ord 11 1868 brought together the law on criminal procedure. On the reliance on the individual in criminal prosecutions, see Morgan, QA, to CS, 6 Feb 1872, SLNA6/A3646.
19 At the beginning of the nineteenth century several types of currency were in common use, the most prominent of which was rix-dollars. After 1825 all government transactions were expressed in sterling, but Indian currency was widely used. In 1872 the government switched from sterling to the Ceylon rupee, which was valued at two shillings. In the years after this change the value of the rupee deteriorated. Around the turn of the century it was worth sixteen pence. Shenoy, *Ceylon Currency and Banking*.

20 Clarence to Douglas, 25 May 1881, E, CO54/532(135); *Law Reform in Ceylon*.
21 Longden to Hicks-Beach, 24 July 1878, CO54/514(243); *SP 23 1879*, 19; E1, CO54/522(514).
22 Dickson, *AR Kandy 1883*, 11A; *SP 12 1874*, 19.
23 Ord 11 1868; Clarence to CS, 15 Oct 1874, *SP 12 1874*, 28. Later all district court cases had a crown prosecutor. C. Longden to CS, 11 Jan 1906, SLNA6/13924.
24 Ord 18 1871; Ord 3 1883.
25 Capper, *Old Ceylon*, 112 – 13.
26 Douglas to Kimberley, 31 May 1881, CO54/532(135); Burrows, *AR Matale 1889*, C23; Berwick, *AR DJ Kandy 1868*, 41. In the twentieth century provision was made for the payment of expenses for witnesses in district court cases. *SP 7 1921*, 7.
27 C. R. de Silva, 325 – 8; Nadaraja, 232; Thomson, 239 – 40.
28 Samaraweera, 'British Justice', 110 – 11; Ord 11 1868.
29 *SP 18 1867*, 9.
30 Clarence to Douglas, 25 May 1881, E, CO54/532(135).
31 Lee, *vyavastha sangrahava muladanin visin*, 1 – 5.
32 *SP 23 1884*, 11.
33 *SP 17 1889*, 7, 31, 69 – 70; Wace, D, 20 Apr 1894, SLNA38/5; Alexander, D, 22 Feb 1904, SLNA30/25.
34 Pippet.
35 Quoted in ibid., 122.
36 For developments in India at this time, see Griffiths, *To Guard My People*, 67 – 91.
37 Pippet, 339 – 45.
38 Information on the structure of the force during Campbell's tenure is found in the annual *AR P*s. Also see Pippet, 246 – 57, 280 – 4; Campbell to CS, 10 Apr 1878, E1, CO54/514(235); *SP 17 1889*.
39 E, CO54/645(78).
40 Pippet, 228.
41 Dep, 27.
42 Campbell, *AR P 1869*, 242; Campbell to CS, 23 Feb 1872, 13 Mar 1872, SLNA6/A3635; Dep, 28 – 9, 49 – 50, 60, 61 – 2, 66, 111 – 12, 114, 164, 179, 192, 221, 285 – 6, 327.
43 *SP 17 1889*.
44 Dep, 289 – 92.
45 *SP 17 1889*, 12 – 13, 58; Havelock to Ripon, 16 Sept 1892, CO54/603(362). Civil servants took police appointments for a brief period during the first decade of the twentieth century. Dep, 410 – 11.
46 Dep, 304, 410; Woolf, *Growing*, 47; Blake to Lyttelton, 28 Sept 1904, *SP 5 1905*, 3.
47 *SP 23 1892*; Dep, 300 – 4.
48 Elliott, *AR Colombo 1893*, B7.
49 D, 23 Apr 1896, SLNA33/19.
50 CS to GAs, circular, 12 Sept 1898, SLNA59/644. In many districts the policy set out in this circular was not implemented. See, e.g., Vaughan, D, 31 May 1904, SLNA30/25.
51 Ellis, *AR Colombo 1900*, B12.
52 Wace, D, 20 Apr 1896, SLNA38/5; Short, D, 11 Dec 1896, SLNA34/27.
53 Fox, D, 3 Apr 1901, SLNA30/23; Burrows, D, 5 Dec 1902, SLNA38/10 & 6 Jan 1903, SLNA38/11; C. Longden to CS, 11 Jan 1906, SLNA6/13924.

54 Knollys to CS, 20 Apr 1894, SLNA6/10114.
55 Dep, 343, 370 – 4, 400 – 2.
56 Knollys to CS, 25 July 1901, SLNA6/13318; Ellis to CS, 14 July 1901, SLNA6/13318.
57 *Standard*, 31 Aug 1904, 5 Sept 1904. Figures on police recruitment by caste are in the *AR P*s for 1897 – 1904.
58 *AR Galle 1904*, D4.
59 Blake to Lyttleton, 28 Sept 1904, *SP 5 1905*, 2; Saxton, D, 13 Feb 1895, SLNA34/26; M Hevagam Korale to GAWP, 5 Feb 1895, SLNA33/2784.
60 Blake to Lyttelton, 28 Feb 1904, *SP 5 1905*, 1. Also see Ridgeway to Chamberlain, 1 Sept 1903, CO54/683(384).
61 Dep, 404 – 12; *SP 5 1905*.
62 Dep, 409, 446 – 9, 462.
63 Dowbiggin, *AR P 1927*, B21 & *AR P 1924*, B22; *Headmen's Commission*.
64 G. Baumgartner, *AR Badulla 1898*, I6; Hill, *AR Kagalla 1900*, J12; Burrows, D, 11 Feb 1903, SLNA38/11; Saxton, D, 17 Sept 1897, SLNA34/27.
65 Wace, *AR Kalutara 1881*, 19A; P. Templer, *AR Galle 1890*, E3; Alexander, PO, *AR Galle 1905*, D3; *Examiner*, 22 Jan 1891; *Lakrivikirana*, 2 Dec 1871.
66 For examples, see the various *AR P*s for the 1920s and 1930s.
67 Ord 26 1871.
68 Samaraweera, 'The "Village Community" and Reform in Colonial Sri Lanka'.
69 Ibid.; Digby, 'A Home Rule Experiment in Ceylon'; Gregory, *Addresses Delivered in the Legislative Council of Ceylon*, II, 271.
70 Byrde, *AR Matara 1878*, 24; Ferdinands, *AR QA 1878*, 1B; Hume, *AR Galle 1878*, 11; Campbell to CS, 6 Oct 1879, SLNA6/5784; *SP 17 1889*, 49; Burrows, D, 24 Sept 1896, SLNA34/27.
71 Fisher, *AR Matara 1875*, 22.
72 Hill, D, 9 Mar 1904, SLNA42/1760.
73 Dickson, [1880], E1, CO54/528(152).
74 Cameron, D, 21 July 1899, SLNA38/7.
75 Samaraweera, 'Litigation, Sir Henry Maine's Writings and the Ceylon Village Communities Ordinance of 1871', 200 – 1; Digby, *Forty Years*, II, 107 – 17; *Lakrivikirana*, 23 Sept 1871, 14 Jan 1871, 2 Dec 1871; *Messenger*, 18 Jan 1876, 24 Mar 1876, 4 Apr 1876; *Native Opinion*, 13 July 1900.
76 Ord 2 1883; Ord 3 1883.
77 Longden to Hicks-Beach, 24 July 1878, CO54/514(243); Longden to Kimberley, 23 Sept 1882, CO54/541(404).
78 Stark, 'On the State of Crime in Ceylon', 96.
79 Ord 16 1889; Ord 4 1891; Ord 15 1896.
80 O. Morgan, *AR CC Midland Circuit 1886*, 20C.
81 Ord 27 1892.
82 Ord 8 1896.
83 Pippet, 82 – 3; *Law Reform in Ceylon*, 90 – 1; Pereira, *Out-door Proctor*; *SP 23 1884*, 15; PM Colombo to AG, 28 Nov 1892, SLNA59/19; *perakadoru hatane*. The terms 'outdoor proctor' and 'petition-drawer' were sometimes used interchangably. These men should not be confused with 'village proctors', who were villagers familiar with the courts through their own extensive experience with litigation.
84 Pagden to AG, 6 Nov 1893, SLNA59/19.
85 Peter de Saram to CS, 23 Apr 1894, SLNA59/19.
86 Layard, *CH 1897 – 8*, 68; Bonser to Havelock, 5 July 1895, SLNA59/19; Wace, *AR Kalutara 1881*, 20A; *SP 17 1889*, 74 – 5; Correspondence

between Burrows and Andrew Wijesinha, petition-drawer, 1888–90, SLNA42/738.

87	Conolly, PM, quoted in Pereira, 2 & *SP 23 1884*, 15.
88	*SP 23 1884*, 6.
89	*Lakrivikirana*, 21 May 1869.
90	Letters in SLNA59/19. Also see *Examiner*, 23 July 1895.
91	Lee, 25 July 1897, E, CO54/645(81).
92	Ord 15 1898.
93	Seneviratne, *CH 1897–8*, 68.
94	Layard, *CH 1897–8*, 68.
95	Ord 6 1891.
96	Ord 15 1898.
97	Ridgeway, *Adminstration of the Affairs of Ceylon, 1896 to 1903*, 87.
98	Ord 17 1894; Ord 11 1897; Ord 7 1899.
99	Fernando, 'The Ceylon Civil Service'; Warnapala, *UCHC*, III, 411.
100	Samaraweera, 'Litigation and Legal Reform in Colonial Sri Lanka'; Maitland to Windham, 28 Feb 1807, CO54/25; Mendis, 122, 396; QA to Anderson, 22 Dec 1853, E2, CO54/309(49).
101	*AR P 1867*; King, *AR DJ Badulla 1869*, 192; *AR P 1869*.
102	Ord 18 1871; Cayley, *AR QA 1877*, 5B & 28 Aug 1877, E1, CO54/508(150); C. P. Layard, *AR SG 1888*, 1C.
103	*SP 8 1898*. Judicial statistics were published annually in the *AR*s.
104	Campbell, *AR P 1879*, 32B; *SP 17 1889*, 33–4; Capper, 'A Statistical Enquiry into the State of Crime in Ceylon', 294.
105	King, *AR DJ Badulla 1869*, 192; Morgan, [1873], E, CO54/494(26); Ramanathan, *SP 8 1898*, 2; F. Templer to CS, 15 June 1880, SLNA6/5908; Longden to Kimberley, 20 Sept 1880, CO54/528(152); David de Saram, PM, *AR P 1867*, 167; Ferdinands, *AR QA 1878*, 2B; *Bi-Monthly Examiner*, 29 Jan 1868.
106	*AR P 1867*, 198.
107	*AR Matale 1891*, C14.
108	Blake to Lyttelton, 19 Dec 1903, CO54/685 (Conf).
109	G. Baumgartner, D, 30 Mar 1894, SLNA33/75.
110	Campbell, *AR P 1879*, 27B, 32B.
111	Sitting Magistrate Colombo, 10 Sept 1829, CO416/14.
112	Beven, *AR Matara 1902*, E37.
113	Stark, 94–5.
114	Pippet, 124; *SP 17 1889*.
115	*Lakrivikirana*, 14 Jan 1871; *Independent*, 4 Apr 1895; *Pradipaya*, 5 Sept 1895, 7 Sept 1896; Blake to Lyttelton, 28 Sept 1904, CO54/637(156); Dep, 252, 310, 435–7, 478.
116	van der Aa, *Ile de Ceylan, croquis, moeurs, et coutumes*, 123; Corner, *Ceylon*, 180–94; Dep, 200–1, 258–9, 333–4, 357.
117	Campbell to CS, 7 Nov 1879, SLNA6/5785; Dep, 171.
118	Campbell to CS, 26 Feb 1878, SLNA6/5540; Dep, 55–7, 106–8, 171–6, 249–50.
119	*Lakrivikirana*, 14 Jan 1871; *Sandarasa*, 28 Feb 1888; *Pradipaya*, 5 Sept 1895; *Independent*, 4 Apr 1895; Ellis, *AR Kalutara 1883*, 87A; G. Templer, *AR Ratnapura 1884*, 17A; Lushington, *AR Puttalam 1883*, 32A; Giles, *SP 17 1889*, 31–2.
120	Blake to Lyttelton, 28 Sept 1904, *SP 5 1905*, 2; *Sandarasa*, 5 Feb 1904; *Headmen's Commission*.
121	Lushington, *AR Puttalam 1885*, 32A; *Independent*, 17 Mar 1891; *Pradipaya*, 7 Sept 1896; *Lakrivikirana*, 14 Jan 1871; *Sandarasa*, 28 Feb 1888.

122 J. Templer to CS, 19 June 1880, SLNA6/5908; Hill, D, 6 Mar 1900, SLNA30/22; *Headmen's Commission*.
123 D. de Saram, *AR DJ Kurunagala 1869*, 198 – 9; Lawson to Robinson, 25 July 1870, SLNA6/3442; F. Campbell, *AR DJ Tangalla 1874*, 57; Atherton, *AR Ratnapura 1874*, 20; Conolly, *AR DJ Negombo 1875*, 25; Lushington, *AR Puttalam 1885*, 32A; Byrde, *AR Negombo 1887*, 59A; *Pradipaya*, 7 Sept 1896; CS to Wace, 12 Dec 1902, E, CO54/683(Private); Woodhouse, PM, *AR Matara 1899*, E38; *Observer*, 3 Aug 1854; Campbell, *AR P 1869*, 222. Also see Chapter Three.
124 Morris to CS, 7 Mar 1866, SLNA6/2293; Elliott, *AR Galle 1886*, 80A; Hay, *AR SG 1891*, A1; Brodhurst, D, 23 Dec 1892, SLNA35/8; Peter de Saram, 15 Aug 1895; SLNA33/2784; Alexander, PO, *AR Galle 1906*, D11; G. Baumgartner, D, 7 May 1894, SLNA33/75.
125 Gordon to Derby, 25 Apr 1885, CO54/558(186). Also see Dep, 259 – 62; Alexander, D, 11 Mar 1904, SLNA30/25; *Independent*, 17 Mar 1891.
126 Digby, *Forty Years*, I, 303.
127 *SP 23 1884*, 4 – 7; *Observer*, 3 Sept 1866; *Lakrivikirana*, 23 Sept 1871; Douglas to Kimberley, 3 May 1881, CO54/532(95); Petition 5 Sept 1854, E5, CO54/309(49).
128 D, 23 May 1903, SLNA38/11.
129 Wickremeratne, *The Genesis of an Orientalist*, 20. Also see Capper, *Old Ceylon*, 114.
130 'Public Meeting', 24 Aug 1854, E1, CO54/309(48); *Observer*, 16 Oct 1854; Dep, 109; Morgan to CS, 5 Jan 1872, SLNA6/A3646; *Law Reform in Ceylon*; *Bi-Monthly Examiner*, 7 Aug 1869; Pereira, 8; Pippet, 110 – 11; *Messenger*, 3 Mar 1874; Wickremeratne, *The Genesis*, 109 – 39; Capper, *Old Ceylon*, 114.
131 Quoted in Longden to Hicks-Beach, 24 July 1878, CO54/514(243).
132 Quoted in Peebles, 'Governor Arthur Gordon and the Administration of Sri Lanka, 1883 – 1890', 96.
133 Layard, 16 Mar 1893, E, CO54/607(113). Also see Fernando, 'The Ceylon Civil Service', 77 – 9.
134 *SP 17 1889*, 48; Clarence to Douglas, 25 May 1881, E, CO54/532(135).
135 Campbell, *AR P 1869*, 225; Hay, *AR Northern Circuit & WP 1886*, 25C; Petition, [1883], E, CO54/549(206).
136 *SP 17 1889*, 46, 73.
137 Contrast D. de Saram, *AR DJ Kurunagala 1869*, 199 with G. Templer, *AR Ratnapura 1884*, 17A.
138 *AR Colombo 1899*, B21.
139 Clarence to Douglas, 25 May 1881, E, CO54/532(135).
140 Ibid.; Also see *SP 18 1867*, 9.
141 Gordon to Holland, 10 Feb 1888, CO54/576(70); Ferdinands, SG, to Grenier, 15 Dec 1886, E, CO54/571(218).
142 Ord 3 1883 reduced the jury size to nine, and Ord 1 1888 to seven, except for murder cases. There was no special provision for jury trials when the defendant was European. Folklore among planters reflected their unease at the prospect of being tried before a jury dominated by Sri Lankans. Several such stories are recounted in Corner.
143 E2, CO54/309(49).
144 Gordon to Holland, 25 Oct 1887, CO54/572(Conf).
145 Ridgeway to Chamberlain, 1 July 1903, CO54/683(274); Ridgeway to Chamberlain, 16 Sept 1903, CO54/684(411); Ridgeway to Lyttelton, 23 Oct 1903, CO54/684(Tel); Fowler, D, 4 Dec 1902, SLNA33/25; Blake to Lyttelton, 19 Dec 1903, CO54/685(Conf).

146 Samaraweera, 'British Justice'.
147 Hayley, 104.
148 Quoted in Dep, 101.
149 The autobiography of an early forest officer includes many incidents of conflict between the state and people over the use of Crown land. See F. Lewis, *Sixty-four Years in Ceylon*. Also see *SP 2 1922*, 9; Banks, *AR P 1939*, A4.
150 Hayley, 111; Caste continued to play a role in popular definitions of crime. *Bi-Monthly Examiner*, 9 Mar 1869; Jayetileke, *AR DJ Kurunagala 1872*, 561; C. de Saram, *AR DJ Kandy 1870*, 243 – 4; *AR Colombo 1904*, A30.
151 Hartshorne, *AR Nuvara Eliya 1873*, 53.
152 Hayley, 129.
153 Petition 363, 7 Sept 1829, CO416/31.
154 Fowler, *AR Kalutara 1889*, B27. Also see Gillman, DJ, *AR P 1867*, 194; Dep, 24.
155 *AR Hambantota 1904*, D69.
156 *Lakrivikirana*, 3 June 1871.
157 Hayley, 93 – 4.
158 Gooneratne, 'On Demonology and Witchcraft in Ceylon'; Obeyesekere, 'The Buddhist Pantheon in Ceylon and its Extensions'; Gombrich, *Precept and Practice: Traditional Buddhism in the Rural Highlands of Ceylon*, 144 – 213; W. A. de Silva, 'Sinhalese Black Magic'; Hodge, 'Poetry and Magic in Southern Sri Lanka'; 'The King v. Aragama Appoohamy', 1829, CO416/20.
159 Gooneratne, 53.
160 *Messenger*, 6 Mar 1883. There is a possible Indian parallel in the observation of a sessions judge at Agra that alibis fell into three categories: the marriage feast, the purchase of a bullock at a distant fair, and the visit to a medical dispensary. Walsh, *Indian Village Crimes*, 19 – 20.
161 Skinner, *Fifty Years in Ceylon*, 138. This image remained popular among officials throughout British rule. In 1869, for instance, an official noted that 'a suit in Court seems to be looked on as the answer to a want met elsewhere by the Theatre, Opera, Music Halls, etc. and it has the advantage of cheapness.' Morris, *AR Kurunagala 1869*, 120. Also see Dowbiggin, *AR P 1924*, B10.
162 'Going to Law in Ceylon', 80 – 1.
163 Quoted in Panabokke, PM, *AR Matale 1898*, C10.
164 *AR P 1867*, 219.
165 *AR Matale 1898*, C10.
166 *AR Anuradhapura 1896*, H4.
167 Sitting Magistrate Matara, D, 5 Oct 1829, CO416/15. Other references to stereotyped testimony in cattle stealing trials include Dowbiggin, *AR P 1914*, B6; Carberry, DJ, *AR Ratnapura 1908*, I3; Torrington to Grey, 11 Aug 1848, K. M. de Silva, *Letters on Ceylon 1846 – 1850*, 100.
168 Gombrich, 262 – 3. Also see Knox, *An Historical Relation of Ceylon*, 120 – 2.
169 Petition 631, 17 Sept 1830, CO416/32.
170 Vijayatunga, *Grass For My Feet*, 25 – 6.
171 Kidder; Mendelsohn. The difficulties of implementing language reforms in post-independence Sri Lanka are discussed in Cooray, 'The Administration of Justice in Swabasha in Sri Lanka'.
172 Wickremeratne, 'The Rulers and the Ruled in British Ceylon', 220.

CHAPTER 3

CATTLE STEALING

Cattle stealing was one of the more prominent crimes carried out in colonial Sri Lanka. It was described as 'the national crime', the 'great curse of the country', and 'the *bête noire* of the island'. In rural areas it was often labelled the most important crime. With varying degrees of vigour, officials tried to stamp it out. The history of cattle stealing illustrates many aspects of rural life, including the effectiveness of the colonial state in asserting its authority, the impact of changes in land use on village society, and the importance of geographical variations when tracing economic and social trends.

The remarks of officials and newspaper correspondents provide detailed information about the crime. A single comment by an official or letter to the newspaper may have reflected the perspective of the writer more accurately than reality, but when hundreds of such comments from different districts and time periods are examined, chronological and geographical patterns may be discerned. The mobility of officials ensured that a variety of view-points are available for all districts.

Systematic crime statistics were not compiled during the first half of the nineteenth century, but there is some scattered evidence about the extent and frequency of cattle stealing during the early years of British rule. Judicial statistics were first published in 1867, and appeared regularly after 1877. They measured the number of cases brought to court by persons who alleged that their cattle had been stolen. Early in the twentieth century these figures were replaced by police statistics which, unlike the earlier series, included cases for which there was no specific accused person, but excluded cases which the authorities believed were false.

This chapter traces the social and geographical patterns of cattle theft, and relates them to changes in government policy and the rural economy. Administrative attempts to counter cattle stealing were generally ineffective in the nineteenth century, but the crime was not common everywhere. Organized stealing thrived only in certain economic and social conditions. In the 1890s it declined in one of its strongholds, Kurunagala district.

Some ten to fifteen years later a similar decline took place in the other area where it was prevalent, the interior of the Low Country. Although improvements in policing contributed marginally to the decline of the stealing networks, structural change in the rural economy was a more decisive cause. By the late 1920s cattle stealing was of little concern to the authorities, but it underwent a revival with the onset of the depression, and received further impetus in 1936 when various regulations designed to control the movement and sale of cattle were lifted.

The Economic and Social Position of Cattle

According to official statistics there were about 700,000 cattle in Sinhala Sri Lanka in 1870.[1] This figure rose gradually to over 1,000,000 by the turn of the century. Since the human population increased by a similar rate, according to the statistics there was a constant proportion of about three persons for each head of cattle. On the other hand, late nineteenth-century observers believed that the number of cattle was declining, not rising.[2] It is likely that the early figures in particular were underestimates, and that at the mid-century there were only two persons for each head of cattle. In the twentieth century official statistics showed the number of cattle rising at a slower rate than the number of people.

There were two types of cattle, buffaloes and black cattle. Buffaloes were generally stronger, but there was no necessary difference in their value, which depended on the size, strength, age and health of the individual animal. The standard price of village cattle ranged from ten to twenty rupees a head, but those in poor condition could be worth as little as five rupees and bulls from India as much as eighty rupees. By and large there were almost as many buffaloes as black cattle throughout Kandyan districts, but in the Low Country black cattle outnumbered buffaloes by at least two to one and in some districts by as much as ten to one.

There is no evidence of major long-term geographical shifts in the cattle population, but disease or drought could cause sudden local declines.[3] There were recurring epidemics of murrain and hoof and mouth disease, a particularly bad series of which decimated herds in the central highlands in the 1860s. Murrain was usually fatal, while hoof and mouth disease permanently weakened animals without causing death. Though a particular district might remain untouched for years at a time, there was always disease somewhere on the island. The epidemics of the mid-century began around 1840, and were probably transmitted by animals imported from India to transport goods to and from the early coffee plantations. In the more normal years after 1870 annual mortality from disease was about one per cent.[4]

Most village cattle were undernourished and unhealthy, and many contemporaries believed that their condition was getting worse. In the words of one official, they were 'miserable specimens of their class'.[5] Inadequate food and shelter and indiscriminate breeding, as well as disease, were blamed.[6] Because there was a shortage of pasture in many districts, cattle were allowed to wander freely to search for food, especially during the seasons when they were not wanted for agriculture. Often they were not seen by their owners for weeks.[7] Some officials, especially in the lightly-populated dry zone, thought there were far too many useless cattle.[8]

Since males were preferred for agricultural and draught purposes, cows rather than bulls were slaughtered for meat. As a result there were more males than females, unlike Europe where milk was a relatively more important reason for keeping cattle.[9] No attempt was made at systematic breeding, whereby the weaker bulls were castrated when young. Instead, bulls were not castrated until they were between four and seven years old.[10] An official report stated that 'it too frequently happens that one cow will cause a furious stampede of bulls of all ages, the pursued animal suffering severe injuries in the protracted chase.'[11]

There were many complaints that cattle infested roadsides, and their search for food often took them to rice fields and gardens. One official labelled cattle trespass 'the curse of the district', and a *mudaliyar* complained that 'at present there is not a single cow, or a buffalo which has not done more damage to the community at large, than double her worth to the owner.'[12] Throughout the nineteenth and early twentieth centuries land previously used for pasture was gradually given over to cultivation. As more and more land was planted with cash crops, the lack of pasture became a serious problem in many districts.

Cattle, especially buffaloes, were used for cultivating and threshing rice.[13] Often buffaloes were driven back and forth, and their stamping was sufficient to soften and muddy the soil. Otherwise a simple plough was used. Black cattle, when they were used at all, ploughed light sandy soil. In many districts cattle were thought essential for rice cultivation, and when there was a shortage fields lay fallow. In parts of the Southern Province and

central highlands they were little used, and human power was
employed instead. When cattle were not used, groups of men beat
the soil with hook-shaped implements called mamoties.

The poor physical condition of cattle hampered agriculture.
When the only cattle available were sickly, or when the cost of
using cattle was high, human power became more attractive.
Though officials sometimes mentioned that poor peasants owned
cattle, ownership was often concentrated and cattle usually had to
be hired.[14] An example provided by a *kachcheri mudaliyar* shows
that out of a crop which yielded sixty bushels of paddy, a little
over eight bushels was paid for cattle hire.[15] Another observer
thought hiring cattle cost smallholders one-third of their crop.[16]

The island's transportation system depended heavily on cattle.
They were used for both pulling carts and carrying loads. The
introduction of railways did not lead to an immediate decline in
the number of draught animals. Cart transport survived both in
direct competition on shorter routes and by taking goods to and
from railway stations.[17] The steady improvement of roads and the
general increase in commerce helped boost cart traffic. Pack
animals, called *tavalams*, continued to serve villages not on a
road, and cattle were also used to pull carriages. It is unlikely that
there was any drop in the number of draught animals during the
late nineteenth century, but the advent of motor vehicles in the
twentieth century did reduce their importance.

Cattle were also a source of food. Milk was not greatly used by
villagers, partially because of the poor condition of the animals,
but buffalo curd was considered a treat by those who could afford
it.[18] Beef was more important. Although among Buddhists there
was a negative connotation attached to eating beef, contemporaries thought that more and more Sinhalese included it in their
diets.[19] Muslims, Christians and low-caste Tamils had no com-
punctions about eating beef. Demand was strongest in urban
areas, especially Colombo, and the local supply was inadequate.
Of the nearly 18,000 head of cattle imported through Colombo in
1901, over sixty per cent were immediately sent to the slaughterhouse.[20] In 1912 an official estimated that as many cattle were sold
for meat as for transportation and agriculture combined.[21]

In rural areas ownership of cattle was also a barometer of
status. A government report stated that cattle were 'property
which Natives of all classes are ever anxious to possess'.[22] The
owner of a large herd could use it as leverage over poorer
neighbours who depended on his goodwill to hire out cattle during
the agricultural seasons. Some important headmen in Kandyan

districts owned hundreds of animals which were spread over several villages.[23] Ownership was somewhat less concentrated in the Low Country.[24]

The Social Context and Incidence of Cattle Stealing

Patterns of cattle theft were largely governed by rational calculations on the part of the thieves. The proximity of a market, the feasibility of holding the animal for ransom, the likely amount of profit to be earned, the value of the animal to thieves if kept for personal use or consumption, and the likelihood of discovery and punishment were among the considerations which were taken into account.

The great majority of thefts were carried out in the villages. Cattle owned by the peasantry were easy to steal because they were rarely folded at night. The difficulty for the thieves was not to gain possession of the animal, but to arrange for its profitable disposal. Draught animals, though frequently more valuable, were stolen less often partly because they were more closely looked after, and partly because carters had a reputation as a violent class of men. Draught cattle owned by households were more often subject to theft. In Colombo they were sometimes openly attached to carriages and driven off.

Stolen cattle were often sold. Usually the animals were spirited away some distance to prevent detection; many ended up at the Colombo slaughterhouse. Others were purchased cheaply for agricultural use by villagers who were willing to do without the sale vouchers which were sometimes required by the government. In some places such thefts were relatively casual. One official wrote that the missing cattle 'have probably been driven off some distance by some of the bolder spirits of the village, and hired out for the season to some not over-scrupulous cultivator, with instructions to let them go loose when done with. The man whose own animals are missing when wanted has, in his turn, to "hire", and so there is a continuous round of misappropriation, to which the whole community is more or less privy.'[25]

A variation was to try to extract a ransom from the owner for the return of the animal. A Government Agent at Kurunagala thought that 'the philosophy . . . is somewhat akin to that of dog-stealing in England.'[26] Cattle stealing for ransom was the most common form in many districts. Officials often complained that the victim of cattle theft preferred paying the ransom to instituting a court case. Thieves who stole for ransom usually had some other use for the animal in case the owner was unwilling to pay for the recovery of his property.

Cattle could be stolen for the personal use of the thieves, often as beef. One young magistrate commented: 'An animal is stolen, killed, and consumed by half a dozen people in a single night — by morning not a vestige of the animal is to be found.'[27] Though in theory taking life was contrary to the tenets of Buddhism, it was considered more shocking to kill animals for other persons, or for their hides, than to kill for a meal.[28] Though most cattle thefts were committed by Sinhalese, Tamil plantation workers occasionally stole an animal in order to obtain beef.[29] Thieves could also take cattle for their own agricultural purposes. Aelian King, when District Judge at Badulla, wrote that it was common 'for the people, at the season for ploughing and preparing the soil for sowing, to help themselves without their neighbour's leave to the labour of their neighbour's buffaloes, which they find roaming at large.'[30] More serious were instances when a group of villagers raided a nearby district for cattle. These expeditions were usually carried out in remote, sparsely populated areas.[31]

Finally, cattle could be stolen for adventure, often tinged with a desire for revenge. Some administrators drew parallels from British society. G. S. Saxton thought that cattle stealing was 'indulged in as pure mischief, as naughty boys used to wrench off knockers. . . . the idea being "Here is our enemy's bull, let us eat it".'[32] King believed that Kandyans regarded it as 'an act of daring, largely partaking the character of a dangerous field sport'.[33] The excitement of cattle stealing was thought by Charles Liesching to be 'as fascinating to the Sinhalese as to the Borderers of old'.[34]

It is important in any analysis of a crime such as cattle stealing, in which individual cases are not of great significance, to assess the frequency of the offence. If there had been very few cases, the crime would not have had much importance. It has already been noted that contemporaries complained of the prevalence of this crime. It is necessary to find out as precisely as possible how often it was committed, whether or not there were regional variations in its frequency, and if there were changes over time. For the first half of the nineteenth century the evidence is sparse, but some generalizations may be made. More detailed material is available for the late nineteenth and early twentieth centuries.

Cattle theft was recognized as a problem in the early years of British rule. In 1814 an official proclamation noted that 'the practice of Stealing and Privately killing Cattle has become very prevalent throughout the British settlements in Ceylon.'[35] In 1829 the Supreme Court judges wrote that cattle stealing was 'very common'.[36] That same year judicial officials were asked which crimes were most prevalent in their districts. Their replies indicated that cattle stealing was more common in the Low Country and Intermediate areas than in the Interior region.[37] Accounts from the 1840s and 1850s show that cattle stealing was thought by the authorities to be a serious problem in many areas.[38] Kurunagala and parts of the districts bordering it were singled out as suffering from an inordinate amount of cattle theft.

The judicial statistics of the late nineteenth century provide more precise information, but they must be carefully assessed in light of the social, economic and administrative settings which produced them. Because the circumstances of many cattle thefts did not encourage people to initiate prosecutions, the statistics greatly underestimated the extent of the crime. When the owner had no idea who had stolen his animal, there was no advantage in reporting the loss. When he suspected a specific person, it was his responsibility to find witnesses to support his case. The nearest court was often twenty or thirty kilometres distant; sometimes the journey was much further. It was inconvenient for a villager to walk that far to report a theft, especially since he often had to make the trip several times if he wanted to complete a prosecution. Since government did not pay for the expenses of witnesses, this cost also fell on the cattle owner. In one instance the complainant and his witnesses each had to walk over three hundred kilometres back and forth from the court because the case was postponed several times.[39] It was often more rational for the cattle owner to accept the loss, or to take a different course of action.

Very often cattle owners negotiated with the thieves, usually through intermediaries, who were sometimes village headmen.[40] When there was little evidence, a 'reward' or ransom of about five rupees was paid for information about the location of the lost animal. Criminal plaints were sometimes filed against the thieves in order to reduce the amount of ransom, or to get a couple of rupees compensation for an eaten animal. Out of court settlements were consistent with Sinhalese norms. In the pre-colonial Kandyan courts persons found guilty of cattle stealing were not imprisoned, but were instead required to render compensation to the injured party.[41]

Another factor which affected the likelihood of a case being reported was intimidation by the cattle stealers.[42] Especially when the complainant's village was relatively remote and the headmen themselves in league with the thieves, the long trip to court with little prospect of success was made even more unattractive by the possibility of violence. Officials complained that cattle stealers often harassed the complainant and members of his family, sometimes by the institution of false criminal charges.

False cases offset under-reporting to some extent. Officials varied widely in their estimates as to their extent. Some seem to have thought that if a case could be traced to a feud, it was false. This assumption was not necessarily justified, for the feud may have been a motive for the theft, or it may have determined whom the complainant decided to accuse in a case of real theft when the thieves were unknown. Other accusations were the result of disputes over the ownership of animals. The authorities considered these cases suitable for civil, not criminal, legal proceedings.[43] There were also cases which had nothing to do with cattle. P. W. Conolly, when District Judge at Negombo, wrote that 'when parties quarrel and assault each other, it is no uncommon thing for the person who has got the best of the struggle to have an animal brought to the spot, and a charge of cattle stealing is preferred against the unfortunate man who has been assaulted.'[44] To bring false charges against one's enemy, backed up by witnesses, was to cause him great inconvenience and expense. Still other cases resulted from trespass. It was legal to seize cattle which were trespassing on fenced land, but such action could lead to an accusation of theft. In addition, when cattle got lost, or were eaten by wild animals, their owners sometimes assumed that they had been stolen and instituted a prosecution against known cattle thieves.[45]

Despite all these shortcomings, the number of reported cases of cattle theft is valuable evidence. The first period for which there is a consistent series is from 1872 to 1905.[46] There were variations in the accuracy of these figures according to time and place, but these evened out over fairly large geographical areas and periods of time. For instance, if a magistrate dismissed most cases because he thought they were false, the proportion of thefts which were reported in his district might decrease because people would decide that it was useless to report them. But over time all regions would have such magistrates. Similarly, although a smaller percentage of cases were reported from places some distance from a court, all regions included such localities. The reported number of cases underestimated the actual frequency of the crime, but it bore a reasonably constant relationship to the real frequency.

Over the period between 1872 and 1905 it is probable that increased facilities for reporting and prosecuting cattle theft resulted in a gradual increase in the proportion of crimes which were reported.

For the purpose of statistical analysis I shall use the three geographical divisions discussed in the first chapter. The annual average number of cases reported between 1873 and 1905 was 1,121 in the Low Country, 454 in the Intermediate region, and 253 in the Interior area. Depending on the region and year, there were between one and sixteen cattle thefts reported annually for every 10,000 inhabitants (Table 3.1). Because the concern here is with general trends and not annual variations, the rates are calculated for five year blocks.

Table 3.1. Average Number of Thefts of Cattle Reported Annually per 10,000 Inhabitants, 1873 – 1905

	Low Country	Intermediate	Interior
1873 – 77	8.5	15.9	5.2
1878 – 82	8.8	11.2	5.1
1883 – 87	9.3	12.5	4.8
1888 – 92	8.1	10.8	3.0
1893 – 97	8.9	7.9	2.7
1898 – 1902	5.1	7.9	1.6
1903 – 05	6.4	3.8	1.4

Source: *Administration Reports.*

An alternative method is to measure thefts against the cattle population (Table 3.2). This approach is less accurate because the cattle returns are not as reliable as the census figures, but it is valuable because the presence of a large urban population can mask a high rate of cattle theft in the rural parts of a region. When interpreting these tables it should be remembered that no matter how many animals were stolen at a time the case was recorded as one theft.

Both sets of figures give a similar indication of the trend in any one region. The main difference is that the rates for the Low Country were proportionately higher in relation to the cattle population than to the human population, because there were more humans per cattle in the Low Country. The tables show that an animal was at greatest risk of being stolen in the Low Country, but until around 1895 a person was more likely to steal an animal in the Intermediate area. How great a chance was there that an animal would be stolen? The statistics are not reliable enough to answer this question with any confidence, but an estimate may be made given certain assumptions. These are threefold: (1) that the number of cases reported represented one-fifth the true rate, (2) that an average of two head were stolen in each theft, and (3) that the hypothetical animal had a life span of ten years. If these assumptions are correct, and the cattle returns accurate, an animal's chance of being stolen during its lifetime ranged from forty per cent in the Low Country around 1880 to three per cent in the Interior region at the end of the century. The first assumption listed above is inevitably arbitrary and is conservative. In areas where cattle stealing was highly organized and ransoming common it is likely that the proportion of cases reported was very much smaller. The odds cited above would have given little comfort to the man in Kurunagala who, during a rash of cattle thefts, had to pay a ransom for the same animal seven times before finally selling it for the paltry sum of two rupees.[47]

Table 3.2. *Average Number of Thefts of Cattle Reported Annually per 10,000 Cattle, 1873 – 1905*

	Low Country	Intermediate	Interior
1873 – 77	33.0	28.5	18.2
1878 – 82	39.5	16.5	17.5
1883 – 87	41.8	17.8	16.7
1888 – 92	36.8	17.6	9.7
1893 – 97	34.0	11.2	8.0
1898 – 1902	23.2	5.0	4.6
1903 – 05	21.4	6.0	4.2

Source: *Administration Reports.*

Administrative changes during the late nineteenth century should have resulted in a higher proportion of cases being reported. After 1885 the cost of prosecuting was less because cases were tried in police courts instead of district courts. The use of itinerant magistrates gradually increased, making prosecutions

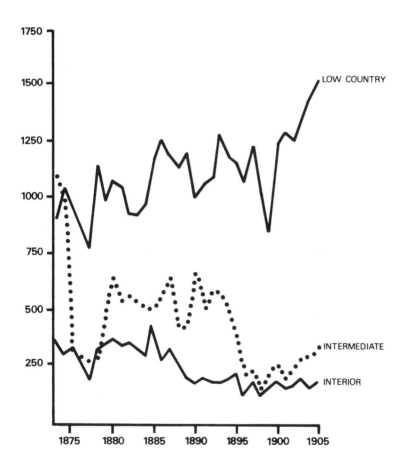

Fig 3.1: Reported thefts of cattle, 1873-1905.

more convenient. Moreover, in the 1890s the British for the first time consistently encouraged headmen to report all cases. This increased activity led to additional prosecutions. In the face of these changes, the decline in the rate of cattle theft is convincing evidence of a real decrease in the incidence of cattle stealing. The theft rate began to drop first in the Interior region and then in the Intermediate area. The decline in the Low Country started later and was less sharp than in the other two regions. The absolute number of cases reported in the Interior area remained fairly constant until 1885, and then fell gradually, levelling off again after 1900 (Figure 3.1). In the Intermediate region the numbers were constant until 1893, with the exceptions of dips in 1875 – 9 and 1888 – 9, both of which were caused by special government measures. After 1893 the number of cases dropped sharply, though there was some recovery after 1901. In the Low Country the number of reported thefts increased very gradually, though not as quickly as the human population.

The comments of officials and newspaper correspondents are consistent with the conclusions drawn from the statistics, and show more precisely the areas where cattle stealing prevailed. There was some casual cattle theft virtually everywhere. The variations in the overall rate were mainly accounted for by organized networks for cattle stealing which extended for scores of kilometres. There were two main areas where organized stealing was carried out. I have chosen to call them the Northern and Southern Bands (Map 3.1).

The Southern Band stretched across the interior of the Low Country, from the Matara-Hambantota border in the south to Siyane Korale, in Colombo district, to the north.[48] Its leaders were local magnates who co-operated with each other by exchanging and transporting stolen cattle. F. R. Saunders, when Government Agent of the Western Province, described the system in some detail in his annual report for 1889.[49] He wrote that there were well-to-do and respectable men in each district who either planned or were informed of all cattle stealing in their localities. When an animal went missing, the owner visited such a man to arrange a price for the restoration of the animal. If they agreed on a sum, an appointment was made to pay the money to an intermediary. If no deal was made, the animal was spirited away to another district. The local managers of cattle stealing operations ex-changed purloined cattle to prevent them from being identified. These men also bailed out the thieves if they were arrested, and arranged for lawyers, false evidence, and the intimidation of

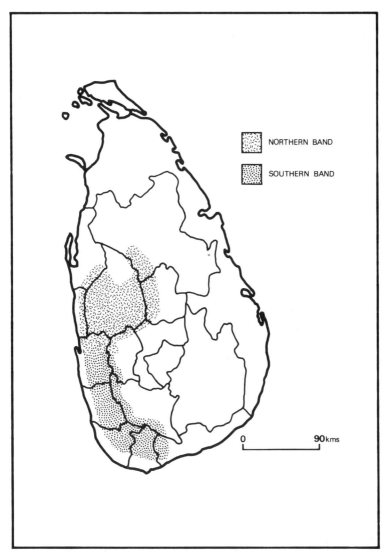

NORTHERN BAND

SOUTHERN BAND

0   90kms

Map 3.1: Organized cattle stealing, 1865-90.

witnesses. The thieves were kept under control because the organizers had evidence which could get them convicted. Saunders concluded his account by observing that evidence could never be found against the organizers themselves.

It was not uncommon for stolen animals to be transported along paths and roads for as far as fifty kilometres. Local networks often took advantage of kinship ties. Members of the Kotalawala family, living along the roads of Rayigam Korale, were thought to control the movement of cattle.[50] E. B. Alexander, the Police Magistrate at Panadura, drew a map showing places where the members of this family lived; Map 3.2 is a revised version of his sketch. It was alleged that the animals were passed from one family member to another. Those animals not ransomed were usually sold cheaply to cultivators or butchers who knew full well the origins of the animal. It appears that a relatively small proportion of cattle stolen in the Southern Band ended up as beef, for there were ready markets for agricultural and draught purposes, especially in the Western Province. Most profit was probably made from ransom payments.

The Northern Band was centred in Kurunagala district, which was long considered the hotbed of the crime.[51] Its organization was similar in that it was controlled by persons of relatively high social status, that ransoming was a major source of profit, and that the transporting of animals over long distances was usual when a payment was not forthcoming. Charles Liesching, when District Judge at Negombo, wrote that 'the distance to which cattle are transported in a single night by relays of men, is almost incredible.'[52] Less traditional modes of transportation were sometimes used. In one case, ten head of cattle were stolen, taken to Polgahavela railway station and that same night put on a cattle truck bound for Colombo.[53]

Although some of the animals stolen in the Northern Band were sold for agricultural use, especially in Chilaw and the Western Province, a high proportion of those not ransomed were sold for beef in the Roman Catholic villages on the littoral, and more importantly, in Colombo. The slaughterhouse of the capital city tried to establish the origins of the animals it accepted, but with little success. Kurunagala district was poorer than the Low Country; the one-way illicit trade in cattle not only enriched the thieves but brought money into the district. By contrast, in the Southern Band cattle were generally exchanged between districts, though there was probably a net movement from the Southern to the Western Province. Goyigama Buddhists normally organized

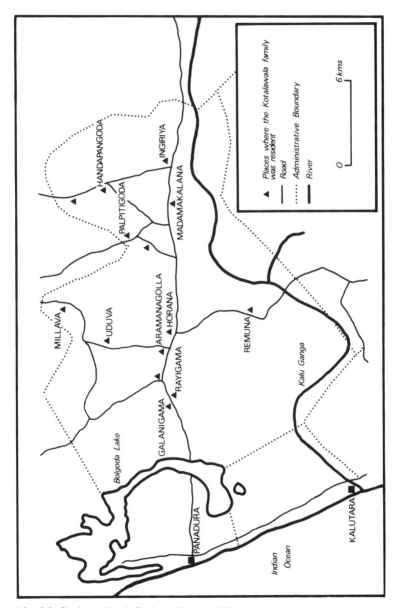

Map 3.2: Cattle stealing in Rayigam Korale, 1900.

thefts in both areas, but Muslim or Sinhalese Roman Catholic
traders usually took control of the animals for the last stages
before the slaughterhouse. One cattle trader suspected of dealing
in stolen animals was Liyange Sardial Perera, a Karava from
Dandugama near Negombo.[54] He was accused, along with two
local men, of stealing cattle from the village of Vadigamangama in
Puttalam district near the border with Kurunagala. When a
warrant was issued for his arrest, the *Hue and Cry* listed among
his friends four headmen and an ex-headman. One of his alleged
accomplices lived in the house of the headman of the village where
the theft took place.

The only available detailed information about the social
characteristics of persons involved in cattle stealing was published
in the *Hue and Cry*.[55] Ninety-six per cent of those accused were
Sinhalese, and ninety-one per cent were Buddhists. Of the
Sinhalese, seventy-five per cent were Goyigamas, nine per cent
Vahumpuras, nine per cent Karavas, Salagamas and Duravas, and
seven per cent members of other castes. Fifty-eight per cent of the
alleged cattle thieves were identified as cultivators; this proportion
was higher than that for any other crime. Just over half the wanted
men were in their twenties. Over thirty per cent were in their
thirties.

This social profile indicates that cattle stealing was not
primarily a crime of the depressed classes. Goyigamas were
substantially over-represented, a fact which cannot be accounted
for entirely by their agricultural pursuits. Some non-Goyigama
villages near the coast, such as Magalkande, Indisgastuduva, and
Pohoddaramulla, had reputations as centres of cattle stealing, but
in the interior relatively wealthy persons and their poorer kin and
clients were the main beneficiaries.[56] The Kotalawalas and the
Kannangaras, who were said to be the organizers of cattle stealing
in Rayigam Korale, were both upwardly mobile Goyigama
families with much local influence.[57] The head of a local network
in the Northern Band, Rajaruwo, literally, 'King', was related to a
middle-level headman in a region where such appointments were
always limited to the respectable and wealthy.[58] The frequent links
between organized cattle stealing and headmen is strong evidence
of the high social position of those responsible for this crime. The
illicit trade in cattle may have played an important role in
providing an economic base for certain upwardly-mobile Goyigama families. Judging from the value of each ransom payment,
usually about five rupees, some stealing networks must have
earned thousands of rupees profit annually.

Around the turn of the century officials noted that the scale of cattle stealing in Kurunagala had declined.[59] Their observations were only partially based on the fall in the number of cases brought before the courts. In 1899, when there was a sharp increase in the number of reported cattle thefts, H. W. Brodhurst, the Government Agent, attributed it to false cases which were instituted because the magistrate was inexperienced: 'I therefore attach little importance to this apparent recrudescence of a crime which was once the curse of the Province, but has been little heard of in late years.'[60] Three years later one of Brodhurst's successors, commenting on another increase over the previous year, noted that 'there has been no return to the systematic trade in stolen cattle.'[61] Although some of the official assessments of cattle stealing in Kurunagala at the turn of the century may have been over-optimistic, it is clear that the level of the crime in the district, and more generally the Northern Band, was much less than it had been in the 1880s and earlier.

In the Southern Band the number of cattle-stealing cases reported to the courts failed to keep pace with the increase in population, but there was no general decline at this time. This situation lasted only a decade; after 1908 the rate dropped sharply, in a way reminiscent of its earlier decline in the Northern Band. The number of 'true cases of cattle theft', that is the number of cases known to the authorities less those in which it was determined that no crime had been committed, declined in the Southern and Western Provinces from 1,160 in 1908 to 394 in 1914.

Throughout the nineteenth century there was some casual cattle stealing in most districts. Villagers stole cattle for beef, for a ransom payment, or in some cases for ploughing or local sale. But most cattle thefts were carried out in the interior of the Low Country, Kurunagala, and in the districts bordering these two areas, where they were organized by wealthy and powerful men. After 1893 the crime declined in Kurunagala, but not in the Low Country, where organized networks of thieves continued to operate for another fifteen years. Before entering into a discussion of the reasons for the decline of the organized networks, and of the patterns of cattle theft in the first half of the twentieth century, I shall first discuss in some detail the administrative policies which affected cattle stealing in its heyday.

Government Policy towards Cattle Stealing

The authorities sought to suppress cattle stealing by punishing thieves and regulating the ownership of cattle. In trying to bring cattle thieves to justice they faced not only the usual difficulties but a certain amount of popular tolerance of the crime. In the Kandyan Kingdom cattle theft was a legitimate way for a person to retaliate against an injustice, such as an unpaid debt or insult.[62] In 1819 the Board of Kandyan Commissioners stated that this 'practice is sanctioned by such long usage that, until by some proclamation it is declared illegal, it might be deemed harsh to visit the act by punishment.'[63] It is not clear to what extent this view was held in the Low Country, but in Kandyan districts at least it survived the early years of British rule. In 1886 King wrote that the 'crime is not, it is to be feared, regarded with sufficient gravity among Kandyans, except by the person victimised.'[64] This last qualification was not unimportant, and violence sometimes ensued when cattle thieves were caught in the act. On the other hand cattle stealing did not rouse general moral indignation. In 1850 A. O. Brodie, who had been specifically appointed a justice of the peace to investigate the extent of cattle stealing, observed that witnesses, without intending irony, often made statements such as 'so and so is a man of good character — he deals in stolen cattle.'[65] Some twenty years later the District Judge at Kagalla found similar attitudes: 'It is a common occurrence for persons to see an animal being driven away under very suspicious circumstances, and yet, although perhaps living within a stone's throw of the owner, they take no trouble to go and tell him what they have seen, and probably say nothing about it until they meet him looking for his stolen animal, three or four days afterward; of course then the recovery is hopeless!'[66]

The attitude of more highly-educated persons towards cattle stealing was often less tolerant. The Buddhist intelligentsia associated it with beef eating, gambling and the consumption of arrack, activities which were frowned upon by those influenced by Buddhist revivalist ideas but which were perceived as regrettably common among the masses.[67] The Buddhist press paid more attention to gambling and drunkenness than it did to cattle stealing, presumably because most newspaper correspondents lived in towns, where cattle stealing was a relatively infrequent occurrence.

In the previous chapter it was pointed out that testimony in cattle-stealing cases was particulary prone to stereotyped ritual delivery. The main reason for this tendency was the lack of true evidence. Thefts were often carried out at night when there were no witnesses. The prosecution case, even if it was brought against those believed responsible, was very often fictional. In prosecutions for many other crimes, for instance assault, testimony varied more because it built on actual incidents.

The conviction rate of persons accused of cattle stealing rose during the late nineteenth century (Table 3.3.). The increase may be largely attributed to the penal code of 1885, which stipulated that most cattle thefts be tried in police courts rather than district courts. Although the maximum length of imprisonment was thereby reduced from one year to six months, and flogging was no longer a possible part of the punishment, trials took place much sooner, and sometimes at a locality closer to the complainant's home. The expense of prosecuting was reduced. This change made compromise less attractive for the complainant when he had strong evidence.

Table 3.3. Conviction Rates for Cattle Stealing

	1872	1882	1892	1902
	(%)	(%)	(%)	(%)
Persons	4.1	5.8	11.5	11.8
Cases	—	—	18.2	19.8

Source: *Administration Reports.*

Convictions were less likely in areas where cattle stealing was rampant. For instance, 441 cases with 1,374 accused persons were instituted at Kurunagala Police Court in 1886. Only twenty-three persons were convicted, less than two per cent of those charged. Casual cattle stealers ran more risk than those involved in organized thievery. The local magnates who did not personally carry out thefts were very rarely tried, although some middle-level headmen were convicted for forging sale vouchers.[68]

Some officials thought that increased flogging was the only way to reduce the crime.[69] Whippings in Sri Lanka were carried out with a cat-o-nine-tails and flayed the back of the prisoner, scarring him for life. One official later described the punishment as 'the most disgusting and barbarous thing I have ever seen', thus it is not surprising that another official wrote that 'the native has a wholesome dread of the lash.'[70] Before 1885 lashes could be inflicted in ordinary cattle-stealing cases. After this date, only repeated offenders or those convicted when the value of the cattle was more than fifty rupees were subject to this punishment.

Particularly efficient or harsh repression could temporarily
suppress cattle stealing. In 1828, after a period when cattle stealing
had been rarely and lightly punished, the Supreme Court in session
at Matara convicted a number of men, including some headmen,
and sentenced each to five years imprisonment and two hundred
lashes. For three months cattle stealing in Matara declined sharply,
and stolen cattle were returned to their owners or set free.[71]
Similarly, in 1888 a Southern Province *mudaliyar* attributed a fall
in the crime to a magistrate 'who was really a terror to evil-doers'.[72]
The efforts of F. R. Ellis, who was given special powers to itinerate
through Kurunagala from 1874 to 1879, illustrate a more sustained
approach.[73] At each locality which he visited, people brought cattle
to him for a decision on ownership. Ellis compared the brands of
the animal to the claimant's name, and if he was satisfied, as he
was in about two-thirds of the cases, he issued the claimant a
certificate of ownership. If the claim was rejected, the animal was
sold, with the proceeds going to the government. While in
Kurunagala Ellis also established a cattle voucher system whereby
headmen had to certify all sales of cattle. He checked the books of
headmen, searching for irregularities. During Ellis's tenure at
Kurunagala cattle stealing went into a sharp decline, but as soon as
he left the district it revived.[74] There was a similar drop in cattle
stealing in 1888, when an additional magistrate, L. F. Lee, was
given the power to order public floggings. Again, as soon as he left
Kurunagala, the crime recovered to its former level.[75] Cattle
stealing could be stopped, but some administrators had reservations. J. O'K. Murty, the Assistant Government Agent at Matara,
wrote in his annual report for 1902 that 'it is true that cattle
stealing can be and has been suppressed by drastic measures, such
as wholesale convictions, involving both innocent and guilty, and
by the application of the lash, but I cannot conscientiously
recommend this procedure.'[76]

A more long-term official approach was the regulation of cattle
through registration, branding, sale certificates, removal permits,
and butchers' licences. Various regulations were proclaimed from
the early years of British rule, but they remained dead letters for
most of the century.[77] Ellis was the first person to enforce them
with determination, but in the end he failed because there were no
corresponding regulations in the districts bordering Kurunagala,
and because the rules could not be enforced without the very
energetic supervision which was lacking after his departure.

A catalogue of regulations mentioned in a handbook published
for headmen in 1873 illustrates the difficulty of enforcing such

rules without a reliable rural bureaucracy.[78] In January of each year cattle owners were supposed to make out and give to the village headman a certificate describing the appearance, sex and brand marks of their animals. Each time a head of cattle was sold, the headman was supposed to certify a receipt which included the signature of the previous owner, the brand marks of the animals, and the signature of a witness. The headman was then supposed to send a copy of the receipt to the police magistrate. Anyone who wished to slaughter an animal was required to request permission in writing from a headman at least forty-eight hours in advance, noting a full description of the animal. The headman was supposed to check the accuracy of this information before giving his permission for the butchering, and he was also expected to send copies of the permits which he had approved to the magistrate at the end of each month. The handbook also included detailed regulations concerning cattle trespass and disease.

Throughout the late nineteenth century spasmodic efforts were made in individual districts to enforce some of these regulations.[79] Similar rules were made by some village committees and municipalities. After about 1870 printed vouchers were used as sale certificates in order to make forgeries more difficult.[80] Only specified headmen were empowered to certify vouchers. The numbered counterfoil of each certificate was returned to the *kachcheri* by the headman. The system was meant to provide for the quick identification of stolen animals.

The lack of a widely-used system of branding hampered official efforts to hinder the disposal of stolen animals.[81] Sinhalese cattle medicine called for branding the animal with particular designs in order to give it strength or to cure it of various illnesses. Ornamental brands were also common. These brands obscured those placed on the animal for the purpose of identification, which sometimes included caste brands as well as the name of the owner and his village. The British wanted to limit branding to the owner's initials and locality, and to require variations between the brands of an animal and the name of the owner to be explained by sale vouchers. There were many difficulties in enforcing such a system. It was not easy to store the counterfoils of sale vouchers out of the range of white ants.[82] The brands on buffaloes were difficult to read after a couple of years, and thieves were ingenious at altering them.[83] Above all, there was no popular consensus that systematic branding was necessary. When the Chilaw *kachcheri* queried a sale voucher counterfoil submitted by a headman, it was explained that the seller had branded the

animal with his grandfather's name, Nicholas, because he believed
it a lucky name in cattle breeding.[84]

Another weakness of these regulations was their dependence on
efficient and honest enforcement. Headmen were frequently
suspected of involvement in cattle stealing, and a number were
regularly dismissed as a result.[85] Former headmen were known to
be important organizers of the illicit trade in stolen cattle.[86] Even
headmen not in league with cattle thieves had little interest in
strictly enforcing the regulations. One *mudaliyar* reported that
'the minor headmen though repeatedly and strictly warned rest
satisfied if the number of permits or vouchers and the number of
cattle agree, without examining brandmarks.'[87] The authority to
issue cattle vouchers enhanced the power and status of a headman,
but many of those assigned to this task could not see why they
should take the trouble to inquire into the origins of the cattle
concerned.[88] Vouchers were issued on the payment of a fifty cent
fee, which was kept by the headman, but blank vouchers were
sometimes sold to thieves for three rupees or so.[89] The large
number of forms in circulation made it difficult for the authorities
to keep track of them. In 1903, for instance, the Galle *kachcheri*
issued over 5,000 voucher forms and 1,500 removal permit
forms.[90]

There were difficulties enforcing regulations at the Colombo
slaughterhouse. Forged vouchers were sometimes detected, but
usually there was no way for the slaughterhouse manager to know
whether or not an animal was stolen. When cattle with brand
marks not corresponding with the name of the seller were rejected,
the owner went with a friend to a headman, and stated that he
wanted to sell the animals to his friend. The headman issued
vouchers, and the animals were brought back to the slaughterhouse with their papers in order.[91] Headmen also issued vouchers
upon the statement that an animal had been born in the fold.
Butchers in small towns were even less likely to reject cattle on the
grounds that they might be stolen.[92] The authorities sometimes
turned down applications for butcher's licences because they
feared that the presence of such establishments would lead to
increases in cattle stealing.[93]

Other government regulations could be manipulated by thieves
for their own advantage. It was legal for landowners to seize and
take to specified headmen or the village committee headquarters
cattle which were found straying on cultivated or fenced land.[94]
The cattle owner was held responsible for any damage done by his
animal. As the possession of documentation for stolen cattle

became important, thieves began to turn stolen animals in as strays. If the animal had been stolen from another district, and its owner did not as a result claim it, thieves could buy the fully-documented animal for a nominal sum.[95] A variation was to drive cattle on to cultivated land, and then have damages assessed at the full value of the animals. The owner of the cattle had to pay the inflated damages or lose his animals.[96]

Another flaw was rooted in the structure of the administrative system. At every level the lines of communication were with the central authority, not with the official who was doing the same job in the adjacent district. Thieves could evade an efficient system by taking stolen cattle to another district for sale. Even if the other district had its own system, it was unlikely that there was much communication between the two sets of officials over such matters. Headmen communicated with each other through their superiors, and often sought to blame crime on persons outside their own jurisdiction. In 1895, when the *ratemahatmaya* of Katugampola Hatpattu in Kurunagala complained that Low Countrymen from Chilaw district were stealing cattle and removing them to their own district, the Low Country *mudaliyar* concerned replied that the charge was false, and that Kandyans were involved in the few cases of cattle stealing.[97]

Legislation was passed in 1898 which attempted to provide for the co-ordination of the various regulations.[98] The Governor was given wide powers to make rules concerning the branding, sale, and transfer of cattle. The ordinance envisioned a common and compulsory branding system which would make possible the easy identification of cattle from anywhere in the island. On one side of the animal there were to be letters and a number which would identify the revenue district, sub-division and village of the animal. The owner's initials were to be branded in Sinhala script on the other side. Persons tending cattle were to be required to have certificates for animals found outside of their branded sub-divisions. In practice this ordinance brought about little immediate change because it was introduced piecemeal into various districts. As late as 1905 there were no branding or registration rules in Sabaragamuva.[99]

Two trends in cattle stealing during the late nineteenth century showed that government regulations had some success. As sale voucher schemes were extended, the crime was more and more concentrated near district borders. If thieves had to transfer cattle out of the district to avoid detection, it was easier to steal animals from these areas. Cattle stealers fully understood the efforts of

the administration to thwart them. In the early 1890s thieves stole
cattle in an area of Anuradhapura which bordered on Kurunagala, drove them across the district border, carried out false sales
there with the help of some headmen, and sent the animals to the
Colombo slaughterhouse.[100] The counterfoils, which contained
descriptions of the animals, were returned to the Kurunagala
kachcheri by the slaughterhouse. Since the animals had been
stolen from Anuradhapura, the descriptions were not recognized
as those of stolen animals, and the system continued undetected
for some time.

The other trend was towards immediately killing the animal. It
was no longer possible for casual thieves to take an animal for
their own use, or to sell it for agricultural purposes in a village five
or ten kilometres distant. Cattle killing became the most common
form of the crime in areas where there were no organized networks
for stealing.[101] The increase in cattle killing was due to the sale-
voucher systems making it more difficult for casual thieves to keep
or dispose of stolen animals.

Government policy in the nineteenth century was important,
but it did not determine the extent and geography of cattle
stealing. It reacted to the crime, and its attempts to suppress it
succeeded only in forcing cattle stealers to adjust to administrative
policies. Headmen were enlisted to issue false sale vouchers,
casual thieves feasted so that the animal could not be identified,
and the stealing networks paid special attention to areas near
district boundaries. Government policy does not explain why the
organized networks only covered certain areas, or why the illicit
trade declined in Kurunagala at the end of the nineteenth century,
but continued to thrive for another fifteen years in the Low
Country before suffering a similar decline.

Cattle Stealing in the Twentieth Century

The picture of cattle stealing which has been built up thus far has
emphasized its institutional nature. In many districts the normal
response when one's animal was missing was to visit a person well
known to have connections with local thieves, and give him a
chew of betel, a wad of tobacco, and five rupees. The intermediary would then send a boy or servant with the cattle owner to
'search' for the missing animal, which would be found tied to a
tree in a nearby forest. In other areas at other times, the missing
animal might have been quickly spirited away to another district

for sale to a cultivator or butcher. When this was the case, the owner had no option but to accept his loss or institute a court case. Although his prosecution, normally based on false evidence, had little chance or success, it was a weapon which could cause expense and bother to those he thought responsible. The organizers were rarely charged in court, probably because such a prosecution would have met with an unpleasant response. Casual thefts, which were increasingly carried out for beef, accounted for a minority of stolen cattle except in districts where there was no organized stealing.

The decline of organized networks around the turn of the century was the single most striking change in patterns of cattle theft during the British period. Any interpretation should be able to explain why the decline came fifteen years later in the Southern Band than in the Northern Band. It also should help determine why there was little organized stealing in the central highlands in the second half of the nineteenth century. What administrative, economic or social conditions already present in the central highlands appeared in the Northern Band in the 1890s and in the Southern Band around 1910? The answer may be found through an examination of trends in land use. Though the areas with organized cattle stealing ranged from some of the least to most prosperous in Sri Lanka, they had in common an economy based largely on the production of rice and other grains for local consumption. They also had relatively easy access to markets for stolen cattle and a reasonable amount of forest land in which to hide and transport animals. The declines of both networks coincided with extensive changes in land use in their areas of operation.

Kurunagala, the centre of the Northern Band, remained an economic backwater in the 1860s, but in the late 1880s and 1890s coconut plantations were established there on a large scale. There were several ways in which the widespread introduction of coconuts into the district interfered with cattle theft. Forests disappeared, reducing grazing areas and possibly the number of cattle.[102] There was no longer as large an area in which to transport cattle secretly away from the scene of the crime and in which to hide animals being held for ransom. The presence of coconut estates also forced cultivators to look after their cattle more closely because plantation managers were inclined to shoot cattle or bring charges of trespass against the owners of animals found on their land.[103] Incidentally, the decreased mobility of cattle thwarted thieves.

Equally important were social changes which accompanied the introduction of coconut plantations. The world which had been dominated by subsistence agriculture crumbled. Peasants put more energy into growing coconuts and garden produce for the market. Land grabbing, often supported by forged documents, and coconut stealing provided alternative disreputable activities for those so inclined. The large-scale immigration of Low Country Sinhalese disrupted the local social structure. Cattle lost some of their importance.

Rubber, tea and other cash crops made similarly rapid and extensive inroads in much of the Southern Band in the first decade of the twentieth century. The social impact of this structural change had been foreshadowed by the temporary effects of the graphite boom of 1898 – 9, when relatively high wages became available to many previously underemployed people. Many of the graphite pits were in the Western and Southern Provinces, and a large proportion of miners who worked in other districts came from these areas. The Government Agent of the Southern Province wrote in his report for 1899 that the 'great feature of the year has been the rush to plumbago [graphite]. Paddy lands have been largely neglected, and the poorer classes have sought employment in the plumbago mines, preferring the certainty of regular and ample wages to the prospective reward of a crop in the fields often liable to damage from floods and other causes beyond their control.'[104] In the provinces most affected by the wave of prosperity the number of cattle thefts reported in 1898 – 9 was twenty-seven per cent less than in 1897 and 1900 (Table 3.4). The men who lived at the graphite pits in 1898 – 9 were the same persons who would be likely to get up in the middle of the night to help take stolen cattle five kilometres to the next relay team, thereby earning a little money and easing the tedium of village

Table 3.4. Reported Thefts of Cattle, 1897 – 1900

	WP & SP	Other Areas	Total
1897	1,123	531	1,654
1898	940	372	1,312
1899	793	455	1,248
1900	1,235	466	1,701

Source: *Administration Reports.*

life. When the price of graphite fell in 1900 and the mines closed they returned to their villages; one result was an increase in the number of cases of cattle stealing in the Western and Southern Provinces of fifty-six per cent over 1899.

The graphite boom temporarily reduced the social and economic importance of subsistence agriculture in the Low Country. By around 1910 the cultivation of rubber and tea had brought about a more permanent change. Many plantations were established in Pasdun Korale and the eastern part of Rayigam Korale, those parts of Kalutara district which were furthest inland. Pasdun Korale, a relatively lightly populated division which bordered Sabaragamuva, had served as a transit area for the illicit cattle trade between the Southern and Western Provinces, and from Sabaragamuva to the Western Province. Increasingly, tea and rubber plantations reduced the number of places where cattle could freely wander, thus making it more difficult for animals to be stolen, hidden and transported. One result was the virtual end of the traffic in stolen cattle between the Southern and Western Provinces. The change from a rural economy largely dominated by subsistence agriculture to one with a greater emphasis on cash crops also led to social changes in the interior of the Low Country similar to those which accompanied the spread of coconut plantations in Kurunagala district. Immigrants, some of them Indian Tamils, arrived to work on the new estates. Peasants also sought and obtained employment in the cash economy, often on a seasonal basis. Some villagers, those with capital, established rubber smallholdings, or grew other crops for the market.

The relationship between land use and cattle stealing helps explain why the crime was carried out relatively less often in the central highlands in the nineteenth century. The steep hillsides made it more difficult to hide and transport cattle, and after the establishment of coffee plantations and gardens in the 1840s the crime must have become more difficult to carry out profitably. Some stolen cattle were transported from the Northern Band to supply the beef market at Kandy; the Moors of Akurana, a few kilometres north of Kandy, were said to be involved in this trade. But most cattle theft in this region was casual, and increased vigilance on the part of the authorities succeeded in reducing its level in the late nineteenth century.

The decline of the networks roughly coincided with reforms of policing in rural areas, but the economic and social consequences of changes in land use were more significant than the hazards of the new policing systems. The attempt in the 1890s to turn headmen into policemen in Kurunagala was widely considered a failure, and even officials responsible for the province at the time emphasized the importance of coconut plantations in the decline of cattle theft. In the Western Province, where the police reforms of the 1890s were implemented with more vigour than in Kurunagala, organized stealing did not decline.

The evidence is slightly stronger for a link between the establishment of rural police stations in 1906 and the decline of organized cattle stealing in the Southern Band around 1910. Cattle transport routes were taken into account when the authorities decided where to open police stations, and efforts were made to enforce branding and voucher regulations.[105] For the first time details of serious crimes, including all cases of cattle stealing which village headmen chose to report, were investigated by a police force which could in theory take quick and decisive action. Nevertheless, administrative change was not the main reason for the decline of the networks in the Southern Band. In its early years the new police force had poor relations with headmen, and there is no indication of any general decline in crime at this time. Thieves deliberately transported cattle across the boundaries of the police jurisdictions, and senior police officers did not exercise enough supervision to ensure that adjacent stations co-operated with each other.

The stealing networks did not disappear entirely in the early years of the twentieth century, but their geographical range and the extent of their operations was sharply curtailed. Even in their heyday they had been fluid entities which could be dormant in specific areas for years at a time, but the decline at the turn of the century was much more widespread than earlier fluctuations. Areas which had previously been central to the stealing networks were affected. In Rayigam Korale, between Pasdun Korale and the coast, a local network survived, but it did not import cattle from the Southern Province because the Kalu Ganga made transportation from that direction impractical. Instead cattle which were not ransomed were sent to Salpiti Korale in Colombo district, and cattle were also received from that area.[106] Organized stealing also appears to have continued in parts of Siyane Korale in Colombo district, along the borders between Kurunagala and the North-Central Province, and between Kurunagala and Kagalla.[107] The authorities continued to feel frustration with cattle owners who refused to report their losses. H. L. Dowbiggin, the Inspector-General of Police, cited one case in Rayigam Korale where twenty-seven buffaloes were stolen from an owner who preferred to pay ransom rather than place the case in the hands of the police.[108] Nevertheless, in the 1920s the police made some progress towards directly deterring cattle stealing. Branding and voucher regulations were enforced much more consistently than in earlier years. Night patrols were introduced in many districts, and some cattle thieves were caught transporting stolen animals. In 1921, for instance night patrols made thirteen arrests for cattle stealing in the Southern and Western Provinces.[109] In the nineteenth century such arrests were almost unknown.

After the declines in organized stealing around the turn of the century, the number of cattle thefts known to the authorities remained at a low level, with some fluctuations, until the onset of the world depression in 1930 (Table 3.5). The official statistics for this period are not directly comparable with those of the nineteenth century because they represent all cases known to the authorities less those cases which the police believed false. The earlier figures measured the number of cases which were instituted before a magistrate or a justice of the peace.

Table 3.5. *Average Number of Thefts of Cattle Reported Annually per 10,000 Inhabitants, 1914 – 48*

	WP	SP	NWP	Sab	CP	Uva	NCP
1914 – 18	2.7	2.7	3.3	1.4	0.4	1.8	1.2
1919 – 23	2.3	4.1	3.3	1.7	0.7	2.7	0.5
1924 – 28	1.1	1.2	1.4	0.6	0.1	0.6	0.5
1929 – 33	1.8	2.0	2.4	1.7	0.3	0.9	1.9
1934 – 38	3.5	3.2	4.3	2.3	0.4	1.0	5.5
1939 – 43	4.3	4.4	7.4	2.3	0.7	1.5	4.9
1944 – 48	5.1	3.9	5.7	3.7	0.5	1.4	4.1

Source: *Administration Reports.*

Note: Figures for 1942 and 1945 were not available.

Cattle stealing was more sensitive to economic fluctuations in the twentieth century than it had been earlier. The severe depression of 1878 – 83, which was longer and deeper in the coffee-growing Central Province than elsewhere, had little effect on cattle stealing (Table 3.6 and Figure 3.1). Officials in the worst hit areas reported an increase in cattle killing, but the number of court cases did not increase sharply in any district.[110] There were only thirteen per cent more cattle theft cases in the Central Province during the height of the downturn than during the years immediately preceding and following it. The equivalent figure for the rest of Sinhala Sri Lanka was five per cent. The coffee crash was felt strongest in areas where there was less cattle stealing, and where most of the stealing was casual. Although all parts of Sri Lanka were affected by the depression, the areas covered by the organized networks were less integrated into the market economy, and were affected less by the coffee crash, than either the central highlands or the coastal strip. The commercial depression in Colombo and other towns may well have decreased the demand for beef, making the shipment of stolen cattle to butchers less profitable.

Table 3.6. Reported Thefts of Cattle, 1874 – 86

	CP	Other Areas	Total
1874	266	1,232	1,498
1875	323	1,130	1,453
1876	—	—	—
1877	190	942	1,132
1878	314	1,380	1,694
1879	341	1,195	1,536
1880	353	1,375	1,728
1881	336	1,258	1,594
1882	339	1,164	1,503
1883	315	1,168	1,483
1884	294	1,153	1,447
1885	418	1,340	1,758
1886	279	1,405	1,684

Source: *Administration Reports.*

Note: The figures for Kurunagala have been excluded because of distortion caused by special administrative policies.

During the years 1918 – 21, a period of severe food shortages, there was a large increase in cattle theft. The number of reported cases was thirty-eight per cent higher than during the years 1916 – 17 and 1922 – 3 (Table 3.7). The increased sensitivity of cattle stealing to hardship may be largely accounted for by the fact that at this time more cattle stealing was carried out casually, mostly for immediate consumption as beef.[111] As soon as the price of food fell, cattle theft declined. During the prosperous 1920s, a time when the acreage devoted to cash crops expanded, cattle stealing nearly disappeared. In the period 1925 – 9 an average of only 400 cases annually were reported in Sinhala Sri Lanka. Under the more inefficient system of the late nineteenth century, it was not unusual for over 2,000 cases to be reported in a single year.

Table 3.7. Reported Thefts of Cattle, 1916 – 23

1916	862
1917	836
1918	890
1919	1,293
1920	1,014
1921	1,008
1922	772
1923	568

Source: *Administration Reports.*

The beginning of the depression coincided with a sharp increase in cattle stealing. The number of reported cases rose from 434 in 1929 to 650 in 1930 and 813 in 1931. It held steady thereafter until 1935, the year of a devastating malaria epidemic, when the number of cases increased to 1,020. Officials attributed these increases to persons who killed cattle for beef.[112] The next year, 1936, all government regulations concerning the branding, movement and sale of cattle were lifted.[113] In the new political climate of the Donoughmore Constitution these restrictions were seen as a restraint on the economic freedom of the peasantry. The number of cattle-stealing cases doubled, reaching 2,020 in 1938, five times the level reported ten years earlier. Unlike the increases of the early 1930s, this jump was caused by the revival of stealing networks, mainly in those areas where they had prevailed in the nineteenth century.[114] The high rate of the North-Central Province, for instance, is an indication that the old trade on the border between this province and Kurunagala had been revived. Urban

consumers of beef benefited; within eighteen months of the lifting
of the regulations the price of beef fell by half.[115] The number of
reported cattle thefts increased still further during the Second
World War, when food prices increased dramatically. The number
of reported cases peaked at 3,547 in 1944, then fell to below 1,500
in the late 1940s. A combination of administrative and economic
factors favoured the revival of organized stealing during the final
decade of British rule, but given the growth of population and the
more efficient reporting system the extent of the crime was not as
great as it had been before 1890.

Conclusions

One temptation is to characterize cattle stealing as a traditional
activity, and to argue that it was the victim of modernization. This
assertion would be misleading, for not only was cattle stealing not
primitive, but when organized it was a rational economic business.
The expansion of the market economy in the nineteenth century at
first stimulated the crime by providing markets for stolen cattle.
Although there may have been a trade in illicit cattle across the
border between the Dutch and Kandyan territories in the
eighteenth century, the large-scale networks were probably a
product of the early and middle nineteenth century, made possible
by the increased demand for cattle for transportation and meat. It
was only when cash crops reduced the importance of subsistence
agriculture and the amount of forest land declined in districts
adjacent to the areas where the new markets had been created that
the market economy began to work against the crime.

Cattle stealing was an institution which provided benefits to
different groups. To village youths, whether they were acting as
minor cogs of a cattle relay team or stealing a disliked neighbour's
bullock, it provided both adventure and a small additional
income. There were few other sources of economic mobility or
excitement in rural areas. For a smaller group, it provided a
living. Certain villages were strongholds of cattle thieves and their
residents derived a significant portion of their incomes from the
cattle trade. More significantly, in many districts there were in
most villages several households which depended on cattle
stealing for their livelihood. Butchers who regularly received
stolen cattle benefited, as did consumers who were able to buy
cattle cheaply and peasants who killed cattle for food at times of
hardship.

Cattle theft must also have brought about a measure of loss equal to the gain of those who profited. It is likely that among the rural population this loss was more widely distributed than was the gain. Thieves probably benefited from a certain popular tolerance which dated back to the time when individual thefts of cattle were a legitimate means of pursuing a dispute. The cultural stereotype of cattle stealing as an exciting, adventurous activity may also have contributed to its acceptance. In addition, the organized networks could to a certain extent rely on intimidation and social pressure. The high social and economic position of the organizers made people reluctant to confront them. Each local network of cattle stealing provided an alternative system of power and wealth in that locality. The local magnates exercised a limited but real authority entirely independent of the colonial administration.

Cattle stealers had to outwit a government with a modern, bureaucratic structure. That they were usually successful indicates that the thieves understood the workings of the colonial bureaucracy, and that government did not function in the way intended by higher officials. Indeed, the colonial system of the nineteenth century was a sort of polity which was particularly vulnerable to an illegal activity like cattle stealing which could not be carried out without the connivance or at least tolerance of a large segment of the population. A more authoritarian regime could have simply imprisoned the organizers. Officials usually knew who they were, though they could not obtain the evidence needed to convict them in the courts. In the twentieth century a combination of economic change and government regulations reduced the profitability of cattle stealing, and when the crime revived in the 1930s there was little the authorities could do in face of nationalist feeling and the economic pressures of the depression.

Over the long term cattle theft was dependent on the position of cattle, the major form of mobile wealth in a rice-based economy. The non-subsistence sector of the economy needed cattle for transportation and food. At the same time the quality of cattle was declining and any increase in their numbers did not keep pace with demand. Cattle stealing provided certain groups in rural areas with an opportunity to benefit from the economic changes along the coast and in the central highlands, but it did not long survive as an organized business once a district was penetrated deeply by plantations. The revival of the 1930s and early 1940s was temporary, brought on by extreme hardship, the temporary decline of the market economy in some rural areas, and the inability of an administration in the last stage of colonial rule to adjust. When the importance of cattle declined in the local economy, so did cattle stealing.

NOTES TO CHAPTER 3

1   The cattle returns were published in the annual *Blue Books*. They were based on reports supplied by headmen.
2   W. A. de Silva, *An English Translation of a Pamphlet on the Treatment of Cattle*, 2: d'Alwis, 'Brand Marks on Cattle', 62; *SP 26 1883*, 6 – 7; Burrows, *AR Matale 1887*, 95A; *Messenger*, 11 Nov 1887; *Sandarasa*, 28 Aug 1891: *Independent*, 1 Apr 1891; Vigors, D, 8 June 1896, SLNA26/154.
3   *SP 4 1867*, 6, 38, 47, 52, 54; *SP 20 1869 – 70*; Saxton, D, 9 Nov 1894, SLNA34/26; Murray, D, 9 Nov 1889, SLNA41/260; H. Baumgartner, *AR Matara 1890*, E17; Longden to Kimberley, 6 Dec 1880, CO54/529(244); Hodson, *AR Kurunagala 1929*, F4; Woolf, *Growing*, 187 – 200. An exception was the decline in Uva after the rebellion of 1817 – 18, a consequence of the scorched earth policy of the British. C. R. de Silva, 200.
4   Sturgess, *AR Veterinary 1903*, N2; *SP 7 1903*, 3 – 5.
5   Elliott, *SP 4 1867*, 102.
6   *SP 20 1869 – 70*, vii; Sturgess, *AR Veterinary 1905*, G4; *SP 26 1883*, 6; Crawford, *AR Kurunagala 1901*, G6; W. A. de Silva, *An English Translation*, 1 – 2; Wace, *AR Galle 1898*, E4.
7   *SP 20 1869 – 70*, vii; Sharpe, *AR Kandy 1886*, 28A; Freeman, *AR Puttalam 1903*, G20; Wace, *AR Galle 1896*, E4; Woodhouse, PM, *AR Matara 1900*, E29.
8   Ievers, D, 20 Nov 1888, SLNA41/260; Nevill, *AR Anuradhapura 1893*, H2, H5 – 6; Booth, *AR Anuradhapura 1901*, H14; Bowes, *AR Puttalam 1904*, F26; Wedderburn, *AR Galle 1929*, C6; Hodson, *AR Kurunagala 1929*, F4.
9   *Messenger*, 11 Nov 1887; Turnour, Agt of Govt Ratnapura, to Rev Cmr Kandy, 18 June 1824, CO416/20.
10 *SP 20 1869 – 70*.
11 Ibid., vii.
12 Brodhurst, *AR Kalutara 1897*, B31; *SP 4 1867*, 155.
13 Ludovici, *Rice Cultivation*, 155; *SP 4 1867*; P. Templer, *AR Galle 1890*, E4; *SP 38 1880*, 2; *SP 26 1883*, 2; *SP 25 1884*, 4; *Sandarasa*, 28 Aug 1891; White, D, 16 Apr 1891, SLNA26/150; *SP 4 1890*, 2; *SP 6 1908*, 7; *Messenger*, 13 July 1883; R. Lewis, 'The Rural Economy of the Sinhalese', 35 – 7; *SP 20 1869 – 70*.
14 *SP 20 1869 – 70*; Ludovici, 155; *SP 40 1880*, 4.
15 *SP 4 1867*, 76.
16 Ludovici, 155.
17 Wickremeratne, *UCHC*, III, 310.
18 *SP 26 1883*, 2 – 7; Nevill, *AR Anuradhapura 1893*, H2; Booth, *AR Anuradhapura 1903*, H3; Dawson, *AR Colombo 1895*, B3; Crawford, *AR Kurunagala 1901*, G5 – 6; *Messenger*, 11 Nov 1887; *Sandarasa*, 28 Aug 1891; *SP 27 1925*, 8.
19 Saunders, *AR Colombo 1883*, 69A & *AR Colombo 1887*, 9A; Dawson, *AR Colombo 1895*, B3; Fowler, *AR Colombo 1899*, B5 & *AR Colombo 1905*, B2; Pinto, PM, *AR Ratnapura 1904*, I7; Vigors, *AR Kalutara 1902*, B39;

Byrde, PM, *AR Kurunagala 1903*, G8; *Messenger*, 11 Aug 1887; *Sandarasa*, 28 Aug 1891; d'Alwis, 'Brand Marks', 60 – 2.

20   Sturgess, *AR Veterinary 1901*, K2.
21   Denham, 451.
22   *SP 4 1867*, 6.
23   *Report of Committee on Cattle Trespass*, 1853, E5, CO54/309(60); *SP 20 1869 – 70*; *SP 4 1867*.
24   *SP 4 1867*, 177; Fowler, *AR Galle 1900*, E14 & *AR Colombo 1902*, B4; Brodhurst, *AR Colombo 1908*, A3.
25   Elliott, *AR Galle 1886*, 80A.
26   Wright, *AR Kurunagala 1871*, 221.
27   Carberry, PM, *AR Matara 1897*, E19.
28   R Dambadeniya, *AR Kurunagala 1894*, G6.
29   *Report of the Committee on Cattle Traspass*, vi, 1853, E5, CO54/309(60); *Lakrivikirana*, 12 Nov 1870; Meyer, 'The Plantation System', 41.
30   *AR DJ Badulla 1869*, 191.
31   G. Baumgartner, *AR Badulla 1899*, E39; Short, *AR Nuvara Eliya 1900*, C25; Burrows, *AR Nuvara Eliya 1898*, C21; Bartlett, *AR Nuvara Eliya 1908*, B35.
32   *AR Matara 1899*, E39.
33   *AR Badulla 1886*, 101A.
34   *AR DJ Negombo 1873*, 29.
35   Regulation 3 1814, CO54/53.
36   SC Judges to Gov, 29 May 1829, CO416/13.
37   CO416/14; CO416/15.
38   Pippet, 186 – 7, 205; *Observer*, 9 Jan 1854; Torrington to Grey, 11 Aug 1848, K. M. de Silva, (ed.), *Letters on Ceylon 1846 – 50*, 100: Anderson to Grey, 4 Jan 1851, CO54/278(2); Colepeper, PO, to QA, 21 Apr 1859, E, CO54/347(137).
39   Burrows, *AR Matale 1889*, C23.
40   *Lakrivikirana*, 30 Aug 1867, 12 Nov 1870, 14 Oct 1871; *Pradipaya*, 11 June 1896; *Bi-Monthly Examiner*, 22 Aug 1868; *Sandarasa*, 14 Aug 1891; *Native Opinion*, 30 Mar 1900; Guruva Naide, petition, 29 Mar 1892, SLNA42/952; Crawford, D, 17 Dec 1887, SLNA35/5; P. Templer, *AR Kurunagala 1886*, 44A; Knollys, *AR P 1892*, B5; Saxton, D, 12 Aug 1893, SLNA34/26; Brodhurst, *AR Kalutara 1894*, B14 & *AR Galle 1902*, E9; Lushington, *AR Galle 1905*, 21; C. Longden, *AR P 1905*, B8; J. de Saram, DJ, *AR P 1867*, 219; H. Baumgartner, *AR Matara 1887*, 153A; R Moravak, *AR Matara 1888*, 171A.
41   Hayley, 118; R. Pieris, *Sinhalese Social Organization*, 143 – 4.
42   Twynam, GANWP, to CS, 28 Aug 1869, E, CO54/448(143); Morris to CS, 11 Sept 1869, E, CO54/448(143); Police *vidane* Kirimatiyana, petition, 30 July 1888, SLNA42/952; Petitions of 28 Feb 1890 & 13 Aug 1890, SLNA33/2758; R Katugampola to GANWP, 23 Oct 1895, SLNA42/952; Le Mesurier, D, 17 – 24 Feb 1892, SLNA26/151; Brodhurst, *AR Galle 1902*, E9.
43   J. de Saram, DJ, *AR P 1867*, 219; King, *AR DJ Badulla 1869*, 191; Giles, *SP 17 1889*, 36; Wace, *AR Galle 1896*, E4; Hornsburgh, *AR Hambantota 1899*, E32; Brodhurst, *AR Puttalam 1900*, G19.
44   *AR DJ Negombo 1875*, 26.
45   Ellis, *AR Colombo 1900*, B12; Fowler, *AR Colombo 1904*, A6.
46   From 1872 to 1896 only prosecutions were recorded. After 1896 some cases without a specific accused person were included. These latter cases have been eliminated from Tables 3.1 and 3.2 in order to maintain the comparability of

the statistics. The proportion of cases with no accused was 5% in 1897, and increased annually thereafter, reaching 33% in 1905.

47   P. Templer, GANWP, *AR AG 1887*, 1C.
48   This account of the Southern Band is mainly based on: Fowler, *AR Galle 1900*, E14; L. Liesching, *AR DJ Galle 1871*, 308; C Liesching, *AR DJ Negombo 1873*, 29; Crawford, *AR Kalutara 1888*, 59A & D, 6 May 1889, SLNA35/7; Saunders, *AR Colombo 1889*, B12; P. Templer, *AR Galle 1889*, E9; Nell, *AR CC Southern Circuit 1891*, A11; Elliott, *AR Galle 1895*, E8; Lushington, D, 10 Jan 1895, SLNA26/153; Murray, *AR Hambantota 1891*, E14; Thorpe, PO, *AR P 1896*, B12; Wace, *AR Galle 1898*, E6 & *AR Galle 1896*, E4; Ellis, *AR Colombo 1898*, B22; Bailey, *AR Kalutara 1898*, B33; Fox, D, 15 Sept 1900, SLNA35/14 & *AR Kalutara 1900*, B51; Ekanayake, PM, *AR Galle 1902*, E11 – 12; Saxton, D, 20 Feb 1902, SLNA35/16 & *AR Ratnapura 1903*, K10; Fowler, *AR Kalutara 1890*, B19; Plant, *AR Kalutara 1912*, A22; *Messenger*, 4 Mar 1873; G. Baumgartner, *AR Badulla 1899*, 110.
49   *AR Colombo 1889*, B12.
50   Fox, D, 15 Sept 1900, SLNA35/14. Alexander's map is bound in with Fox's diary.
51   This account of the Northern Band is mainly based on: Jayetileke, *AR DJ Chilaw 1871*, 328; Dawson, *AR Kagalla 1875*, 67 – 8; Lushington, *AR Puttalam 1886*, 56A; P. Templer, *AR Kurunagala 1886*, 44A; Moysey, *AR Matale 1886*, 32A & *AR Negombo 1889*, B17; Ievers, *AR Anuradhapura 1892*, H4; Bowes, PM, *AR Anuradhapura 1894*, H2; G. Baumgartner, *AR Puttalam 1896*, G17; Noyes, *AR Puttalam 1897*, G12; Alexander, D, 8 Mar 1904, SLNA30/25; Burrows, *AR Kurunagala 1904*, F8 & D, 3 Oct 1902, SLNA38/10; Cameron, *AR Anuradhapura 1895*, H5; D. de Saram, PM, *AR P 1867*, 219; C. Liesching, *AR DJ Negombo 1873*, 29; Byrde, *AR Anuradhapura 1897*, H4 & D, 10 Jan 1899, SLNA41/266; *Messenger*, 15 Nov 1889; *Bi-Monthly Examiner*, 2 Oct 1869; Twynam to CS, 28 Aug 1869, E, CO54/448(143); Morris to CS, 11 Sept 1869, E, CO54/448(143); Eaton, PM, *AR Matale 1890*, C16; Dyke to CS, 16 May 1849, E3, CO54/278(2); Brodie, [1850], E2, CO54/278(2); Correspondence in SLNA42/951, SLNA42/952 & SLNA42/962.
52   *AR DJ Negombo 1873*, 29.
53   Bailey, *AR Kurunagala 1889*, G10.
54   *Hue and Cry*, 14 July 1899.
55   The geographical distribution of the cattle thefts committed by the 393 persons listed in the *Hue and Cry* between 1896 and 1905 accurately reflected that of the 16,500 cases reported to the courts during this period.
56   Jayetileke, *AR DJ Kalutara 1872*, 561; Crawford, D, 14 Feb 1889, SLNA35/7; Brodhurst, D, 31 May 1894, SLNA35/10; *Lakrivikirana*, 30 Aug 1867; *Bi-Monthly Examiner*, 28 June 1868; Dep, 320; Dowbiggin, *AR P 1920*, B16. These three villages were largely populated by Vahumpuras, Demala Gattaras, and Salagamas respectively. All are in Kalutara district.
57   Fox, D, 15 Sept 1900, SLNA35/14.
58   Burrows, D, 3 Oct 1902, SLNA38/10.
59   King, *AR Kurunagala 1896*, B5 & *AR Kurunagala 1898*, G6; Crawford, *AR Kurunagala 1901*, G10; Burrows, *AR Kurunagala 1903*, G9.
60   *AR Kurunagala 1899*, G4.
61   Crawford, *AR Kurunagala 1902*, G8.
62   Hayley, 81.
63   Ibid.
64   *AR Badulla 1886*, 101A.

65 [1850], E2, CO54/278(2).

66 Mainwaring, *AR DJ Kagalla 1872*, 567.

67 *Lakrivikirana*, 19 Mar 1869, 14 Oct 1871, 30 Dec 1871; *Sandarasa*, 14 Aug 1891; Petition from Ragama Pattu, 28 Feb 1890, SLNA33/2758.

68 D. de Saram, *AR DJ Kurunagala 1871*, 318; Saunders, *AR Colombo 1889*, B12; Fowler. *AR Galle 1900*, E14; Vigors, *AR Anuradhapura 1906*, G4.

69 Burrows, *AR Matale 1887*, 91A; King, *AR Badulla 1886*, 101A; Crawford, *AR Kalutara 1887*, 63A; Carberry, PM, *AR Matara 1898*, E18; Brodhurst, *AR Kalutara 1897*, B31.

70 Woolf, *Growing*, 166; Byrde, *AR Anuradhapura 1896*, H4.

71 SC Judges to Gov, 29 May 1829, CO416/13.

72 M Four Gravets, *AR Matara 1888*, 171A. For another example see Pippet, 205.

73 Ellis's diary for part of this period is in SLNA38/1.

74 Morris, *AR Kurunagala 1874*, 127 – 8, 137; Campbell, *AR P 1880*, 27B.

75 Gordon to Holland, 23 Jan 1888, CO54/576(48); P. Templer, *AR Kurunagala 1887*, 178A; Bailey, *AR Kurunagala 1889*, G5; Campbell, *AR P 1887*, 37C.

76 *AR Matara 1902*, E36.

77 Pippet, 10 – 11, 61, 205; Sitting Magistrate Kandy, 26 Sept 1829, CO416/19.

78 Lee, 14 – 16, 22 – 3, 43, 46 – 8.

79 'Report of the Cattle Commission', 15 July 1897, SLNA59/285; Lee, *AR Kagalla 1871*, 30 – 1; *SP 26 1883*, 2; Ord 24 1889, H. Baumgartner, D, 27 Feb 1890, SLNA26/150.

80 Lee to CS, 2 Nov 1871, *AR Kagalla 1871*, 31; Morris, *AR Kurunagala 1874*, 128; *Messenger*, 29 May 1874.

81 Ellis, D, 23 Mar 1900, SLNA33/23 & PM, D, [1875], SLNA38/1; 'Cattle Branding Rules, Chilaw District', 1898 & 1899, SLNA42/969; Chinniah, 'The Branding of Cattle', 288, 362; Pohath-Kehelpannala, 'Brandmarks on Kandyan Cattle'; *Overland Observer*, 24 July 1875; Fowler, D, 27 May 1902, SLNA33/25; *SP 38 1925*, 3 – 4.

82 Unsigned note, 17 Aug 1893, SLNA42/969; Ellis, [1905], SLNA6/13653.

83 Mainwaring, *AR DJ Kagalla 1872*, 567; Ekanayake, PM, *AR Galle 1902*, E12; Crawford, D, 21 Sept 1904, SLNA43/12; 'Report of the Cattle Commission', 15 June 1897, SLNA59/285; Chinniah, 362.

84 M PkN, 16 Nov 1899, SLNA42/969.

85 D. de Saram, *AR DJ Kurunagala 1871*, 318; L. Liesching, *AR DJ Galle 1871*, 308; Dickson, *AR DJ Anuradhapura 1873*, 16; Moysey, *AR Matale 1886*, 32A; Jayetileke, PM, *AR P 1867*, 219; Eaton, PM, *AR Matale 1890*, C16; H. Baumgartner, D, 12 Feb 1890, SLNA26/150; Lushington, D, 10 Jan 1895, SLNA26/153; Cameron, *AR Anuradhapura 1895*, H5 & D, 24 Mar 1899, SLNA38/7; Brodhurst, D, 7 June 1894, SLNA35/10; R Demala to AGA Puttalam, 7 Oct 1894, SLNA42/952; R Katugampola to GANWP, 23 Oct 1895, SLNA42/952; Hill, D, 3 Aug 1899, SLNA30/21; Wace, *AR Galle 1896*, E4 & D, 17 Sept 1896, SLNA38/5; Le Mesurier, D, 17 – 24 Feb 1892, SLNA26/151; Ramanathan, *CH 1897 – 8*, 100; G. Baumgartner, *AR Badulla 1899*, I9; Crawford, D, 6 Oct 1904, SLNA43/12; Murray, D, 20 July 1901, SLNA38/9; Burrows, D, 3 Oct 1902, SLNA38/10 & D, 17 Oct 1905, SLNA38/13; Fowler, D, 4 Oct 1905 & 17 Nov 1905, SLNA33/26; Vigors, *AR Anuradhapura 1906*, G4; Brodie, [1850], E2, CO54/278(2); Dep, 194; *Observer*, 9 Jan 1854; *Lakrivikirana*, 19 Mar 1869; *Bi-Monthly Examiner*, 2 Oct 1869; *Messenger*, 4 Mar 1873; *Native Opinion*, 10 Aug 1900.

86 Weeraperumal, PO, 20 Aug 1879, SNLA6/5973; Crawford, *AR Kalutara 1888*, 59A; Murray, *AR Hambantota 1891*, E14; Byrde, D, 10 Jan 1899, SLNA41/266.
87 M PkS to AGA Chilaw, 31 Jan 1898, SLNA42/962.
88 M PkS to AGA Chilaw, 10 Oct 1893, SLNA42/952; Petition of 18 Dec 1899, SLNA42/969.
89 'Report of the Cattle Commission', 15 June 1897, SLNA59/285.
90 Brodhurst to CS, 26 Aug 1904, SLNA6/13599.
91 Epps, slaughterhouse keeper, to Secretary Colombo Municipal Council, 18 Feb 1886 & 5 Nov 1886, SLNA33/538.
92 Petition, Feb 1868, SLNA6/3180; Crawford, D, 27 Sept 1888, SLNA35/6; Lee, [1897], SLNA59/285.
93 A. A. Fernando, petition, 17 Jan 1889 & M PkS, 6 Feb 1889, SLNA42/951.
94 Ord 9 1876; Ord 24 1889.
95 Crawford, *AR Kalutara 1888*, 59A; Byrde, *AR Anuradhapura 1896*, H4; 'Report of the Cattle Commission', 15 June 1897, SLNA59/285; Elliott, *AR Colombo 1894*, B5; Thorpe, PO, *AR Colombo 1896*, B12; Fowler, *AR Galle 1900*, E10; Lee, PM, 13 May 1888, SLNA42/952; Saxton to Dunuwille, 11 Apr 1888, SLNA42/952; Dowbiggin, *AR P 1921*, B20.
96 Crawford, *AR Kurunagala 1902*, G8.
97 R Katugampola to GANWP, 23 Oct 1895, SLNA42/952; M PkC to AGA Chilaw, 2 Dec 1895, SLNA42/952. Also see Saxton, D, 12 Aug 1893 & D 10 Sept 1893, SLNA34/26; Ievers, D, 21 Nov 1887, SLNA41/260; R Demala to AGA Puttalam, 7 Oct 1894 & 18 Nov 1894, SLNA42/952; Dep, 330.
98 Ord 10 1898; 'Report of the Cattle Commission', 15 June 1897, SLNA59/285; Ramanathan, *CH 1897–8*, 92–3.
99 Alexander, *AR Kagalla 1903*, K21; Saxton, D, 26 Apr 1905, SLNA45/37.
100 Bowes, PM, *AR Anuradhapura 1894*, H2; Cameron, *AR Anuradhapura 1895*, H5; Ramanathan, *CH 1897–8*, 100.
101 Gooneratne, PO, 23 Aug 1878, SLNA6/5542; Moysey, *AR Matale 1878*, 45; Wace, *AR Ratnapura 1886*, 160A; Sharpe, *AR Kandy 1886*, 28A; Bailey, *AR Kandy 1898*, C5; Wace, *AR Galle 1899*, E15; Beven, PM, *AR Kurunagala 1905*, F3 & PM, *AR Matara 1901*, E35; Allnutt, *AR Hambantota 1904*, D63; C. Longden, *AR P 1908*, B4; *Messenger*, 25 Feb 1887; *Standard*, 30 July 1904; *Native Opinion*, 10 Aug 1900.
102 *SP 6 1908*, 13; R Veudavili, *AR Kurunagala 1895*, G4; Saxton, *AR Kurunagala 1907*, F2.
103 R Veudavili, *AR Kurunagala 1895*, G4; King, *AR Kurunagala 1897*, G6 & *AR Kurunagala 1896*, G5; Murray, D, 11 Aug 1902, SLNA38/10; Saxton, *AR Kurunagala 1907*, F2. Also see Fowler, D, Oct 1890, SLNA35/8; Fox, D, 10 Mar 1901, SLNA30/23; Hellings, *AR Ratnapura 1907*, I2.
104 *AR Galle 1899*, E15.
105 Lushington, *AR Galle 1906*, D8.
106 Plant, *AR Kalutara 1912*, A22; Dowbiggin, *AR P 1914*, B6, *AR P 1918*, B11, *AR P 1919*, B10 & *AR P 1921*, B20–1; Gottelier, *AR P 1929*, A15.
107 Dowbiggin, *AR P 1916*, B6, *AR P 1917*, B6, *AR P 1919*, B10, *AR P 1921*, B20 & *AR P 1923*, B13.
108 Dowbiggin, *AR P 1933*, A19.
109 Dowbiggin, *AR P 1921*, B20.
110 Moysey, *AR Matale 1881*, 62A & *AR Matale 1884*, 64A; King, *AR Badulla 1878*, 37 & *AR Badulla 1887*, 218A; Fisher, *AR Badulla 1888*, 223A. Also see *Messenger*, 23 Feb 1883.

111 Fraser, *AR Colombo 1919*, A7; Brown, *AR Matara 1919*, C10; Forrest, *AR Chilaw 1919*, F14; Dowbiggin, *AR P 1919*, B7 & *AR P 1920*, B15.
112 Dowbiggin, *AR P 1931*, A15 & *AR P 1935*, A23; Rodrigo, *AR Kurunagala 1935*, F10, F15.
113 Davidson, *AR Matara 1936*, C22.
114 Banks, *AR P 1937*, A14 – 15, *AR P 1939*, A8 – 9 & *AR P 1940*, A7 – 8.
115 Banks, *AR P 1937*, A15.

CHAPTER 4

HOMICIDE

In modern times Sri Lankan élites have consistently perceived homicide to be a major problem.[1] The aim of this chapter is to examine and interpret the rate and social pattern of this crime during the British period. A main argument is that, in contrast to cattle stealing, the incidence and nature of homicide cannot adequately be explained by reference to long-term social and economic change, and still less by government policy. With few exceptions patterns of homicide changed little during colonial rule, or at least after 1860, a fact which is remarkable given the degree of population growth and other social and economic developments. Another distinctive feature of homicide in Sri Lanka was that the social profile of those who committed it was in many ways similar to that of the adult male population at large. There were however significant geographical variations in the incidence of homicide, and the crime was also sensitive to economic fluctuations.

Although there are some indications of the extent and nature of homicide during the first half of the nineteenth century, systematic evidence of its incidence is available only for the second half of the British period. Official statistics, first compiled for 1867, provide an annual frequency count by province. Other information, such as the ethnic breakdown of offenders and the number of times various types of weapons were used, was sometimes tabulated by the authorities. These data, while essential, are not sufficient for a full study of homicide. Fortunately, for two periods, 1883 – 9 and 1900 – 4, narrative descriptions of homicide cases were printed in the annual *Administration Reports*. These accounts provide information on the circumstances of the crimes, as perceived by the police, and many list the name, ethnic group, occupation and age of both the accused and deceased.[2] The accounts from 1900 – 4 are generally less detailed than those for the earlier period. Therefore, although for many purposes it has been possible to combine the two blocks of data and use them as a sample for homicide during the mature colonial period, for questions involving ethnicity, occupation and age a restricted sample of cases from 1883 – 9 has been used (Appendix B). There are 1,482 cases in the general sample and 730 cases in the restricted sample.

No comparable set of descriptions is available for the period from 1905 until the end of British rule, but a government-sponsored survey collected detailed information about all homicides known to have been committed in 1956. The findings of this survey are accessible through the work of the American criminologists Arthur Wood and Herbert Bloch, both of whom also carried out research of their own on homicide in the 1950s.[3] Although the survey was taken several years after independence, there is no evidence to indicate that patterns of homicide underwent significant change at this time. The data presented by Wood and Bloch have been taken as broadly representative of homicide in the mid-twentieth century, including the closing years of colonial rule.

The first section of this chapter treats the incidence of homicide and the social characteristics of assailants and victims. It is shown that Sri Lanka had a moderately high rate of homicide by comparative standards. Unlike many societies, offenders and victims were not clustered at the lower end of the socio-economic scale. Another distinctive feature was the relatively high age of those involved.

The second section examines the proximate causes of the crime. No one set of circumstances, such as land disputes or conflicts over women, accounted for a dominant proportion of violent deaths. Few homicides were carried out for economic gain, and lack of premeditation was the rule. When there was planning, it was seldom of long duration. Homicides sprang from normal social intercourse, and the types of incidents which led to them changed very little during the second half of colonial rule.

The final section seeks to explain this distinctive pattern of homicide. Theories based on culture conflict and on subcultures of violence are rejected as not fitting the Sri Lankan evidence. Another hypothesis, that homicide was the product of inadequate mechanisms for dispute settlement, is discarded because no causal link between homicide and the failure to resolve disputes can be established. Instead, homicide is seen as a product of stress which was in turn the result of the emphasis on status and social competition in Sinhalese society.

The Social Geography of Homicide

Scholars generally accept that official statistics for homicide are more accurate than those for other crimes. Although the conviction rate for homicide is often low, the fact that it was committed usually comes to light. In Sri Lanka the authorities occasionally discovered a murder which villagers had concealed for months, but the factionalism present in most parts of the colony worked to the advantage of officialdom. Charges of serious crime were important weapons in disputes, and a violent death could not be hushed up if it provided one party or another with an opportunity to do damage to an opponent. Homicide statistics were also more accurate because accusations made when no crime had been committed were easier to weed out for homicide than for other crimes.

G. W. R. Campbell, the long-serving Inspector-General of Police, was the first person to try to compile information about the annual tally of homicides.[4] He believed that his initial enumerations, carried out in the late 1860s, failed to include all cases which occurred in rural areas. After 1879, when he began to publish regularly the number of homicides by province in his *Administration Report*, his figures may be taken as an accurate reflection of homicides known to the authorities. During the last two decades of the nineteenth century it is possible that a higher than average number of deaths were concealed from officials in some of the less policed areas, such as parts of the North-Western and North-Central Provinces and Sabaragamuva, but during the twentieth century there was probably little regional variation in the number of homicides which were hushed up.

Homicide rates by province are shown in Table 4.1. Between 1879 and 1905 the annual average number of homicides in Sinhala Sri Lanka known to the police was 4.7 per 100,000 inhabitants. The rate did not increase in the early twentieth century; between 1915 and 1929 it was 4.8 per 100,000 persons. But after 1929 it rose sharply, and remained high throughout the depression and war years, averaging 6.8 per 100,000 inhabitants between 1930 and the end of British rule.[5] In the years immediately following independence the rate declined to 5.3 per 100,000 residents. With the exception of the increase during the 1930s and 1940s, the homicide rate for Sinhala Sri Lanka as a whole remained stable between the 1860s and 1950s. Although there is no evidence with which to determine reliable homicide rates for the early nineteenth century, analysis of the frequency with which homicide was tried in the courts in the early years of British rule suggests that the overall rate at this time was not radically different from that of the later colonial period.[6]

The seriousness of homicide in Sri Lanka depends upon which base of comparison is used. International comparisons of crime rates are always difficult, in view of differences in levels of police efficiency, in judicial systems, and in methods of recording statistics. Homicide is however the most suitable crime for this purpose. When the number of homicides known to have been committed, rather than some judicial statistic, is used as the measure, comparisons between countries with stable, bureaucratic governments which officially process most homicides may be made with some confidence.

Table 4.1. Annual Average Rates of Homicide per 100,000 Inhabitants, 1867 – 1955

	CP*	CP	Uva	NCP	NWP	SP	WP§	WP	Sab	Total
1867, 1869	3.7	—	—	0.6	4.3	4.3	4.1	—	—	3.9
1879-83	5.2	—	—	0.9	4.2	3.0	4.7	—	—	4.3
1884-88	3.8	—	—	0.3	5.4	4.2	5.8	—	—	4.7
1889-95	3.3	3.6	2.5	1.6	6.6	4.1	4.9	5.6	2.7	4.5
1896-1900	2.5	2.6	2.5	3.0	5.1	4.1	5.1	5.2	4.2	4.1
1901-05	2.3	2.2	2.9	3.3	7.2	5.6	5.0	5.3	4.0	4.6
1915-19	2.3	2.1	3.0	2.7	4.8	4.9	5.1	4.9	5.4	4.3
1920-24	2.2	2.2	2.4	4.4	7.2	5.9	5.1	5.3	4.5	4.8
1925-29	2.0	2.1	1.8	6.0	6.3	5.8	4.7	4.6	5.2	4.4
1930-34	2.9	2.7	3.4	4.5	8.2	6.8	7.0	6.8	7.4	6.0
1935-39	2.8	2.6	3.6	7.3	7.6	7.5	6.8	7.0	6.3	6.3
1940-44	3.7	3.4	4.5	7.5	11.4	9.7	8.3	8.6	7.4	7.6
1946-48	3.5	3.4	4.0	11.5	9.9	9.5	9.2	9.1	9.4	7.9
1951-55	2.5	2.2	3.5	6.9	7.0	6.6	6.0	5.5	7.1	5.3

Sources: *Administration Reports*; Wood, 58.

Notes: Statistics are not available for 1890, 1891 and 1942; these years are omitted from the calculations. The period 1906 – 14 is not included because the statistics for most of these years included attempted homicide. The years 1868, 1870 – 8 and 1945 are omitted because information is not available.

* Including Uva. § Including Sabaragamuva.

In the late nineteenth century homicide was three to four times more common in Sri Lanka than in Britain.[7] Germany's rate was similar to that of England, while the French rate, though higher, was still below that of Sri Lanka.[8] On the other hand, the Sri

Lankan rate was lower than those of the United States and Italy.[9] Comparison with India produces a more gloomy picture; the authorities were aware of four times or more homicides in proportion to population than in most parts of India.[10] A. H. Giles, the Bengal policeman who investigated crime in Sri Lanka, believed these differences between Sri Lanka and India did reflect social reality, but further research is needed before one can comment fully on the validity of this comparison.[11] The Tamil-speaking provinces of Sri Lanka also had a lower homicide rate than Sinhala Sri Lanka, though their rate was high by Indian standards.

In the first half of the twentieth century the homicide rate of Sri Lanka remained higher than those of most European countries.[12] The British rate declined during this period, thus the differential between the British and Sri Lankan rates increased. The American rate also declined.[13] In the 1930s it briefly dropped below the Sri Lankan level, but after the decrease in homicide in Sri Lanka in the late 1940s the American and Sri Lankan rates were similar. Most South American and some Asian countries had higher rates at this time.[14] Although the Indian homicide rate gradually increased during the first half of the twentieth century, it remained well below that of Sri Lanka.[15]

Within Sinhala Sri Lanka there were some differences over time and by region (Table 4.1). The North-Western Province stood out with a consistently high rate and the Central Province with a low rate. The Western Province, Southern Province and Sabaragamuva had slightly above average rates, while Uva had a below average rate. The rate of the North-Central Province changed from below average in the nineteenth century to above average in the twentieth century. It is likely that some of the increase for this lightly-populated province was a product of administrative ignorance in the earlier years.

These data on the incidence of homicide by province may be supplemented by district rates for the mature colonial period, drawn from the general sample discussed above (Map 4.1).[16] Although coastal districts generally had above average rates, the highest rate, 7.3 per 100,000 inhabitants, was that of Kurunagala district. If one excludes Kurunagala and the special cases of lightly-populated Anuradhapura district, and Tamil-dominated Nuvara Eliya district, both of which had low rates, district variations were not large, ranging from 3.5. to 5.8. The rate for the city of Colombo was below average, at 4.0 per 100,000 inhabitants.

The homicide rate of the Central Province fell in the quarter-century after 1881. Its high point coincided with the coffee-leaf

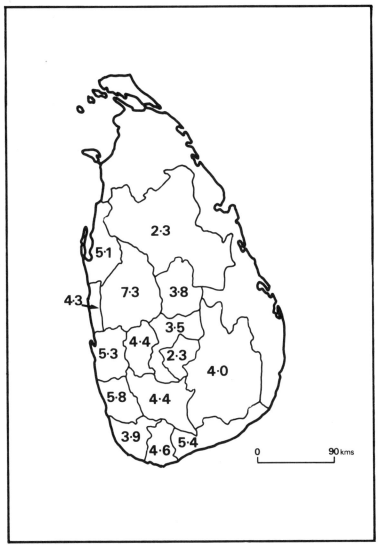

Map 4.1: Annual average homicide rates per 100,000 inhabitants, by District, 1883-9 and 1900-4.

disease depression. Although no homicide statistics were compiled from 1870 to 1878, in 1879 several officials reported an increase in violent crime in the Central Province.[17] These accounts suggest that there was an increase in homicide in the late 1870s, at the beginning of the depression, and that the decline at the end of the nineteenth century was a return to the normal state of affairs. Judicial statistics from the 1870s and the police figures from 1867 and 1869 support this view.

The positive relationship between economic hardship and homicide is borne out by an analysis of other periods when economic conditions changed rapidly. In contrast to the increase in the homicide rate during the coffee-leaf disease depression, the incidence of violent fatalities dropped during the boom of 1898 – 9. The number of homicides reported in the years from 1897 through 1900 was respectively 139, 111, 112 and 135. Again, there was an increase in homicide during the difficult years 1918 – 21. The number of homicides during this period was nine per cent greater than that of the more prosperous years 1916 – 17 and 1922 – 3. As mentioned above, there was also a sharp increase with the onset of the world depression, when the number of homicides increased from 229 in 1929 to 310 in 1930. The homicide rate remained high throughout the depression and during the Second World War, but declined during the prosperous years immediately following independence.[18]

Although there was a significant relationship between economic fluctuations and the incidence of homicide, there was no general correlation between the poverty of a district and its homicide rate. The standard of living was generally higher in the Low Country than in Kandyan districts, but the Low Country rate in the mature colonial period, 5.0 per 100,000 inhabitants, was above average. Within the Kandyan region there were sharp variations, but these did not reflect differences in wealth. The rate for the Intermediate area was 5.7, but the more populous and little or no better off Interior region had a low rate of 3.3. Examination of district rates also shows no relationship between poverty and the incidence of homicide (Map 4.1). Chilaw, the district which probably had the highest standard of living, had a below average rate, but so did all Kandyan districts except Kurunagala, which had a very high rate. One must look elsewhere for an explanation of geographical variations.

With the exception of the sharp increase in the North-Central Province the rank order of provincial homicide rates remained largely intact during the last eighty years of colonial rule. The increase in the North-Central Province was partially a reflection of deeper administrative penetration, but the immigration of Low Country Sinhalese probably increased the rate of violence.[19] There was also a general tendency for homicide to increase in areas which were among the last to become fully integrated within the market economy; rates in the North-Western Province and Sabaragamuva increased in relation to other districts. These increases were not however striking, and may be at least partially due to the increased administrative presence which accompanied the introduction of plantations into these regions. On the other hand there is some evidence that during periods of plantation expansion Low Country Sinhalese emigrants committed a disproportionate number of homicides.[20] None the less, with the exception of the North-Central Province the structural economic and social changes of the late nineteenth and early twentieth century did not cause major permanent changes in the geographical distribution of homicide.

The police reports provide a considerable amount of evidence about many of the social characteristics of those involved in homicide. In addition, officials irregularly compiled statistics about those thought responsible. Detailed information is also available from the 1956 survey.

Table 4.2. Proportionate Responsibility of Each Ethnic Group for Homicide, 1883 – 9

| | Low Country | | Intermediate | | Interior | |
	% of pop	% of hom	% of pop	% of hom	% of pop	% of hom
Sinhalese	88	87	89	90	60	67
Tamils	5	8	7	9	33	27
Moors	6	4	4	2	6	6

(N = 643, MC = 87)

In the late nineteenth century officials pointed out that although the Sinhalese made up only two-thirds of the island's population they committed over eighty per cent of homicides.[21] These findings partially reflected the low rates of the Northern and Eastern Provinces, not differences between the rates of the

Sinhalese and other ethnic groups in predominantly Sinhala-speaking areas. When the two Tamil-speaking provinces are excluded, the Sinhalese fare somewhat better (Table 4.2). Only in the Interior region did the Sinhalese commit more than their share of homicides. Since the overall rate was lowest in this region, it is clear that Indian Tamils, many of whom worked on plantations, had a low rate. These findings run counter to studies in other societies which show that economically-depressed minority groups often have high rates of homicide.[22] In the twentieth century the Sinhalese continued to be disproportionately responsible for homicide, although the rates of the Northern and Eastern Provinces increased.[23]

Religious identity was not a significant independent variable. In the mature colonial period districts with large Hindu concentrations had generally lower than average rates, while those with a significant Roman Catholic population had average rates. Chilaw, the district with the largest Catholic concentration, had a slightly below average rate. Of the 161 persons wanted for homicide who were listed in the *Hue and Cry* between 1896 and 1905 whose religion was known, eighty-one per cent were Buddhists, nine per cent Christians, six per cent Hindus and four per cent Muslims. The religious identity of assailants may be explained by ethnicity and geographical location. Detailed data on homicide offenders in 1956 confirm this conclusion.[24]

The police reports do not in most cases mention the caste of persons accused of homicide. There is no reliable evidence that specific castes were disproportionately involved. Of the 143 Sinhalese listed in the *Hue and Cry* who were accused of homicide, sixty-five per cent were Goyigamas, even though Goyigamas accounted for between only fifty and sixty per cent of the Sinhalese population. The only other available enumeration of the caste of homicide offenders is for 1956 and is more representative than the *Hue and Cry* sample. Of 220 Sinhalese thought to be responsible for homicides that year, fifty-nine per cent were Goyigamas, eighteen per cent Karavas, Salagamas and Duravas, and twenty-four per cent members of other castes.[25] These proportions reflect the strength of these castes among the general population. Homicide was not more common among those of low caste.

About half of all homicides in the sample were committed by persons described as cultivators. Officials believed that the peasantry had a homicide rate at least as high as that of the population as a whole.[26] One small occupational group which stood out with a higher incidence of homicide than its size warranted was carters and boatmen, but they were only responsible for between three and four per cent of violent deaths. The occupations of the assailants reflected male occupations in general.

The overall impression given by the police reports is that the proportion of homicides committed by persons with different degrees of wealth did not differ much from what would be expected from the distribution of wealth in society, with the exception that the urban rich were rarely thought to be involved. This view of the socio-economic position of homicide offenders was confirmed by the 1956 survey, which found that most persons accused of homicide were villagers of typical means for their locality.[27] Most offenders were poor, but they were not poorer than most Sri Lankans. These findings are unusual in that studies of other societies have usually found that homicide offenders are heavily concentrated on the lower end of the socio-economic scale.[28]

In many ways victims appear to have had social backgrounds similar to assailants, largely because homicides tended to arise from normal day to day social intercourse. In over ninety per cent of homicides the deceased was of the same ethnic group as the offender. The occupations of the assailant and victim were also very often identical. In addition, the police reports suggest that the assailant and victim were likely to be of the same general socio-economic status. There were, for instance, few cases between domestic servants and their masters. The more detailed data from the 1956 survey show similar patterns.[29] Although the social position of persons involved in homicide was higher in Sri Lanka than elsewhere, most studies of other societies have also found many similarities between the social profiles of offenders and victims.[30]

Though they had many similar social characteristics, assailants and victims were differentiated by age and sex. Persons in their thirties were the most prone to commit homicide (Table 4.3). There were many more people alive in the younger age brackets, so that the absolute number of homicides committed was weighted more to the younger age groups than is indicated in the table, but homicide was committed mainly by adults, not by youths. The average age of offenders was significantly higher than those found in studies of other societies.[31] Most Sri Lankans lived in nuclear families after marriage; thus those men in the most violent age group, the thirties, normally had financial control and social authority within their own families. Homicide was not the product of frustration resulting from marginality within the household. Victims were distributed more widely across the age spectrum than were offenders. Many more victims than assailants were under twenty or over forty years of age, especially the latter. The survey of 1956 found similar patterns of the ages of both assailants and those persons who were killed.[32]

Table 4.3. Homicide Rates by Age, of Offenders and Victims, per 100,000 Members of the Age Group, 1883 – 9

Age	Offenders	Victims
0 – 9	0.0	0.9
10 – 19	1.6	1.8
20 – 29	8.3	6.3
30 – 39	14.3	10.8
40 – 49	7.2	10.0
50 –	3.5	6.7

Offenders: N = 486, MC = 244; Victims: N = 629, MC = 101)

Very few women committed homicide. There was no female offender in ninety-six per cent of the cases in the sample, and in a further one per cent of incidents a man was the principal accused although a woman was thought to have played a subsidiary role. The proportion of women offenders did not increase in the twentieth century.[33] A woman was the victim in nineteen per cent of all homicides in the sample. Again, this proportion was almost identical in the 1950s.[34] The percentage of homicides involving women, both as assailants and victims, was considerably higher in Europe throughout this period.[35] In late nineteenth-century England well over half of all homicide victims were women.

The police reports indicate that the assailant and victim were related in one out of every five homicides. In six per cent of all cases they were husband and wife. These figures, especially the former, no doubt understate the real incidence. There must have been many cases when kin ties were unknown to the police and when such kin ties were not mentioned in the published reports. In addition, the police definition of marriage was inevitably arbitrary and legalistic; this is shown by the frequent use of the terms 'paramour' and 'mistress'.[36] Nevertheless, it is interesting to note that the ratio of instances when a spouse died to those where another relative was a victim was inversed both among Tamils and in the city of Colombo. The husband-wife relationship may have become stronger in both the urban and plantation settings, resulting in more frequent quarrels. The 1956 survey shows a considerably higher proportion of offenders and victims with kin ties, thirty-eight per cent, but it does not show any change in the proportion of homicides by spouses.[37] Since there is no indication that those who provided information for the police reports were required to mention kin links, it is likely that this change reflects the different procedures by which these data were compiled rather than an increase in the proportion of instances when assailants and victims were related.

Homicide was often committed by a group. The data collected on this subject should be treated with caution because police reports were not consistent in mentioning persons against whom charges were dropped. Many homicides took place in public places where a number of individuals were gathered. It is likely that many persons mentioned in the police reports were associates of the accused who did not actually participate in the fatal assault, and against whom charges were later dropped. The reports mentioned two or more accused in thirty-eight per cent of cases, and four or more accused in seventeen per cent of cases. Cultivators were one-third more likely to commit homicide in a group than persons who pursued other occupations. This reflected the large number of disputes which took place in an agricultural setting, where onlookers joined in the fight, often on both sides. The 1956 survey found that a somewhat smaller proportion of homicides had more than one accused, but no direct comparison is possible because of variations in administrative procedures.[38]

A knife or other sharp instrument was used to inflict death in about half of all homicides. Knives were routinely carried not as weapons but for agricultural and other uses.[39] Blunt instruments, often sticks or rice pounders, accounted for one in five homicides, as did firearms in eighteen per cent of cases. Blows and kicks caused death in one of every twenty instances, while strangulation, poison and other means were employed in the remaining six per cent of homicides.

By international standards colonial Sri Lanka had a high but by no means extraordinary rate of homicide. What was unusual was that its incidence was not concentrated among low-status social groups. In many respects assailants had social characteristics similar to those of the general adult male population. Assuming that he would live the next ten years, a thirty-year-old Sinhalese man had a better than seven out of a thousand chance of becoming involved in a homicide case, either as an offender or victim, before he reached the age of forty.

The social and economic changes of the second half of the British period did not greatly affect either the rate of homicide, the types of people who committed the crime, or the social characteristics of their victims. Geographical, ethnic, sexual and age differences remained constant. The main variations in the incidence of homicide were cyclical. Homicide tended to increase during periods of hardship and fall at times of economic growth.

The Social Circumstances of Homicide

Homicide occurred in many different situations. Before advancing broad interpretations on the basis of quantitative data concerning its incidence among various social groups or by region, it is useful to consider the specific settings of the events themselves. The main body of evidence used in this section is drawn from the police reports.

The various proximate causes of homicide around the turn of the century are listed in Table 4.4. A little more than one-half of violent deaths resulted either directly or indirectly from disputes over land, money or other property or from a desire for economic gain. Material conflict played no direct part in the remainder of incidents, many of which arose from sudden quarrels or disputes about women.

Well under one in ten of all homicides were carried out as part of robberies. They were likely to be committed by a large group; the police reports mention four or more accused in over forty per cent of these incidents. In addition, the victim was three times more likely than in other cases to be over fifty years old, and strangulation, which was a rare way of inflicting death in other circumstances, was favoured in twenty per cent of homicides carried out for robbery. Usually the crime was committed at night in a house where it was rumoured that money and jewellery were hidden:

At Narambedda, Kegalla District, Punchi Banda and Tegis, Sinhalese cultivators, aged 26 and 28 respectively, entered the Buddhist temple, and having tied up the inmates forced the priest, Bayawa Sumangala Unnanse, aged 65, to say where his money was kept. The priest died from the effects of the assault.[40]

Table 4.4. Annual Average Number of Homicides, by Proximate Cause, 1883 – 9 and 1900 – 4

Land Dispute

Property Dispute among Rice Field Shareholders	2
Property Dispute among Garden Shareholders	5
Property Dispute about overall Title to Land	1
Unspecified Land Dispute	8
Total (Land Dispute)	16 (13%)

Dispute about Property other than Land

Dispute over Damage to Property	3
Other Property Dispute, not about Land	5
Dispute over Debt	7
Total (Dispute about Property other than Land)	15 (12%)

Dispute over Theft

Committed by a Thief Surprised in the Act	4
Committed Against a Thief Surprised in the Act	8
Dispute over Theft, Committed by the Alleged Thief	3
Dispute over Theft, Committed against the Alleged Thief	3
Total (Dispute over Theft)	18 (15%)

Unspecified Feud	11 (9%)

Economic Gain

To Ensure Successful Robbery	8
To Claim Inheritance	0
Total (Economic Gain)	8 (6%)

Sudden Quarrel, No Feud Known	23 (19%)
Dispute over Woman	22 (18%)
Infanticide	3 (2%)
Other, including Accident and Insanity	6 (5%)
Total	124

Note: The sum of the individual categories does not add up to 124 because the averages were rounded off.

Sometimes a person was attacked on a road or path:

> In the Badulla district, Mardai a Tamil woman aged around 30, was going along the road selling cakes, when three Tamils and a Bengalee tailor, ages varying from 28 to 35, took her through a jungle to a garden, and there murdered her by cutting her throat. They carried away all the jewellery she had on her person.[41]

There is some evidence that there was an increase in this type of homicide in the Central Province at the beginning of the coffee-leaf disease depression.

A large number of homicides were associated with successful, suspected, or attempted thefts. Very often the property in question was growing agricultural produce, more often garden crops than rice. When the homicide happened during the theft itself, firearms were used in four out of ten cases:

> On June 12, 1886, at midnight, in the Bandarawela district, Menikrala, a Sinhalese cultivator aged 28, was watching his paddy field with a loaded gun. Having noticed some thieves cutting the stalks of paddy, he fired in that direction and killed Siribadu, a Sinhalese cultivator of 28 years.[42]

A free-for-all could develop:

> At Welwitta, in the Colombo district, Baron Sinho, a Sinhalese cultivator aged 29, was seized by the father of Juanis Perera for stealing coconuts from his garden, whereupon Pedro, Juan, and Ellias, Sinhalese cultivators, aged 30, 45, and 16, respectively, came and assaulted Juanis' father. Juanis Perera, aged 17, hearing his father's cry, came to his rescue, and in the struggle, Juanis Perera received several wounds, causing his death.[43]

Usually the value of the produce or property concerned was small, though this may not always have been the perspective of the poor, who lived close to the subsistence level. Sometimes more valuable property such as cattle or jewellery was at stake. Some feuds had their origin in one side suspecting the other of thievery:

> Wedikara Methias Silva, a Sinhalese man aged 35 years, of Kalumodara in Kalutara, bore a notorious character, having stolen cattle belonging to Anthony Durage Arnolis, a Sinhalese man aged 35 years, a

trader of Warapitiya. He was thrashed for the theft. On the day of the murder Methias, the accused, saw Arnolis the deceased in a tavern, and went in and stabbed him to death.[44]

Homicides associated with thefts showed no significant regional or seasonal variations.

Property disputes produced tensions which led to many homicides. A large proportion of these conflicts were about the use of land. Some of them lay in the grey area between theft and dispute:

Hewahakuruge Baronchy, aged 26 years, Sinhalese cultivator, and Gironissa were relations and owned a paddy field in shares, about which a dispute arose; and on Gironissa going to the field to reap corn without the knowledge of Baronchy, who also proceeded there, a fight took place resulting in the death of Baronchy. Hewahakuruge Gironis had been aided by Nadoris, Sanchiya, Jony, Matha, and Podia, aged 30, 28, 26, 19, and 23 years respectively, who were accordingly accused.[45]

Gironissa and Baronchy may have viewed each other as thieves, but any case in which a claim of ownership was made has been classified as a dispute.

Paddy land and gardens were usually held in shares. The produce could be divided, or the right to the land could be rotated annually. It was not so much undefined boundaries as the share system which produced tensions. A man might own, say, 7/58ths of a jak fruit tree. Determining the amount of produce to which each shareholder was entitled was difficult even when the size of the respective shares was agreed. Often very small amounts of produce were at stake, but in many cases these disputes were long-standing affairs, and irritation grew cumulatively until it reached a breaking point and erupted into violence, sometimes leading to death.

Not surprisingly, homicides provoked by land disputes were committed mostly by cultivators. Ninety-one per cent of the accused and eighty-six per cent of the deceased were so classified by the police. Even higher proportions of those involved were Sinhalese. The deceased and accused were known to be kinsfolk other than husband and wife considerably more often than average.

Disputes over money led to a significant number of homicides. In many cases, the amount at stake was only a rupee or two:

Kirihamy, a Sinhalese cultivator aged 40, owed Sadeya, a Moor trader aged 38 years, Rs.1.50 for provisions supplied. On June 30, 1886, when Kirihamy was passing the Moragahamulla bazaar in the Urugala district, Sadeya met him and demanded payment of the debt, and because Kirihami was unable or unwilling to pay he was set upon and severely assaulted by Sadeya and four of Sadeya's friends. The assault caused death.[46]

Gambling, which was common in many districts, led to many disputes, some of which concluded in altercations leading to death. A survey of all homicides from 1896–1902 revealed that two per cent could be traced to gambling disputes.[47] Other homicides arose from more substantial debts:

Pedro Fernando, a Sinhalese man aged 35 years, a trader of Mugona in Kalutara, was the son-in-law of Regina Fernando, a female aged 50 years, Sinhalese, of Kalamulla in Kalutara. P. Fernando, the accused, bore a grudge against his mother-in-law, the deceased, concerning some dowry money due to him. On the day in question, which was the wedding [day] of a daughter of the deceased, the accused came to her house, and without uttering a word stabbed her and her two daughters. The mother died on the spot, but the two daughters recovered.[48]

Few homicides appear to have been provoked by disputes over the long-term debts to traders, landlords or estate foremen which were the burden of a majority of the population.[49] Twenty-two per cent of homicides over money occurred in the month of April, which contained the Sinhalese and Tamil New Year. This concentration could have been because debts often fell due at the New Year, or because people tried to collect unpaid debts at this time due to the expenditure connected with the festivities. Probably more significant was the fact that gambling reached a peak during the holiday season.

Disputes over damage to property, the most common of which were the product of cattle trespass, could lead to violence. Sometimes the damage inflicted was intentional; in these cases bad feelings already existed between the two parties. More often the initial damage appears accidental:

At Eswatta, in Avisawella district, on January 22, 1889. The deceased (Sinhalese, cultivator, male, age 27) and accused (three Sinhalese cultivators) had an altercation, one of the accused having killed two pigs belonging to the deceased, for damaging a field of potatoes belonging to the accused. A quarrel ensued, and the accused who had killed the pigs assaulted the deceased with a club.[50]

Damage to irrigation ditches was another cause of disputes which could end with a fatality.

Most homicides which ensued from material conflict shared some common characteristics. The value of the property at stake was small, and violence appears to have been caused more by deep-rooted ill-feeling between the assailant and victim, or by a sudden outburst of temper, than by intention on the part of the assailant to improve his material position. Only the small number of homicides carried out as part of the commission of robberies were primarily motivated by economic considerations.

Other circumstances led to nearly half of all violent deaths. Eighteen per cent of homicides in the sample were the product of disputes about women, nineteen per cent sprang from a sudden quarrel which had no apparent material cause, and two per cent were cases of infanticide. A minority of the nine per cent of homicides classified as the result of unspecified feuds also fell into the first two categories. It is also probable that infanticide was not discovered by the authorities as often as other homicides.

Sexual jealousy and disputes over women were the causes of one in every five homicides. A woman was the victim in thirty-nine per cent of these cases. Twenty per cent of the victims were the spouse, almost always the wife, of the accused, and many of the other victims were women killed by their lovers. A man who suspected his wife or mistress of infidelity could lash out violently, sometimes at the other man, sometimes at the woman:

Hudi, a Sinhalese washerwoman, aged 14, was kept by Sadris, aged 35, a Sinhalese washer. On discovering that she was on terms of intimacy with another man, Sadris murdered her. The body was found in his house in the Badulla District covered with wounds (about 30), apparently inflicted with some sharp instrument.[51]

Sometimes a woman's lover assaulted her husband:

At Waradala, in the Negombo District, Podinaide, aged 25, and Hysuhamy Appu, aged 40 years, were at enmity in consequence of Hysuhamy Appu's intimacy with Podinaide's wife. Hysuhamy Appu waylaid Podinaide as the latter was returning home one night, and shot him.[52]

Usually there does not seem to have been much premeditation:

> Paulu Perera (35), L. Fernando (30), and Francisco Peris (40), peasants, surprised Selestino Fernando, cartman, in a room alone with Francisco Peris's wife. Peris, Perera and L. Fernando thereupon attacked Selestino, and killed him with a hatchet. They then removed deceased's body two miles, and, tying a heavy log to it, placed it in a stream.[53]

Disputes over women did not necessarily owe their origin to either emotional attachment or concern over unsanctioned sexual relations. Marriage was an expression of a family's social status, and the refusal of a woman's family to accept a marriage proposal could be interpreted as a statement of social superiority:

> At Nivithigala, Ratnapura district, Walawatte Lekamalage Wastulianne, Sinhalese, was deliberately murdered by Makuwattege Malhami, Sinhalese, who smashed the deceased's skull by striking him with a heavy stone in consequence of a grudge he bore him for refusing to give accused his daughter in marriage.[54]

Anthropological research suggests that such situations may have been especially prone to give rise to bitterness when upwardly-mobile persons began to cut kin ties with poor relations.[55]

A less distinct cause of homicide was altercations resulting from sudden quarrels. To the detached outsider the motive often does not seem to in any way warrant serious violence. There was nothing tangible at stake; these quarrels were often started by a slight or a curse. Alcohol may have been a factor, for some disputes began in taverns, but an official survey revealed that the accused had been drinking before only eleven per cent of homicides from 1896–1902, so drink was not the complete explanation.[56] The police reports sometimes hint that the root of the quarrel was the failure of one party to treat the other with the respect the latter expected. Other cases were the outgrowth of family tensions. Spouses died in nine per cent of these homicides, and other relations were known to be the victim in a further sixteen per cent of cases. Women accounted for twenty-two per cent of those killed. The following three examples illustrate the range of seemingly trivial altercations which led to death:

> At Palmada, in the Pasyala district, Punchirala, a Sinhalese cultivator aged 40, while abusing some unknown thieves for stealing his arecanuts,

was stabbed under his ribs by Baba Sinho and in the head by Baronchy, both of whom were neighbours of his. He persisted in using bad language after being requested to desist.[57]

On August 11, at Weligampola, in the Nawalapitiya district, Kiri Ukkuwa and Setuwa (two cousins, both Sinhalese, cultivators, ages 30 and 40) were living together. Setuwa asked Kiri Ukkuwa to go to the field for work. Kiri Ukkuwa refusing, Setuwa struck him on the head with a mamotie, causing his death.[58]

On March 4, 1887, in the Matale district, Appuwa, a Sinhalese cultivator, aged 30, who was drunk at the time, stabbed with a knife and killed his little daughter Kirihami, aged 4 years, owing to a quarrel with his wife for being late in preparing his meals.[59]

Tamils were more likely than the Sinhalese to be involved in this type of homicide. This fact may have been related to occupation, for non-cultivators were more prone to these quarrels than cultivators. This latter association cannot be explained by ethnicity, for among Sinhalese alone it remains strong.

A final type of homicide was infanticide. Although there is evidence that female infanticide was not uncommon in some Kandyan districts in pre-colonial times, infanticide of any type was relatively rare by the late nineteenth century.[60] All of the mothers of the victims were unmarried. The desire to escape shame and, less often, inability to provide for the child were motives given for this crime. The offender was not always the child's mother; other relations, especially the mother's mother, sometimes disposed of the child. Reversing the pattern for all other homicides, eighty per cent of those accused were women, and they accounted for over half the women accused of homicide. The sex of the child does not appear to have been of importance.

From the above accounts it is clear that homicides arose from a large variety of situations. No one category of circumstances, such as disputes over land or women, accounted for more than one-fifth of all homicides. The strongest recurrent themes are the lack of rational motive and, to a lesser extent, the lack of premeditation. Although more than one-half of all homicides stemmed at least in part from disputes with a tangible material cause, in the vast majority of these incidents the crime was not carried out for economic gain, but was instead an expression of aggression and resentment which was only partially the product of economic grievances. Almost no homicides were carried out to claim an inheritance, but there were many deaths in affrays resulting from disputes over small amounts of garden produce or slight damage to property. When there was premeditation, it was rarely of long duration. Most homicides appear to have been the result of the release of pent-up aggression.

The most important exception was homicide committed as part of a robbery. In some instances victims may have been killed to prevent them from identifying the robbers, but often only one resident of a household was murdered; death sometimes ensued from the effects of torture inflicted to find out where valuables were hidden. Robbers often travelled long distances, and they relied on local informants for information about houses where substantial wealth might be found with little risk. This information was more likely to be provided when the potential victims were unpopular; one official thought that death was inflicted only when this was the case.[61]

Another exception to the dominance of irrational and largely unpremeditated motives for homicide was the small number of instances when men unpopular with large numbers of their fellow villagers were eliminated:

At Uggallboda, in the Negombo district, Don Sardial, a Sinhalese money lender aged 40, unpopular in the village from the high interest he charged and his grasping dealings, was one night shot dead in his own compound. Four Sinhalese cultivators, aged between 40 and 16 years, were accused.[62]

The deceased was a troublesome character and litigant in the village, and he was not liked by the people, and had many enemies. On the night in question, when he was in his verandah after dinner, he was shot dead. Eight accused were taken up on suspicion, and on orders of the Attorney-General they were discharged.[63]

In most of these cases it is likely that the crime was carried out by persons who had specific grievances against the victim, but that larger numbers of villagers tacitly approved of their action and refused to give evidence. Those who carried out these crimes may have taken a conscious decision that their lives would be better off with the death of their victim. The premeditated murder of unpopular headmen and 'village bullies' may have increased around the turn of the century, a consequence of widespread land grabbing in some districts.[64] Such crimes were never common, and in no district did they account for a large proportion of homicides.

Officials agreed that most homicides were irrational and unpremeditated.[65] In many cases the assailant made no effort to avoid detection, and there was considerable official success at punishing the crime. It was usually through headmen that cases first became known to the government. Any headman who heard of a death caused by assault was supposed to send a message immediately to a senior official, and then go to the scene of the crime, take charge of any weapon, and note down details of the case. He also had the power to detain suspects.[66] In the early years of British rule chief headmen were often in charge of gathering evidence, but by the second half of the nineteenth century either a member of the civil service or police officer usually directed the investigation. All cases of murder or manslaughter were tried in the Supreme Court. When medical evidence indicated that the victim's death was partially brought on because he was in ill health the assailant was often charged with a lesser crime and tried in a lower court. In the late nineteenth century convictions were obtained in slightly over half of all homicides known to the authorities. Death was the only possible sentence for murder, but this punishment was often commuted by governors to a long term of imprisonment. Until 1885 executions were carried out in public, and they often attracted large crowds.

For most of the nineteenth century government showed no particular concern over homicide, though as early as 1816 a regulation was issued which restricted the carrying of knives because of the frequency with which they were used to inflict injury during sudden quarrels.[67] The implicit official view was that a certain amount of homicide was inevitable, and that the state's responsibility was limited to punishing the guilty. Around 1890 this perception changed, and the level of homicide suddenly became an important issue. The primary reason for this change in attitude was the availability to the Colonial Office and to officials in Sri Lanka of statistics which showed that the rate of homicide was several times greater than that of both Britain and India.[68] Governors began to consider ways in which policy might reduce the annual count of violent deaths. Arthur Havelock believed that the new system of rural policing, established in 1892, would lead to a reduction in violence. He also won approval for an ordinance which placed restrictions on the carrying of knives.[69] This act, like the regulation of 1816, was found to be impractical to enforce.[70] His successor, J. West Ridgeway, also relied on administrative measures. During his governorship legislation was passed which made it easier to station extra police in localities where residents refused to provide evidence in a murder case.[71] Flogging was introduced as a standard punishment for anyone convicted of using a knife with intent to cause hurt, even if the injury was minor.[72] It was thought that this policy would create an 'instinctive fear of punishment' which would reduce the incidence of these cases.[73] Officials soon found this ordinance open to abuse, for some persons cut themselves in order to bring a criminal charge against an enemy.[74] Towards the end of his tenure as Governor, Ridgeway became disillusioned with the policy of corporal punishment. He came to believe that flogging could not have any deterrent effect because the offender normally struck when enraged, and had no time to consider the eventual consequences of his action.[75]

These efforts at prevention failed. S. M. Burrows, the Government Agent at Kurunagala in 1903, noted in his official diary that 'it seems to make no difference whether we catch and hang the murderers or whether we do not. It is rather maddening, because you feel it is a disgrace to the Province and to the Island, and yet it apparently passes the wit of man to devise preventative action.'[76] Most homicides were random, unpremeditated events arising out of everyday social intercourse, and there was little the government could do to stop them.

In the twentieth century officials accepted that administrative measures were unlikely to reduce the homicide rate. H. L. Dowbiggin, the long-serving Inspector-General of Police, believed that fighting was inevitable in all societies, and that the difference between Sri Lanka and Britain was that in Sri Lanka men used knives while in Britain they used fists. He hoped that the introduction of boxing in schools would teach boys to use their fists and eventually reduce the incidence of homicide.[77]

The results of the 1956 survey show that the circumstances leading to homicide changed very little in the last half-century of British rule. The proportion of offences committed to further a property crime remained small, and when premeditation was present it usually was of short duration and motivated by rage rather than any expectation that the crime would improve the assailant's lot in life.[78] Bloch's statement that 'it might also reasonably be argued that land disputes, and even the quarrels over women, may simply provide convenient focal points for the release of accumulated aggression' might well have been made by a reader of the police reports which were compiled at the turn of the century.[79] There was a decrease in the proportion of cases which could be traced to disputes over property other than land, and an increase in the proportion of sudden quarrels where no previous dispute was known. It is possible that this difference was caused by different methods of classifying motives, for when the police reports mention any material cause of the dispute, however trivial or short-lived, the case was classified according to the relevant type of economic conflict. There was also a decrease in the proportion of cases in which thieves were killed; this change cannot be accounted for by different methods of classification and was probably real. On the other hand the proportion of cases caused by disputes over women remained constant, and the frequency with which different types of weapons were used changed only slightly.[80] Interestingly, there was a small decrease in the use of firearms, and a corresponding increase in the proportion of deaths caused by stabbing and cutting.

Social Structure, Social Change and an Interpretation of Homicide

The low rate of premeditated homicide, and even lower rate of homicide carried out for tangible gain, should not be taken to imply that there was a lack of social aggression and conflict which was rational and measured. It is only that such aggression was not often expressed by killing people. The institution of a civil or criminal court case was one alternative. Although the courts, by their failure to administer any popularly-held concept of justice, sometimes served to increase frustrations which led to unplanned outbursts of violence, they may well have served to channel some aggression away from physical expression.

The use of black magic and sorcery may also have reduced the frequency of planned violence. Gananath Obeyesekere has argued that in Sri Lanka sorcery is the sociological equivalent of premeditated murder because the intention of the perpetrators, the rational nature of the acts, and the traditional definitions of the 'crimes' are similar.[81] In the Kandyan Kingdom sorcery, like murder, could be punished with death. Obeyesekere's suggestion that sorcery channelled much aggression away from violence is plausible, though it is probable that undefined misfortune, rather than death, was the usual expected result. The presence of these other ways to express aggression helps explain why such a small proportion of homicides were premeditated in a society where there were many long-running feuds.

Obeyesekere's point, that inferences about personality and social structure that are drawn from analyses of homicide should be treated with caution, is valid. Homicide is not an accurate measure of the quality or quantity of aggression. Not only can aggression be expressed in ways other than homicide and violence, but factors unrelated to aggression, such as the quality of medical care, affect the homicide rate. One cannot, from this study of homicide, deduce that the Sinhalese were generally impulsive, or that there was a low level of measured social conflict. On the other hand, the presence of other forms of premeditated aggression does not negate the significance of the high rate of unpremeditated and irrational homicide.

Any interpretation of homicide in Sri Lanka should be able to explain its distinctive characteristics: the high overall rate, the low rate of the central highlands, the general steadiness of both the overall and provincial rates during the last eighty years of colonial rule, the positive relationship between economic downturns and the incidence of homicide, the unusually high average age of offenders and victims, the unusually high social and economic position of offenders and victims, the generally unpremeditated nature of the crime and the remarkable stability over time of the immediate settings of the crime.

One interpretation often put forward in relation to twentieth-century developing countries is that homicide increases as a result of rapid social change which produces cultural conflict and the disruption of indigenous norms.[82] As more and more persons move to towns and cities, become literate, and participate in a market economy, family ties weaken and traditionally prescribed values are challenged. Arthur Wood has argued that homicide in post-independence Sri Lanka reflected such a pattern.[83] He claims that modernization brought about 'relentless frustration' among persons unable to cope with the new economic and social order, and that this frustration was expressed violently. His thesis rests on two claims, that there was a general upward trend in the homicide rate under colonial rule, and more importantly, that the rate of homicide in the 1950s was higher than average in those areas under the influence of Western ideas and commercial practices.

Wood's evidence of a general rise in the homicide rate depends on statistics compiled by the Department of the Registrar-General which date from 1880.[84] Unfortunately, before 1920 these figures include only a small proportion of violent deaths known to the authorities. Wood does recognize that the early figures underestimate the incidence of the crime, but he concludes that there was a real increase anyway. The data presented earlier in this chapter do not support this conclusion; instead they show that there was no general increase in the rate of homicide from the 1880s to 1929. Although the rate in the 1930s and 1940s was higher than in earlier years, in the 1950s it declined to close to the earlier level. The increase in the last two decades of British rule reflected a cyclical variation brought on by depressed economic conditions; it was not a reaction to increased Westernization.

Wood's argument that there was in the 1950s a positive relationship between the degree of Western cultural and commercial influence and the homicide rate is also faulty. The city of Colombo, the locality most strongly influenced by Western values, had a consistently low homicide rate during the second half of British rule. Wood admits this for the 1950s, but asserts that Colombo is an exception because its residents had already adapted to Western values.[85] His argument rests instead on data which show that the homicide rate was highest in 'urban maritime' areas other than Colombo, followed respectively by areas called 'rural maritime', 'urban interior', 'estate' and 'rural interior'.[86] Leaving aside the fact that the plantations could be considered to be more 'Western' than rural maritime areas, examination of the way these categories are constructed casts doubt on their usefulness. The entire Western Province is classified as urban, even though it includes many agricultural areas. The Kandyan districts of Kurunagala, Ratnapura and Kagalla are classified as maritime and assumed to be more under Western influence than the central highlands. Conclusions based on the use of these categories must be discarded.

Other evidence presented here does not bear out Wood's arguments. Between 1867 and 1956 there was little change in either the social profile of persons involved in homicide or in the types of circumstances which led to violent deaths. According to Wood, social changes in the twentieth century accounted for many of the pressures which caused a high rate of homicide in semi-Westernized areas. The overall steadiness of the homicide rate, the consistent social profiles of offenders and victims, and the lack of change in the types of incidents which led to homicide are all run counter to the culture conflict interpretation.

Another widely-held theory is that homicide may be explained by subcultures within which violence is portrayed as an acceptable mode of behaviour in many situations. This theory is empirically based on cross-cultural findings that young men of low social and economic status tend to have high rates of homicide. It is argued that violence becomes an acceptable response to many social situations among members of the subculture. Marvin Wolfgang and Franco Ferracuti have argued that in developing countries it is not the general disruption of values by social change which causes homicide, but the creation of social heterogeneity and thus subcultural pockets by these forces of social change.[87] Physical aggression becomes a virtue within these subcultures.

This theory appears inadequate to explain homicide in Sri Lanka because offenders and victims had mainstream social characteristics. The generalization about homicide and low socio-economic status does not apply; the social groups on the margins of society did not have high homicide rates. Instead, Sinhalese men in their thirties of typical socio-economic status were the most likely persons to be involved in homicide. One could perhaps argue that it was not the poor or marginal but the upwardly-mobile who were socially disrupted and formed a subculture of violence, but the lack of any correlation between the incidence of homicide and the extent of exposure to the market economy or Western culture is strong evidence against this supposition.

Another common interpretation of homicide is that in some societies dominant cultural values place a positive connotation on violence in a significant number of social situations. The equation of masculinity with physical aggression has, for instance, been thought to contribute to high homicide rates in Latin America.[88] This theory has little relevance for Sri Lanka. Firstly, violence was not considered desirable in Sinhalese culture. The predominant religion, Buddhism, explicitly condemned violence, and the Kandyan state defined homicide little differently from the British colonial one. It is true that Sinhalese mythology and folklore includes many violent stories, but this may be taken only as evidence of a concern or preoccupation with violence, not as a positive cultural attitude towards it. Secondly, homicide was not generally the result of socially-sanctioned violence. Masculine honour did not dictate that the recipient of an insult needed to show off his physical prowess to an adversary. In fact, examination of the circumstances surrounding homicide shows that it is more plausible that aggression was normally suppressed, and that this suppression increased tension which was sometimes suddenly let loose in adversarial situations.

If homicide was not a consequence of social disorganization or of a culture or subcultures which sanctioned violence, but instead the result of the inability to solve festering grievances, why was

this so? L. F. Knollys, Campbell's successor as Inspector-General
of Police, thought that homicides ensued from a lack of control
caused because there was no adequate way for villagers to gain
satisfaction for injury. He believed that neither the courts nor
headmen were able to solve disputes which later led to violence.[89]
Many other officials also cited the lack of effective dispute-
solving mechanisms as either a primary or subsidiary cause of
homicide.[90]

In view of the earlier discussion concerning the perception of
the courts as an amoral source of power, Knollys's explanation of
homicide has some plausibility. There can be no doubt that in
many instances the outcome of court cases escalated hostility.
J. Vijayatunga, writing of the Low Country village where he
grew up in the early twentieth century, described one such
incident which arose from a charge of cattle trespass:

> The Headman's relationship being closer with us and only indirect with
> the Millionaire's family, he tried to pacify the parties, but the eldest son
> of the Millionaire insisted on bringing the case before the Village
> Tribunal at Nagoda. I remember the case was dismissed, and that evening
> as our carts bearing witnesses and partisans overtook those of the other
> party on our return to the village, there was a certain amount of
> boisterous showing-off; especially as the males in our party had
> celebrated too well with arrack. These are the little incidents which,
> beginning between grown-up people in a village, are handed down to the
> uncomprehending young as reasons for hostility and which sometimes
> pass from generation to generation.[91]

The above account illustrates a not uncommon sequel to criminal
or civil charges, and it is not difficult to find in the police reports
homicides which were committed in the aftermath of court cases.
But judicial decisions did not create conflict where there was none
before. Antagonism pre-dated court cases. The lack of effective
dispute-solving mechanisms did not cause homicide, but the way
the courts were used, and the weakness of dispute-solving
mechanisms in Sinhalese society in general, were symptoms of the
same social and economic structural ills which produced a high
number of homicides. As mentioned above, the heavy use of the
court system suggests that it may even have channelled hostility
away from violence. No matter what the judicial outcome of cases
which were the product of feuds, the underlying disputes were not
solved. Neither was it the absence of compromise-oriented institutions which caused disputes to escalate. In the account cited by

Vijayatunga the injured party rejected the offer of the headman to negotiate compensation. The roots of homicide lay deeper than administrative arrangements.

A close examination of the immediate circumstances of homicide suggests that a seemingly inordinate sensitivity to personal status was the cause of many crimes. The importance of status, of 'saving face', has been noted by many observers of Sri Lankan, and especially Sinhalese, society.[92] Sinhala and Tamil both contained numerous terms which allowed the expression of fine gradations of status. Seating arrangements were another public indication of the relative rank of individuals. Restrictions concerning dress and the exchange of food were also common. The kinship system of the Sinhalese was based on the assumption of social inequality; marriage was the ultimate measure of social status. The importance of hierarchy as an inherent, some would argue basic, element of culture is common to most South Asian societies.

Although inferiority and superiority were expressed in everyday social relations, there were many occasions when status rank was ambiguous. Some such ambiguity was present everywhere in South Asia; indeed it was necessary in order to accommodate economic and political change. But among the Sinhalese there were several factors which rendered hierarchy less convincing and thus more sensitive an issue. The combination of these two facts about status in Sinhalese culture, its importance and its ambiguity, produced a degree of stress which led to an annual tally of random homicides greater than that found in most other parts of South Asia.

Buddhism and Christianity, the two religions of the Sinhalese, both accommodated inequality, but neither actively justified it. Hindu ideas of purity and pollution, which were important justifications of caste in India, were weak in Sinhalese society. There were no institutions similar to the caste councils found in India; caste in Sri Lanka was perceived more as a matter of state regulation than of inherent worth. It was viewed as an historical reality, not as a reflection of one's 'substance'. A high-caste woman who married a low-caste man did not necessarily 'lose' caste. Such a marriage was instead intolerable to her relations because the tie created unacceptable affinal kin who diminished the status of the woman's family.

Equally important was the large size of the Goyigama caste, which accounted for over one-half of the Sinhalese population. In most Kandyan districts there were ranked sub-divisions among

Goyigamas, but elsewhere status differentiation depended on the
various degrees of respectability among different families and
lineages. These boundaries were very flexible and there was much
jostling for position. For most Goyigamas social status was not
primarily a matter of caste, for one's caste position was assumed.
Status was instead determined by a combination of variables such
as wealth, occupation and the respectability of kin, all of which
were subject to change. The following account, set in the second
decade of the twentieth century, illustrates the sensitivity among
Low Country Goyigamas to distinctions of status:

> Many a bitter grudge is laid up for future accounting at these weddings.
> A slight oversight is an insult and insults are readier imagined than
> caused. You take some time in going in to eat. For you want to be sure of
> your companions. Heavens! you say to yourself fearing some imminent
> catastrophe, surely not him, not her, to sit at the same table! Why, his so-
> and-so's so-and-so was originally such-and-such. And so-and-so's family
> pedigree is a *Vahumpurage* while you are a true blue *Patabendige*.[93]

The low rate of homicide among Sinhalese in the central highlands
may be related to the fact that relatively clearly defined sub-castes
played a prominent role in the determination of status in that
region.

Another aspect of Sinhalese social organization which contributed to the ambiguity of status was the position of the three
maritime castes. The Karava, Salagama and Durava were never
fully integrated into an overall Sinhalese caste system. There were
no ritual or service relationships among these castes or between
these castes and Goyigamas. The settlement pattern of the Low
Country ensured that most social interaction was with persons of
one's own caste. Again, inequality as an ideal was universal, but
caste was of little help in determining one's effective social
position.

Caste was only one indication of status. Occupation, wealth,
age, family and other variables were also important. The relative
importance attached to each depended on the social context
concerned. When there was inconsistency among variables, there
was likely to be disagreement between the view taken by the person
concerned and that taken by many of his fellow villagers. This was
no less true in the nineteenth century than in the twentieth.

Concern over status led to stress which was translated into
violence in two ways. Casual violence, which was mainly against
persons of clearly lower status, was often the product of insecurity

which built up from the tensions of everyday life. Sometimes it was ongoing and accepted, especially within families, but it accounted for a minority of violent deaths. Persons rarely died after being hit with a fist or stick. Women were often the victims of this type of violence. A larger number of fatal deaths were the result of incidents between persons of relatively equal status, especially when one party believed that he had not been treated with the respect due to him by someone he thought inferior. Although these crimes were not usually carefully planned, they were sometimes the culmination of long-standing disputes. The immediate incident which preceded the homicide was the catalyst which brought stress to the point at which it was unbearable. Land disputes, thefts, quarrels over women and sudden altercations provided the settings in which persons lost control, but they did not cause homicide. These situations were symptoms of continuous social competition; a very small proportion of them ended with a fatality. There was no necessary direct relationship between, say, land disputes, and the number of violent deaths. The level of stress was the more important factor. At times of economic hardship stress increased, and a larger number of violent deaths ensued.

In rural areas disputes were likely to focus on land, even when there was little actual economic interest at stake. In urban or semi-urban localities they were more apt to take the form of sudden petty quarrels. Seen in this light the distinction between homicides which can be traced to material conflict and those which cannot loses much of its significance. Fifty-nine per cent of homicides committed by cultivators were provoked by economic disputes, as opposed to only thirty-seven per cent among non-cultivators. This difference between the two groups was accounted for almost entirely by inverse proportions of crimes motivated by land disputes and by sudden quarrels. Most homicides which resulted from land disputes were not premeditated; like petty quarrels they exploded unexpectedly. Often very small amounts of produce were at stake. Many land disputes were about the respective social positions of the protagonists, and economic concerns were not the prime consideration.[94] The cause of many of these homicides was the same as the cause of those deaths which were the product of sudden quarrels: a high degree of sensitivity to status. The almost complete absence of murders carried out to claim an inheritance supports this view.

Structural change in the second half of the colonial period had contradictory effects on those aspects of religion and caste which

encouraged social insecurity. Religious revival probably channelled some aggression into religious activities, but it also further
undermined hierarchy by encouraging claims to equality. In the
late nineteenth century caste identity may also have become
stronger along the coastal strip, at least at the local level, but
although tensions within caste groups may have declined because
of the creation of negative reference groups, there was a
compensating increase in violence between castes.[95] The trend
towards greater caste solidarity did not continue in the twentieth
century; one result was the virtual disappearance of the small
number of cases where caste affrays led to violent deaths.[96]

Homicides were largely irrational actions, a product of
insecurity over personal status. The economic and social changes
of the late nineteenth and early twentieth centuries had little
impact on the way people judged each other. In many cases the
subject of the dispute which preceded the homicide was not as
significant as the way each party felt he was treated by the other
party. In other instances, particularly when the violence was
against women, homicide was an expression of stress which had
built up in a socially competitive environment. Land disputes were
a constant source of irritation in rural areas, but most homicides
resulting from them were not planned. It is no wonder that
government attempts at prevention failed; to succeed they would
have had to change the basis of social relations.

NOTES TO CHAPTER 4

1   Wood, 'Crime and Aggression in Changing Ceylon', 53; Straus & Straus,
     'Suicide, Homicide, and Social Structure in Ceylon', 461.
2   Another approach would have been to use the transcripts of murder trials
     enclosed in the correspondence between Supreme Court judges and the
     Governor. These are found in SLNA6. Though available for a longer time
     period, this evidence is less representative because it covers only cases when
     there was a death sentence. Such cases accounted for a small minority of
     homicides known to the authorities.
3   Wood; Bloch, 'Research Report on Homicides, Attempted Homicides and
     Crimes of Violence'. I am indebted to Gananath Obeyesekere for lending me
     his copy of Bloch's report. The survey questions are listed in Wood, 120 – 2.
4   *AR P 1867 & AR P 1869.*
5   Slight apparent discrepancies between these rates and those shown in Table
     4.1 are due to the rounding off of decimal points and the use of different
     census years as the base for calculating rates.
6   An annual average of fifteen persons were tried for murder in Kandyan
     districts from 1816 – 29. Assuming that total population was 275,000, an
     average of 5.5 persons per 100,000 inhabitants were tried annually. In the
     maritime provinces, including Tamil-speaking areas, if one assumes a

population of 550,000 an average of 2 persons per 100,000 inhabitants were tried annually from 1802 – 29. Because of differences in judicial procedure, cases were more likely to come to trial in Kandyan districts than in maritime areas when the evidence was poor. Given the quality of information available to the government at this time, it is likely that only a small proportion of homicides came to trial. CO 416/13; CO416/19.

7 Gatrell, 342 – 5.
8 Zehr, 114 – 18.
9 McDonald, 'Death Penalty and Homicide', 106; Lane, 'Urban Homicide in the Nineteenth Century', 92 – 6; Brantingham & Brantingham, 189 – 91.
10 Giles, *SP 17 1889*, 35; Trivedi, 338; Hula, 'Calcutta: The Politics of Crime and Conflict, 1800 to the 1970s', 535, 551; Ridgeway, *Addresses*, IV, 199; Kitts, 2.
11 Giles, *SP 17 1889*, 35. For a dissent from Giles's view that most homicides in late nineteenth-century India were known to the authorities, see Carstairs, *Human Nature*, 257 – 9.
12 Clinard & Abbott, 59; Wolfgang & Ferracuti, *The Subculture of Violence*, 274 – 5; Wood, 55; Gatrell, 342 – 5; Dowbiggin, *AR P 1919*, B9 & *AR P 1933*, A16; Archer & Gartner, *Violence and Crime in Cross-National Perspective*.
13 Zahn, 'Homicide in the Twentieth Century United States', 115 – 17; Brantingham & Brantingham, 189 – 91; Archer & Gartner.
14 Wood, 55; Wolfgang & Ferracuti, 274 – 5; Archer & Gartner.
15 Nayar, *Violence and Crime in India*, 28, 87; Hula, 572; Archer & Gartner.
16 So that these sample-based figures are directly comparable to the provincial rates shown for 1879 – 1905 in Table 4.1, they have been adjusted so that the overall mean is 4.7 per 100,000 persons. The actual mean of the sample is 4.9.
17 Ferdinands, *AR QA 1879*, 4B; King, *AR Badulla 1879*, 59; Campbell, *AR P 1879*, 31B; Longden to Hicks-Beach, 18 Oct 1879, CO54/521(409).
18 Wood also found a positive relationship between homicide and economic conditions (for the period 1928 – 54). Wood, 82 – 3.
19 Wood, 60.
20 Hill, *AR Kagalla 1899*, J13; Byrde, PM, *AR Kurunagala 1903*, G7; Fisher, *AR Badulla 1893*, I3; Massie, *AR Matale 1872*, 62.
21 Ridgeway, *Administration*, 83; Campbell, *AR P 1879*, 28B.
22 Wolfgang & Ferracuti, 263 – 4.
23 Bloch, 311 – 12.
24 Ibid., 313 – 15.
25 Ibid., 320.
26 Campbell, *AR P 1883*, 27; Knollys, *AR P 1896*, B5.
27 Bloch, 324 – 40.
28 Wolfgang & Ferracuti, 260 – 3.
29 Bloch, 377 – 412.
30 Wood, 70.
31 Wolfgang & Ferracuti, 258; Bloch, 299 – 300.
32 Bloch, 299, 378 – 82.
33 Wood, 68; Bloch, 383; Jayawardene & Ranasinghe, *Criminal Homicide in the Southern Province*, 99.
34 Bloch, 382 – 4.
35 McDonald, 96; Pollak, *The Criminality of Women*; Wolfgang, *Patterns in Criminal Homicide*, 60.
36 In 1891 the Census Commissioner noted that 'so long as it is uncertain what constitutes a marriage in Ceylon, it is useless to inquire whether persons are married or not.' *Census of Ceylon 1891*, I, 3.

37 Wood, 70.
38 Ibid.
39 Knollys, *AR P 1896*, B2; Ridgeway, *Administration*, 89; Hay, *AR SG 1889*, A2.
40 *AR P 1888*, 38C.
41 *AR P 1886*, 46C.
42 Ibid., 42C.
43 Ibid., 45C.
44 Ibid., 38C.
45 Ibid., 40C.
46 Ibid., 42C.
47 Ridgeway, *Administration*, 83.
48 *AR P 1886*, 38C.
49 Meyer, 'De la dette interne à la dette externe'; Samaraweera, 'Masters and Servants', 140 – 1.
50 *AR P 1889*, B10.
51 *AR P 1883*, 48C.
52 Ibid., 46C.
53 Ibid.
54 *AR P 1886*, 39C.
55 Yalman, *Under the Bo Tree*, 82 – 6, 155 – 72.
56 Ridgeway, *Administration*, 83.
57 *AR P 1886*, 45C.
58 *AR P 1889*, B11.
59 *AR P 1887*, 44C.
60 C. R. de Silva, 308; d'Oyly, 55 – 6. One official in late nineteenth-century Sabaragamuva thought some infants were deliberately allowed to die. Atherton, *AR Ratnapura 1874*, 19.
61 Dowbiggin, *AR P 1921*, B16.
62 *AR P 1886*, 44C.
63 *AR Kurunagala 1903*, G14.
64 Price, *AR Badulla 1902*, I6; Burrows, D, 22 Oct 1902, SLNA38/10; Pinto, PM, *AR Ratnapura 1903*, K6; Layard, *CH 1896 – 7*, 56 – 7; Dep, 318, 320, 453, 454. For a further discussion of land grabbing, see Chapter Six.
65 Havelock to Knutsford, 20 Oct 1890, CO54/589(415); Knollys, *AR P 1895*, B2; Ramanathan, *SP 8 1898*, 12; Ridgeway, *Administration*, 89; Dowbiggin, *AR P 1924*, B10.
66 Lee, 18 – 19.
67 Pippet, 12.
68 Berwick, Feb 1884, E2, CO54/553(171); Ridgeway, *Administration*, 80; Havelock, *Addresses*, IV, 6; Giles, *SP 17 1889*, 35; *SP 8 1898*, 12.
69 Havelock, *Addresses*, IV, 78; Ord 19 1890.
70 Knollys, *AR P 1895*, B2.
71 Ord 15 1896; Ridgeway, *Addresses*, IV, 200.
72 Ridgeway, *Addresses*, IV, 258 – 9; Ord 15 1896.
73 Knollys, *AR P 1895*, B2.
74 Ridgeway to Chamberlain, 2 July 1898, CO54/647(217); Brodhurst, *AR Kalutara 1897*, B32.
75 Ridgeway, *Addresses*, IV, 377 – 8.
76 Burrows, D, 27 Aug 1903, SLNA38/11.
77 Dowbiggin, *AR P 1924*, B10 & *AR P 1928*, B12.
78 Bloch, 269 – 98.
79 Ibid., 279.

80   Statistics for the weapon used in homicides are given in the *AR P*s of the 1920s
      and 1930s. For the 1956 survey, see Bloch, 261.
81   'Sorcery, Premeditated Murder, and the Canalization of Aggression in Sri
      Lanka'.
82   Clinard & Abbott, 59; Jayawardene & Rajasinghe.
83   Wood.
84   Ibid., 57 – 8.
85   Ibid., 62, 66.
86   Ibid., 58 – 62.
87   Wolfgang & Ferracuti, 269 – 72.
88   Ibid., 259 – 60; Clinard & Abbott, 59 – 60.
89   Knollys, *AR P 1896*, B5.
90   *SP 17 1889*, 34 – 5; Berwick, *AR DJ Colombo 1872*, 552; Havelock to
      Knutsford, 20 Oct 1890, CO54/589(415); Aluwihare, *AR P 1947*, A30.
91   Vijayatunga, 56.
92   See studies by anthropologists on Sri Lanka, e.g. Yalman. For a psychologi-
      cal perspective see Straus, 'Westernization, Insecurity, and Sinhalese Social
      Structure'.
93   Vijayatunga, 63.
94   Selvadurai, 'Land, Personhood and Sorcery in a Sinhalese Village'.
95   See Chapter Five for a discussion of collective violence along lines of religion
      and caste.
96   The 1956 survey found no homicides which were the result of caste tensions.
      In the late nineteenth and early twentieth centuries there were a few such
      cases, often provoked by a slight or curse. For examples, see *AR Kurunagala
      1903*, G13; *AR Colombo 1904*, A30.

CHAPTER 5

RIOTS AND DISTURBANCES

Historians have generally portrayed Sri Lanka as a model colony, free from strife and unrest except for the agrarian rebellion of 1848 and anti-Moor riots of 1915. In particular, scholars have had little to say of riots and disturbances in the period between these two well-known events. Only the 1883 clash between Roman Catholics and Buddhists at Kotahena is mentioned in the *University of Ceylon History of Ceylon.*[1] This overlooks a large number of incidents, some of great significance. A few of the more important of these clashes have attracted the brief notice of scholars, but only as background to other topics.[2]

This chapter seeks to examine both major and minor riots during British rule. The emphasis is on disturbances in the mature colonial period which have not hitherto attracted much attention. I have done little original research on the events of 1848 and 1915, but new light is thrown on these better-known outbreaks by viewing them in the context of long-term patterns of collective violence. Ample and in some instances copious documentation is available for many riots in the late nineteenth and early twentieth centuries. The main sources are diaries of revenue officials, the correspondence of the Colonial Secretary, and newspapers. The latter are especially valuable when they offer opposed interpretations of the same incident.

Unlike homicide, but like cattle stealing, patterns of riot were sensitive to long-term social change. The nature of the relationship was however radically different. Cattle stealing was largely governed by short-term calculations of potential profit. In contrast, riot is by definition a collective act, and most major riots were acts of social expression which reflected the way persons perceived their position in society. Long-term changes in patterns of riot may be traced to economic changes and the new social groups which accompanied them.

Riots in colonial Sri Lanka reflected a bewildering variety of motives and social divisions, but on systematic examination certain common patterns emerge. No claim is made that these patterns necessarily reflected fundamental social divisions. Just as individual aggression and hostility did not necessarily result in homicide, collective frustrations and conflicts did not always lead to rioting. The transformation of social tensions into riot was often dependent on chance. Many riots could have been avoided if an official had acted differently, or if there had been no petty quarrel to set off a general affray. Many potential riots never happened.

The first section of this chapter examines the main disturbances of the early and middle nineteenth century: the rebellions immediately following the assertion of British control, the agrarian unrest of 1848 and the grain riots of 1866. It is argued that these incidents were primarily reactions to political and economic developments which were perceived as undesirable; rioters justified their actions with reference to past practices. In the early years of British rule these disturbances had a strong political content because they looked to the pre-British past, but by the middle of the nineteenth century grievances could at least in theory have been resolved within the colonial framework. The second section discusses the many local riots of the late nineteenth and early twentieth centuries. Some were protests against taxes or high prices, others were caused by ethnic, caste or commercial tensions. None posed any threat to the colonial government. Rioters were unable to obtain effective support for their campaigns from outside their own localities. The third section treats a new form of riot which appeared in the 1880s. These disturbances were sustained by religious ideologies which were systematiclly propagated through preaching, publications and education. They were rightly perceived by the authorities to be dangerous to the colonial order, for the newly-constructed or revived ideology of Buddhism had the potential to unify a majority of the population. Religious revivalism did not object only to specific aspects of society; it was capable of putting forth an alternative vision of the social order. Most religious riots were between Buddhists and Catholics, but there was also conflict between Buddhists and the government. The fourth section examines rioting in the twentieth century, when some Sri Lankans became more conscious of their potential to influence politics. Religious tensions spread from the south-western coastal strip to other regions of the island. A series of procession disputes between Buddhists and Muslims led in 1915 to widespread rioting. The extent and violence of these disturbances were the greatest since the Kandyan rebellion of 1817 – 18, but the forces which prompted them were soon derailed, only to re-emerge after independence. In Colombo economic protest also

sharpened in the early twentieth century. Labour unrest increasingly took the form of strikes, which remained illegal until 1922.
The anti-police riot of 1929, which was the outgrowth of a strike
by tram workers, demonstrates that some workers in Colombo
had developed a sense of solidarity based on their common
economic condition.

The concluding section of the chapter examines the relationship
between the two dominant strands of ideology behind disturbances, the one economic and the other religious. Both currents
were flexible, and both underwent significant changes over time.
In many cases the same social groups were involved in both types
of protest. After around 1880 ostensibly religious protests
dominated, but riots were most dangerous when economic and
religious disaffection were combined.

Protest in the Early Years of British Rule

After the British first seized control of the Low Country, the East
India Company appointed to positions of importance officials
from southern India who were intent on enriching themselves. To
make matters worse, late in 1796 the new authorities imposed
unprecedented taxes on coconut trees and on land which had
previously been held tax-free in return for services. These new
taxes, together with the manner in which they were collected, led
in 1797 to armed opposition in many rural districts.[3] Headmen
who felt that their power was being undermined supported this
resistance, which the British were unable to subdue by military
means alone. Government power was fully asserted only after the
new revenue policies were reversed.

In the former Kandyan Kingdom too there was a major revolt
soon after the assumption of power by the British.[4] Unlike the
earlier rebellion in the Low Country, it was not sparked by harsh
taxation, but like the Low Country unrest it reflected the concern
of powerful headmen that their power was being undermined by
the new rulers. The Kandyan aristocracy had apparently felt that
the British would not seriously interfere in the internal affairs of
their country. The goal of the rebels was to restore the independence of the Kandyan Kingdom. Militarily, this revolt proved
much more serious than the disturbances in the Low Country, and
at one point the British considered temporarily abandoning much
of the interior. In the end the rebellion was crushed through a
ruthless policy of terrorism. Never again was there armed

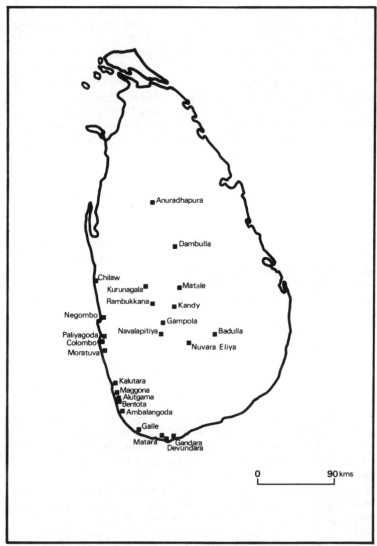

Map 5.1: Locations of riots and disturbances.

resistance which would threaten the sovereignty of the colonial power.

During the first thirty years of British rule there was a series of movements which sought to restore the Kandyan Kingdom.[5] Typically, a pretender appeared in a remote district and moved around the countryside with a number of peasant followers. These movements often received some support from landowners, including headmen. They either faded away or were defused by preventive action by officials; they had no chance of dislodging the British but they did reflect widespread resentment of the new order in many rural districts. The early agrarian policies of the British were mainly limited to extracting revenue, and there was no reason for the peasantry to feel any attachment to the new regime. The partial withdrawal of state support for Buddhism and the negative ecological impact of coffee plantations established in the 1840s also contributed to unease. It was in this context of general dissatisfaction that several new taxes, some of which fell directly on the peasantry, were suddenly announced in June 1848.

There were altogether seven taxes, of which four aroused widespread opposition.[6] Henceforth annual licences were to be required for guns, dogs and shops, and there was to be a poll tax of three shillings imposed on all male residents aged between fifteen and fifty. This latter levy was meant to finance the construction and maintenance of roads. Those who could not afford to pay it were required to provide six days labour on roadworks, a provision which made the tax seem a revival of the system of *rajakariya*, or forced labour, which had been abolished by the reforms of 1833. The gun tax was widely resented because in many rural areas guns were necessary for hunting and to keep wild animals away from crops. The new ordinance required that all guns be taken to the *kachcheri* every year and be licensed at a cost of two shillings and sixpence. The licence had to be applied for on a form printed in English; thus gun owners had to bear not only the annual expense of the licence fee and of travelling back and forth to the *kachcheri*, a journey which in some cases was eighty kilometres or more, but they had to pay a petition-drawer or *kachcheri* clerk to fill out the required form. Most of the guns were worth less than one pound, and had already been subject to import duty. The dog tax, of one shilling a year, had no justification or precedent in rural areas, and was easily subject to abuse by headmen. The shop tax required all retail stores with an annual turnover of five pounds or more to take out each year a licence which cost one pound. Few Kandyans owned such shops, but the tax was widely resented in the Low Country, especially because the burden fell equally on roadside shacks and large commercial establishments. Taken together, these measures affected the peasantry more heavily than other social groups. The British were not unaware of this fact, but they viewed the taxes as a means to force cultivators to enter the market economy, a move which they thought would contribute to the economic progress of the island. Fear and resentment in rural districts was further increased by rumours that still more new taxes were planned. Statistical inquiries going on at the time fuelled this disquiet.

In the Low Country the new taxes were met with protests in the form of public meetings and petitions, but not with violence.[7] A large crowd at Galle gave James Tennent, the Colonial Secretary, a hostile reception when he addressed them on the subject. In Colombo a number of protesters clashed with the police, but they were persuaded before the arrival of the military to present their grievances to the Governor through a petition, and they soon dispersed peacefully. There were also non-violent protests in the interior.[8] In Badulla many persons destroyed their firearms in front of the *kachcheri*, demonstrating their belief that the new tax made gun ownership prohibitive. A large unarmed crowd also gathered in the town of Kandy. Alerted by this demonstration of the widespread disaffection, the authorities arranged for a meeting two days later between Tennent and Kandyan headmen. Tennent harangued the gathering about the benefits of the taxes, but his speech served only to convince those present that the government did not have their interests at heart.

It was not in the Kandyan heartland that armed resistance to the government emerged. Instead, unrest centred upon the remote areas to the north and west of the town of Kandy.[9] Throughout July 1848 the government received reports that a pretender to the Kandyan throne was travelling in the area around Dambulla, gathering villagers on his way. The presence of the pretender, a man of Low Country origin, seems to have been the catalyst which caused peasants concerned about the new taxes and fearful of additional levies to take action. At first the reports of rebellion were not taken seriously, but when the arrival of armed Sinhalese in villages where there was a British presence became imminent, local officials panicked. When peasants approached Matale the magistrate fled, as did many of the coffee planters who lived on nearby plantations. The rebels looted government buildings and shops, and court records were strewn about. Abandoned plantation buildings were also looted, but as in Matale none were put to the torch. A few days later other peasants entered Kurunagala, which had also been abandoned by the British. There another pretender was crowned. Several government buildings and the district court records were destroyed.

Local officials were not the only ones to panic. In Colombo there were rumours that the rebels numbered as many as 50,000, and the British community in places as far apart as Puttalam, Trincomalee, Ratnapura and Kandy feared imminent attack. A detachment of two hundred troops was sent from Kandy to Matale, and martial law was declared. The rebels were easily driven from the village, and expeditions were sent into the surrounding countryside to search for rebels and to confiscate the property of headmen and landowners who were thought to be sympathetic to their cause. Another detachment, made up of only thirty soldiers, was sent to Kurunagala, where again resistance was brief and ineffective. There was no further fighting. One soldier was wounded in these engagements, perhaps from fire originating on his own side. One British estate superintendent, who was said to have 'interfered' with a Sinhalese woman, was found trussed up and bruised. Those coffee estates not abandoned by their managers were not attacked. The only person known to have been killed by the rebels was a Tamil estate worker, but at least two hundred villagers died at the hands of the troops, and others, including the Kurunagala pretender, were executed after trial by courts martial. The Dambulla pretender, who was of Low Country origin, was eventually captured and transported.

The 'rebellion' of 1848 was not more violent, on the rebel side, than many other affrays and riots later in the colonial era. It differed from later disturbances in that the rebels supported the claims of pretenders to the Kandyan throne. Nevertheless, many of those involved must have known that there was no chance of dislodging the British. For these men the 'rebellion' was primarily a protest against unfair taxation. These disturbances are well known mainly because the initial incompetence of a few officials allowed the rebels to seize two villages where there was a British presence, and because the subsequent over-reaction of the colonial authorities led to political controversy which eventually resulted in the retraction of most of the new taxes and the recall of Governor Torrington. The riots illustrate the weakness of the colonial administration in remote rural areas as well as the underlying dissatisfaction of many Kandyans, but they posed no serious political or military threat to the British.

The next major set of disturbances were the grain riots of 1866. They were geographically as widespread as the protests of 1848, but were more limited in their goals and did not pose a direct political challenge to the government. In 1866 poor harvests in India caused a sharp increase in the cost of rice. The standard price in the 1860s was about six shillings a bushel in Colombo and two or three shillings higher in the interior; in September and October 1866 the price fluctuated between twelve and fifteen shillings a bushel in Colombo, and reached twenty shillings in many inland towns. The doubling of grain prices had an immediate effect on the urban and semi-urban poor. They lived close to the subsistence level, buying their food day by day. The high prices meant they could afford only half as much rice as in normal times.

Rioting broke out in Colombo on the evening of 21 October.[10] During the day the price of rice had risen above fifteen shilings a bushel for the first time, reaching twenty-one shillings in some parts of the city. After first demanding rice at a 'just' price, crowds attacked some shops and seized grain. The next morning many merchants agreed to maintain the price at thirteen shillings a bushel, but they soon changed their minds. When as a result rioting was again threatened, they closed their shops. This only exacerbated the situation, because there was no way for people to get food. Shops were attacked in most parts of Colombo. Much plunder was acquired at Sea Street, where the Nattukottai Chettiar merchants were concentrated. One wealthy trader, Anandappa Chetty, lost his entire stock. The crowd not only carried off rice, cloth, silk, money and jewellery; they also destroyed his account books and promissory notes. The value of his losses was estimated at £5,000, a substantial sum in a city where a day labourer, when fortunate enough to find steady employment, normally earned between one and two pounds in a month.[11] The next day, 23 October, the Chettiars and Coast Moors defended their premises more aggressively, and there was more fighting than looting. The final violence in the city was on 24 October, when some residents resisted searches for stolen goods. After the first day of rioting, when the police proved inadequate, the government deployed troops to restore order.

Tensions also developed in the towns of the interior, where prices rose proportionately higher than along the coast.[12] In the town of Kandy the price of rice rose extraordinarily quickly. On the morning of 20 October the price was twenty shillings a bushel, but it rose several times during the day and reached thirty shillings in the evening. When Tamil and Sinhalese labourers found the price at thirty-five shillings the next morning, they began to seize rice.[13] The stores all closed, and a bevy of officials, accompanied by police, arrived on the scene. The Government Agent persuaded the merchants to reduce the price to twenty-one shillings, and the stores reopened. Threatening crowds also gathered in Matale, Kurunagala, Gampola and Navalapitiya, but although there was some minor looting, there were no major incidents.[14] Tamil plantation workers, who consumed a large proportion of imported rice in the interior and who dominated the crowds which gathered in these localities, were somewhat cushioned from the price rise because they were paid partially in rice. Although many plantation managers reduced the amount of rice they provided their workers, employers had to bear some of the increased cost.[15] Officials in Kandyan districts were also able to prevent rioting because the towns of the interior were small and Tamil workers visited the bazaars mostly on weekends.

In the Southern Province port of Galle the rioting was prompted by somewhat different motives.[16] Anxieties developed because of a rise in the price of rice from ten shillings a bushel on 16 October to fifteen shillings on 18 October. On the morning of 23 October a rumour spread through the bazaar that there was a large consignment of rice at the port awaiting shipment to Colombo. A crowd gathered and prevented the steamer from being loaded. They next turned their attention to nearby rice shops. Some two hundred bags of rice were looted. A leading Sinhalese merchant saved his establishment by promising to sell rice at six shillings a bushel. When the military arrived the crowd dispersed, but it soon reformed at the suburb of Kaluvella, where the Chettiars had cloth shops and warehouses. Eight stores were broken into, and over a thousand pounds worth of goods were taken.

Elsewhere in the Low Country action was taken to prevent the export of rice to other districts. At Matara carts carrying grain bound for Galle were halted by a crowd which dispersed only after being promised that the load would not proceed to its destination.[17] Sinhalese carters transporting grain from rice-growing districts south of Colombo were offered the 'value' of their loads; if they refused attempts were made to loot the rice.[18] Fear of similar blockades along the Colombo-to-Kandy road resulted in the refusal of carters to supply Kandy until the government provided them with a military escort.[19]

The rioters in Colombo and Galle were made up of the ordinary poor of the cities and their suburbs. No doubt 'criminals' and 'loafers' joined in, but too many people were involved for their role to have been significant. In Colombo there is evidence that many rioters came from nearby villages, including some where the Vahumpura, a low caste, predominated.[20] But the rioters were not of any particular caste or even ethnic group. In both Colombo and Galle Tamils, Moors and Burghers, as well as Sinhalese, participated in the riots.[21] The Nattukottai Chettiars of Colombo accused other Chettiars of plundering their shops.[22] In Kandyan districts most of the rioters were Tamils. Only on the third day of rioting in one Colombo ward did the violence turn into a general clash between Sinhalese and Moors.[23] The primary cause of the disturbances was clearly outrage at the behaviour of the merchants, who were widely believed to be hoarding supplies in the hope that the price would rise still further. This anger crossed ethnic lines.

There was a widespread belief that the government ought to control the price and distribution of rice. Richard Morgan, the Queen's Advocate, received several threatening anonymous letters because he was held responsible by some for the government's free-market policy, and there were rumours that a mob would attack his house.[24] The belief that the government should intervene was not limited to the poor. The *mudaliyars* of two coastal districts in the Southern Province forbade the sale of rice to Chettiar traders.[25] A friend of Morgan's and fellow Burgher, Adrian Labroy, told Morgan that the government was short-sighted for not itself marketing rice in competition with the Chettiars. Labroy was an old man, and Morgan dismissed his suggestion as 'old-fangled'.[26] More forthright was a correspondent of the *Lakrivikirana*. He argued that the common people provided revenue for the state through the tax on imported grain and through road tolls, and that the government's failure to fix the price of grain showed that it did not care about the poor.[27]

Before the riots broke out there was little official response to the price increase. The Governor, Sir Hercules Robinson, felt that the state should limit itself to 'securing for the operations of trade the fullest protection, leaving prices to adjust themselves by the influence of the natural laws of supply and demand.'[28] A group of leading residents in Colombo, more sensitive to the social consequences, held a public meeting to form a relief fund on 17 October, four days before the first outbreak of rioting.[29] Within a week they raised over £2,000. The committee purchased rice on the free market and then resold it to the poor at a lower price. Although some officials contributed to the relief fund, its efforts found no favour with Robinson.

Many traders, when faced with the threat of looting, abandoned the free market. After the first outbreak of rioting leading Colombo rice merchants held a meeting and decided to set a maximum price of thirteen shillings a bushel.[30] They did not at first keep to this agreement, but the looting in Colombo soon convinced them of its desirability. For security reasons much of this rice was sold at the Colombo *kachcheri* and at police stations. At Galle the trader who had saved his stock from looting by promising to sell for six shillings set his price at ten shillings, still three shillings less than what he could have obtained on the free market.[31] Other Galle traders later agreed to join him in selling rice at a subsidized price.[32] The disturbances succeeded in bringing down the price of rice.

Apprehended rioters were tried in police courts, and were generally sentenced to short terms of imprisonment and to receive lashes.[33] Corporal punishment was administered publicly, and the sight of eighty-odd persons being whipped in the streets of Colombo must have deterred further rioting. The lowering of prices by merchants and the activities of the relief committee also helped defuse the violence. In early November increasingly large supplies of rice arrived from India, the price of rice fell, and by the end of the month the crisis was over.[34]

Early disturbances under British rule were essentially reactions to unwanted political and economic change. In the Kandyan countryside dissent was linked to the restoration of the Kandyan Kingdom, but after the failure of the rebellion of 1817 – 18 the overwhelming dominance of the British was clear to most. Thirty years, later, when a number of new taxes were suddenly imposed, some peasants rallied to the support of pretenders, but their action was more a protest than a rebellion. In the Low Country, which had long been subject to foreign rule, protests were aimed against specific economic grievances, such as new taxes or high prices. The grain riots of 1866 reflected not only the increased reliance of the island on imported rice but a newly-found official faith in the merits of the free market. In the early years of British rule government had followed the Dutch practice of regulating the price and distribution of rice when there was a shortage.[35] In 1866 the British were no longer interested in such paternalistic exercises. Consumers responded by rioting to force the price down.

Local Riots in the Late Nineteenth Century

In the years following the relatively widespread disturbances of 1848 and 1866 there were no riots which spread beyond any one

district. Grievances over high food prices and new taxes
occasionally surfaced, but the ensuing protests were weak. There
were also series of riots along caste, ethnic and factional divisions
during this period; these too remained local and parochial.

Indian crop failures continued to affect the price of rice in Sri
Lanka, most notably in 1878 and 1897, but prices never quite
doubled. In 1866 serious rioting did not usually break out until
prices tripled. Although Sri Lanka's dependence on imported rice
increased steadily, the supply and distribution proved adequate.
Minor disturbances revealed that resentment and distrust of
traders remained. These clashes were usually brought about by
high food prices, and were more likely to occur when shopkeepers
were Moor or Chettiar and consumers Sinhalese.[36]

The 1897 – 8 disturbances in Chilaw district contained many
elements of grain rioting, but ethnic factors played a more
prominent role than in 1866. Some tension between the Sinhalese
and Moors was long-standing in Chilaw town, as elsewhere. The
trading and money-lending activities of Moors were two of the
main points of contact between these groups. Disputes over
relationships between Moor men and Sinhalese women had made
ethnic relations particularly sour in Chilaw town.[37] When the price
of rice rose all over Sri Lanka in 1897, the position of Moors as rice
retailers increased Sinhalese resentment. It was widely believed
that the traders had banded together to keep prices artificially
high.

A few days before Christmas 1897 a notice appeared in the
bazaar which threatened looting unless the Moors lowered their
prices.[38] The local authorities took little notice, but on 26
December a 'petty quarrel' between a drunken Sinhalese and a
Moor threatened to develop into a more general disturbance. A
crowd with hundreds on both sides gathered. Three Moor shops
were slightly damaged. There was no looting; instead the crowd
threw curry stuffs on to the road, and poured kerosine on them.[39]
Headmen and the Assistant Government Agent, C. R. Cumberland, were quickly on the scene. Although both sides were armed
with clubs, serious violence was avoided. Tension remained high
for some time. On 27 December rumours spread that armed
Moors were arriving in town from outlying villages. With the
approvalof the local priest church bells were rung, and the
Sinhalese,who in Chilaw were mostly Roman Catholic, gathered
to oppose the supposed invasion. Cumberland sped off to the
north of town and found a large crowd of Moors who had collected because they believed the ringing of the bells to be the signal

to commence looting.[40] The authorities defused the situation, but it was several days before the Moors reopened their shops, partially because of the fear of looting, and partially in response to a Sinhalese threat not to sell them fish.[41] Special police were quartered on the town for six months, at the expense of the Moor and Sinhalese inhabitants.

In Chilaw town the high price of grain was the catalyst which set off limited violence against Moors. In early January rioting spread to two small towns nearby.[42] In both cases headmen avoided serious violence by convincing traders to lower prices. The only case of actual looting, at Nattandiya, was against a Sinhalese-owned shop, even though the rioters were Sinhalese and only two of the five shops in Nattandiya were Sinhalese-owned. Chillies, salt and curry stuffs were strewn about, not stolen, showing again that this was a protest rather than a desperate act by starving men. At Madampe, where a crowd of about a thousand gathered, the leaders claimed success after the *mudaliyar* ordered the Chettiar traders to reduce their prices. Although in Chilaw town the rioting followed ethnic lines, in the surrounding countryside anger at the price of grain dominated the disturbances.[43]

There was a degree of general antipathy between the Sinhalese and Moors which could lead to violence.[44] In the nineteenth century this conflict rarely took place on religious grounds, and confrontations involving large numbers of persons were neither frequent nor serious. Although tensions were often produced by economic grievances, sometimes the loss of a woman to the other group was the catalyst for such affrays. A clash in Colombo in 1870, in which the government was perceived by Moors as siding with the Sinhalese, may serve as an example.

On 24 February a twenty-five-year-old man, a Karava carpenter, Roman Catholic and native of Moratuva, eloped with a young Moor girl, Minakshi, who lived with her mother on the outskirts of Colombo.[45] The elopement was felt to be a blow to many Moors in Colombo, and charges of abduction and theft were brought before a justice of the peace. Only after putting much pressure on the Moratuva headmen was the government able to take custody of Minakshi. The girl's family brought a writ of *habeas corpus* before the Supreme Court to take charge of her. The hearing was held in a disorderly atmosphere, for some of the Moors present were in an aggressive mood. Minakshi's mother and uncle were allowed to visit her while she was in custody, but she remained adamant in her desire not to return to her family. On 27 April the judges decided to free her, mainly because they

felt that her safety could not be guaranteed if she returned to her
mother. They did not announce their decision in open court, but
Minakshi's family was informed that evening. The next morning a
crowd of several hundred Moors gathered in the mosque grounds
opposite police headquarters, where Minakshi was being held.

During the afternoon the crowd grew until it numbered about a
thousand. They apparently hoped to seize Minakshi when she left
the barracks with her lover. The noise disturbed G. W. R.
Campbell, the Inspector-General, who was at work in his office.
Finally, late in the afternoon, he went outside and addressed the
crowd as if they were children: 'I told them forcibly, but civilly
and even kindly, that they would gain nothing whatever by
assembling and making a noise.'[46] The crowd responded by
throwing bricks, stones and sticks. One of the bricks hit
Campbell. The police in the building at the time, who numbered
about twenty, then charged the crowd with the aid of European
and Sinhalese bystanders. About seventy persons were arrested,
some of them inside the mosque. The mosque lamps and furniture
were smashed.

It transpired that the brick which had hit Campbell had been
thrown by John Hogan, a former soldier and police constable who
had been discharged from the Ceylon Police for drunkenness. It
was not uncommon for down-and-out Europeans to be converted
to Islam.[47] There were altogether eight European Muslims in the
crowd, but there were also Moors of very high social status. One
thousand pounds was accepted as bail for one rioter.[48] During the
Supreme Court deliberations Abdul Raheman, the Turkish
Consul, was willing to stand security for the good treatment of the
girl.[49] In the end she was smuggled back to Moratuva and married
her lover.[50]

Clashes between the Sinhalese and Moors demonstrated that
relationships between members of the two ethnic groups were
strained. The position of many Moors as money-lenders and
traders, cultural differences, and the lack of social ties were
among the causes. This is not to say that violence was always
imminent, for this tension was accepted, and the level of violence
when it did occur was not serious. On the other hand, given a
catalyst, local solidarities could emerge vigorously. In the aftermath of the riot over Minakshi Moor shopkeepers in Colombo
were threatened and blackmailed, and there was some minor
looting.[51] In the weeks after the Chilaw disturbances, brought on
by high rice prices, a group of Moors sang indecent songs near
Sinhalese houses at night, and a picture of a pig was alleged to

have drawn on a mosque wall.[52] But these conflicts were never in any danger of spreading geographically; the protagonists viewed each other as local entities.

Most riots were confined to one ethnic group. Fights between factions of Moors were frequent, both in places where they formed a large proportion of the population and where they were a small minority. In most localities there were two factions, each of which included wealthy and influential men.[53] Control of a mosque was often the focus of these clashes, which on occasion resulted in fatalities.[54]

Among the Sinhalese many local riots followed the boundaries of caste. In some instances caste status was the explicit point of conflict. Low-caste persons who lived near the south-western coastal strip attempted to gain social status by adopting customs similar to those of high-caste persons; the aim was to challenge specific hierarchical relationships, not hierarchy itself. They justified their claims through myths which explained how they lost their formerly high positions.[55] The locally-dominant high caste sometimes responded with violence; the aim of the rioters was to restore the status quo. The elopement of a high-caste woman with a low-caste man could also provoke an affray. These disturbances pitted Goyigamas, Karavas or Salagamas against Hunus, Hinnas, Henas or Olis.[56]

There were also caste riots caused by a more general local antipathy. These disturbances, like those provoked by attempts to adopt new customs, were limited to the south-western coastal region.[57] They were often set off by insults or coarse language. The more violent of these clashes were between Karavas and Salagamas or Duravas in the Southern Province, but most other castes with a presence near the coast were also involved. An incident at Modara (Mutwal), a ward of Colombo, may serve as an example.[58] On 5 May 1887 two boys, one a Karava and the other a Salagama, quarrelled. The police, anticipating trouble, brought in additional men in case there was a disturbance. On the following Sunday, after church services, 300 Karavas and 150 Salagamas assembled; each side threw stones and tiles at each other. Women collected the missiles. The police and a priest were soon able to disperse the men.

There was no consistent policy towards caste riots. Generally officials adopted a legalistic perspective, but there were exceptions. In 1887, for example, men from an élite Oli family from just south of Colombo planned to attend a marriage ceremony wearing combs in the Goyigama style. The local Goyigamas successfully prevented them from doing so, and an Oli was killed in the affray.[59] Although the police detective who investigated the case believed that local headmen were behind the crime, Arthur Gordon, the Governor, opposed taking any action against them. He believed that the Olis had provoked the riot by giving 'grievous offence', and commented that 'they have no doubt a *right* to wear combs or whatever other article of ornament or dress they please, just as a man has a right to go to an Irish Nationalist meeting dressed in an Orange coat.'[60]

Riots concerned explicitly with economic interests also remained local, and were usually of concern only to narrow social groups or factions. In 1883 men in the pay of fish merchants assaulted Modara fishermen who had sold their catch to outsiders willing to pay a better price.[61] There was a riot in 1890 when rival coach operators fought over the right to carry passengers from Alutgama to Galle.[62] At Devundara (Dondra) in 1893 there was violence between landowners when a dispute arose about the location of shops which were to be built to serve the crowds expected for the annual fair.[63] In 1904 Moor and Sinhalese traders clashed at Rambukkana after the Sinhalese began to deal in plantains, a business which had previously been a Moor monopoly.[64] The most common type of economically-motivated riot was committed to assert a claim over disputed land; this phenomenon was referred to by contemporaries as land grabbing.[65] There was also periodic conflict over fishing rights. One source of tension was the presence of Indian fishermen who migrated seasonally to exploit coastal waters.[66] On other occasions only Sinhalese were involved; sometimes these disputes followed caste lines.[67]

The authorities were not usually overly concerned about fighting motivated by parochial economic interests unless the government's authority was explicitly challenged. In 1874 the villagers of Gandara objected to the use of fishing nets by the inhabitants of nearly Devundra in a bay near Gandara.[68] Traditionally only rod-and-line fishing was allowed in the bay, which was a source of small fish used for bait. The Assistant Government Agent, Edward Elliott, ruled that the Devundara villagers could use nets in the bay during certain hours. When it became clear that the Gandara villagers would resist his order, he proceeded to the scene with headmen and police. When the Devundara people began fishing, the Gandara villagers intervened, Elliott was jostled, and the police had to retreat. Twelve men were later convicted of riot and assault and sentenced to terms ranging from three to five years imprisonment.

Increased taxation could lead to dissatisfaction. No major direct taxes were introduced in the years after the unhappy experience of 1848, but as government services were expanded in specific localities taxes linked to these services were imposed. In the 1870s the Colombo Municipal Council increased taxes to pay for piped water and gas. These levies remained a sore point in the Modara division of Colombo for over a decade. In the 1880s the predominantly fisherman population refused to pay their municipal assessment for six years, arguing, no doubt accurately since they were unable to afford the service fees, that they had received no benefit from water or gas.[69] A majority of the fishermen were Roman Catholic, and they were supported to some extent by Catholic members of the Colombo élite. On 9 July 1888 a municipal tax collector was assaulted when attempting to collect goods in lieu of the unpaid taxes. Police were called in to confront a crowd numbering about 1,000, but serious violence was avoided when members of the Municipal Council calmed the protesters with assurances that their grievances would be considered.[70] When the police withdrew the crowd jeered and clapped their hands.

When a community resisted paying a tax the authorities were usually able to overcome the initial opposition tactfully and avoid violence. The government had overwhelming force at its disposal, and the people knew it. One case, at the seaside village of Ambalangoda, ended tragically.

In 1898 the government decided to impose a sanitary rate on the village under an ordinance which had been designed to provide for such services in places not yet considered ready for an elected local board.[71] There were immediate objections from the villagers, expressed through petitions to the government. By 1899 the rate and assessment were decided, but the levying of the tax was delayed because of continuous protests. In June 1900 the residents of three nearby hamlets were excluded and the ordinance confined to the town proper.[72] Recovery of the tax was postponed to 1901; meanwhile an Ambalangoda Association was formed to oppose the tax. Ambalangoda was a large village with a high rate of literacy and was populated primarily by Karavas. Among its residents were men of English-language education and relative wealth. J. P. Gunesekera, the Secretary of the Association, was a pharmacist.[73] The Association's aims undoubtedly had general support. The sanitary rate was collected as a poll tax, so it affected all villagers. It is probable that the poor resented similar taxes in small towns, but where there was a local board it was unlikely that wealthier men would organize opposition, for local board elections and politics could give them an outlet for their political ambitions. At Ambalangoda there was to be no local control over how the funds were to be spent.

In April 1901 the *mudaliyar* attempted to collect the tax, but only 122 of the 1,137 men liable paid up.[74] Under the ordinance, the government had to distrain the movable or if necessary immovable property of defaulters. This was a time-consuming and complicated task, especially since so much property was jointly owned. Nevertheless, on 24 September 1901 George Fowler, the Government Agent of the Southern Province, accompanied by one hundred policemen, began this operation. A hostile group of men, numbering about one hundred or perhaps somewhat more, immediately approached him.[75] The crowd was in the form of a Buddhist procession, but Fowler had had reports that the resistance to his operations would be in this guise. He ordered the crowd to disperse, and when it paid no attention the police moved to arrest two men at the front of the demonstration.[76] Stones were thrown and Fowler's hat was knocked off by a fish gaff. Suddenly, some of the policemen opened fire. Two persons were killed outright and four others wounded. Two of those injured died soon afterwards. Among those shot was a woman who had been watching from her own verandah. After the crowd fled Fowler spent the remainder of the day distraining property. Troops were summoned by telegraph, but soon returned to Colombo because they found on arrival that there was no need for them.

The men who made up the procession were a cross-section of village society. Of the thirty-eight whose descriptions were published in the *Hue and Cry* in connection with the disturbance, there were sixteen fishermen, six carpenters, five traders and two contractors.[77] Occupations with one representative were petition-drawer, pharmacist, mason, tailor, fish seller and tavern keeper. Two of the thirty-eight were wealthy enough to be included on the jury list for the district.[78] All but one of the men was born in Ambalangoda, but many were often employed away from the village. Eighteen were said to 'haunt' localities outside the Southern Province.

If Fowler had handled the situation differently there would not have been any serious violence. There is no evidence to suggest that the crowd was in a frenzied state. The villagers expected some trouble, for the shops were shut and some leading residents were careful to be away, but if the crowd had been intent on violence its members would have carried more effective weapons than stones, one fish gaff, and several sticks. The villagers were very surprised when the police opened fire. Many of them believed that the police could not shoot unless martial law was proclaimed and a red flag hoisted.[79] Nobody took responsibility for ordering the police to shoot, though a police officer admitted that he shouted 'don't fire, don't fire', an order which was perhaps foolish given that the scene was confused and noisy.[80] In fact, the police weapons were not even supposed to have been loaded.[81] Despite this, Fowler did not attempt to find out which policemen had opened fire. In the immediate aftermath of the riot some of the police involved received special rewards, but a later investigation, the findings of which were not made public, concluded that the police had not been justified in using firearms.[82]

There were no more violent confrontations, although passive resistance to paying the tax continued for some time.[83] A punitive police force was stationed in the village for a year. In December, after a week-long trial, six men were convicted of riot, and Gunasekera of abetting riot, and all were sentenced to two years rigorous imprisonment.[84] Six other men tried with them, who were not at the scene of the riot but who were accused of having organized it at a meeting of the Ambalangoda Association a few days earlier, were acquitted. After this long trial a second batch of accused, members of the crowd, pleaded guilty and were fined ten rupees each.

The Buddhist press criticized officials for over-reacting, but it thought the villagers foolish and did not launch any sustained campaign on their behalf.[85] The Catholic *Nanartha Pradipaya* openly attacked the government in an editorial entitled 'Murder at Ambalangoda', but there were very few Catholics in the Southern Province, and no effective support for the villagers ensued.[86] The incident was soon forgotten, except in Ambalangoda itself.

The disturbances discussed in this section were essentially reactions to events. Not only were they confined to one locality, but their aims were local and parochial. Grain riots reflected the belief that food prices should be kept stable irrespective of market conditions. The riot by Moors over Minakshi showed that the loss of a woman to another community was resented. Increased taxation for new, unwanted or unneeded services were opposed, as were attempts by low castes to adopt high-caste customs. At Ambalangoda, an association modelled on British lines was established, but it was used only to oppose the levying of a local tax. In none of these clashes were the protesters able to garner effective support for their aims from outside their own locality. These riots were either isolated reactions against unwanted economic and social change or other protests which did not threaten the social order.

The Emergence of Religious Riots

In the 1880s a new and potentially more dangerous form of riot appeared dramatically on the scene. On Easter Sunday, 25 March 1883, at Kotahena, a ward of Colombo, some two thousand Roman Catholics, white crosses painted on their foreheads, attacked a Buddhist procession, killing one man and several bullocks.[87] The Buddhists fought back, and dozens of men on both sides were injured. Both the scale of the clash and the form in which religious passion was expressed were unprecedented in Sri Lanka under the British.

In the early nineteenth century, despite vigorous Protestant missionary efforts, most Buddhists took little interest in Christianity. Around the mid-century, however, some Low Country Buddhists began to organize religious activities along missionary lines, partly as a response to assaults on their cultural heritage by missionaries, and partly to gain social status commensurate with their economic status. Buddhist-owned newspapers appeared in the 1860s, and they devoted much space to religious affairs, both Buddhist and Christian. The revival gained further momentum with the addition of the organizational skills of the American Theosophist Henry Olcott after 1880.

That the first religiously-motivated violent clashes were between Buddhists and Catholics, not Buddhists and Protestants, may be partially explained by the relative size of the Catholic and Protestant communities. There was no numerically significant Protestant community with which to do battle. There were religious controversies in the 1870s between Buddhists and Catholics as well as between Buddhists and Protestants. Catholic tracts attacked Buddhists and vice versa.[88] One Buddhist pamphlet which particularly infuriated Catholics was entitled *A Curious Virgin*.[89]

The heightened tension in Kotahena, which led to the riot, was not of long duration. Catholics and Buddhists had lived together without incident. More than half of Kotahena's population was Catholic, and only about one-quarter was Buddhist. In 1870 the Catholics began work on St Lucia's Cathedral, which was in use but still unfinished in 1883. Nearby, four hundred metres away,

was a Buddhist temple which was controlled by Migettuwatte
Gunananda, the controversial anti-Christian orator. In January
1883 the Buddhists decided to hold celebrations to mark the
completion of this temple. These consisted of frequent processions
to the temple from various villages on the outskirts of Colombo.
To reach the temple these processions inevitably passed through
the Roman Catholic neighbourhood of Kotahena. Irritation
among Catholics mounted in February 1883, and the priests began
to worry as the holy season of Easter approached. On 6 March
Father Massillamany wrote to the police, asking that Buddhist
processions not be allowed on Palm Sunday, Good Friday and
Easter Sunday. He received the reply that permits for processions
would be issued to the first group which requested them, and that
no applications had yet been received. The priest immediately
applied for permits for the Roman Catholics.

Nevertheless, because of confusion among police officers, the
request of some Buddhists who a few days later applied for a
permit to hold a procession on Palm Sunday was granted. This
procession was stoned by a group of Catholics as it passed a street
corner in Kotahena. In itself the incident was not serious; the
police were present but did not make any arrests. Included among
the images which were carried was a female figure, which many
Catholics believed represented the Virgin Mary.[90] Two days later,
when the police issued a permit for Buddhists to hold a procession
on Good Friday, which was also a full-moon day, many Catholics
were furious. An anonymous letter taunted Louis Mendis, a
prominent Catholic well known for his proclivities for violence,
with a note informing him that 'on your funeral day we intend to
celebrate our wedding day.'[91]

By this time it was apparent even to the police that serious
trouble was possible. On Thursday evening they cancelled the
permit for Friday's procession, and rescheduled it for Sunday
after the services in the cathedral were over. This arrangement had
the approval of the bishop, Monsignor Pagnani. Nevertheless, on
Good Friday a number of Roman Catholics gathered near St
Lucia's to oppose any Buddhist procession. Again, the police
made no attempt to disperse the crowd, which by all accounts was
in an ugly mood.

The authorities took some precautions for the Sunday procession. Aware that there were rumours that images insulting to
Christianity would be carried, police officers, including a Roman
Catholic, inspected the procession before it set off. They found
no such images. But as the procession approached Kotahena, the

bells of St Lucia's began to ring, and churches in Modara responded. Two or three thousand Roman Catholics assembled near St Lucia's. Meanwhile, rumours spread among those in the Buddhist procession that Catholics had assaulted a monk. Men began to pick up makeshift weapons from a timber factory. At this point the police accompanying the procession, about seventy in number, attempted to turn it back, but the crowd's emotions had been aroused and the efforts of the police were ignored. Other police tried to disperse the Catholic crowd, but they were forced to retreat by a shower of bricks and stones. When the procession reached St Lucia's Corner, the Catholics attacked and the Buddhists countered by attempting to drive through the Catholics with their bullock carts. They did not succeed and their carts and images were smashed. The police were caught in the middle and sent a message asking for the military. By the time the troops arrived most of the fighting was over, mainly due to the cooling effects of a sudden downpour.

Sporadic trouble continued for several days after the riot.[92] On Easter Monday two previously planned Buddhist processions, for which licences had been obtained, assembled at the outskirts of Colombo and headed towards Kotahena, where the cathedral's bells were ringing and a crowd gathering. The military were called out to turn the processions back. Members of one of the processions, from Paliyagoda, were armed with clubs, cartloads of stones, and six loaded muskets. On the same day the Roman Catholic chapel at Dehivala, just south of Colombo, was burnt down. There were other attacks on Catholic property over the next few days, and a Church Missionary Society chapel was also put to the torch. Religious tension was high where Roman Catholics and Buddhists lived in proximity. At Ratmalana, south of Colombo, Buddhists paraded a cross after hearing rumours that Catholics had gone in procession carrying yellow cloth, a Buddhist symbol, on a pole. At Kandana, to the north, a monk was said to have had his robes torn off. In Colombo itself scattered cases of assault for religious reasons lasted several days. Five days after the riot there was a rumour that 5,000 Catholics were coming from Negombo, a Catholic centre north of Colombo, with the intention of burning down the Kotahena temple and murdering Migettuwatte.

The immediate cause of the riot was the firm belief among Catholics that Buddhists were carrying images insulting to Christianity. Pagnani believed that such images were carried, and the *Catholic Messenger* reported that processionists had carried a monkey nailed to a cross.[93] Catholics felt that Buddhists were invading their sacred space. Many Catholics were fiercely attached to their faith, which had survived Dutch persecution, proximity to the majority Buddhists, and often indifferent priestly leadership. Few Catholics may have read the religious tracts, mutually insulting, which were exchanged between Buddhists and Catholics, but all had heard stories about Migettuwatte trampling on a Bible while lecturing inside his Kotahena temple.[94]

This was tolerable as long as it was limited to clearly Buddhist space. Pagnani told the commission which inquired into the riot that 'the Roman Catholics would not take into serious consideration anything inside the walls of Kotahena temple. . . . The offence on the part of the Buddhists consisted of their taking the images so near the cathedral.'[95] The use of bells to summon the faithful, and their quick arrival, many with crosses already painted on their foreheads, indicates that resistance to the procession was planned. Afterwards a priest admitted that this was so, though he said that he did not know who was behind the organization.[96] In fact, it is clear that the Catholic hierarchy did not have full control over their flock. It had already been decided in Rome to remove Pagnani and his predominantly Italian missionaries from Colombo because they were unable adequately to serve the Catholic community.[97]

The ferocity of Catholic feelings clearly took the priests by surprise, but the desire of Pagnani and his colleagues to use their authority to defuse the situation may also be questioned. They were sitting in the bishop's quarters smoking after-dinner cigars when the bells of St Lucia's began to toll. Although the priest who went outside was unable to stop them ringing, Pagnani did nothing.[98] In the weeks after the riot, the *Messenger*, while deploring violence, was not in the least penitent. In fact it took satisfaction from the Catholic success in smashing up the Buddhist procession.[99] Both Christopher Bonjean, the new bishop who arrived later in 1883, and senior British officials felt that Pagnani's conduct had lacked foresight.[100]

In the longer run, Kotahena was a Pyrrhic victory for Catholics. Bonjean, who had long been posted to Jaffna and was experienced in dealing with the colonial government, was conscious of the Catholic position as a minority religion. He attained greater control over Catholic affairs than had Pagnani, and acted to suppress the more crude publications which attacked Buddhism.[101] His efforts did not succeed in defusing Buddhist anger. Kotahena spurred Buddhists into asserting their identity more forcefully than before.

One Buddhist response to their humiliation was provoked by the failure in the courts of all prosecutions of rioters. The Queen's Advocate felt that the witnesses were biased. He wrote that 'each accused should be proved to have taken an active part and to have been seen doing so by at least two disinterested witnesses.'[102] No Catholic could be found to testify against Catholics and Buddhist witnesses were considered biased. Altogether four legal proceedings were instituted: by the police, the widow of the dead man, a group of Buddhists, and a group of Catholics. By 8 June all charges had been dismissed, the evidence produced being contradictory. The British felt that both sides used false evidence to charge prominent men who were not on the scene but who were thought to be instigators. This explanation was unsatisfactory to many Buddhists, who felt that justice had been denied.[103] A rumour circulated that the charges had been dropped because the new Queen's Advocate who arrived in Sri Lanka shortly after the riot was himself a Roman Catholic.[104] Buddhist leaders complained to Longden, the Governor, but received no redress. On 28 January 1884 they formed the Buddhist Defence Committee, which decided to send Olcott to the Colonial Office in London to plead their case.[105] The new Governor, Gordon, was more sympathetic than Longden, but he felt that too much time had passed for him to do anything.

The other Buddhist response was to increase the number of processions through Catholic neighbourhoods and by churches; these processions became a permanent source of contention in the years after the clash at Kotahena.[106] F. R. Saunders, the Government Agent of the Western Province, wrote in his report for 1889 that whenever there was a procession 'it requires the greatest care and circumspection on the part of all concerned to prevent some trivial and accidental action from giving serious offence and leading to riot.'[107] In 1890 a *mudaliyar* pointed out that 'it must be understood that since the Kotahena riots assemblies between the aforesaid parties [Buddhists and Catholics] whenever they meet together do not go quiet.'[108] Members of Buddhist processions liked to slow down in front of churches, increase the tempo of their drumming, and shout *sadhu, sadhu*. In 1889 the *Messenger* stated that no Buddhist procession was 'thought meritorious that does not pass before the Catholic church and offer some insult to the Catholics of the place.'[109] Bonjean felt that any violence was detrimental to the Church's interests, and tried to restrain the response of Catholics.[110] Nevertheless, on some occasions there were fatalities.

The extension of sacred space by Buddhists was not directed only against Catholics. The revivalist movement led to awareness of Sri Lanka's Buddhist past. Land, trees or stones which were perceived as being historically imbued with a sacred nature were also claimed for Buddhism. Since sacred qualities were not recognized in colonial law, conflict with the government was inevitable. In Kandyan districts the extent of temple land, which had a special tax-exempt status, had been decided in the mid-century by the Temple Land Commissioners. These tracts were endowments and not inherently sacred; otherwise there was no particular legal provision for religious land. Around the turn of the century some Buddhists began to assert claims to certain Crown land on the grounds of its inherent sacredness as shown by ancient texts.[111] The most important of the claims was at the ancient city of Anuradhapura, but it was at the Low Country town of Kalutara where violence first broke out.

There had long been an oral tradition in Kalutara that the Dutch Fort had at one time been the site of a Buddhist temple.[112] This land was used by the British for government offices and official residences. In the late 1880s some Buddhists applied to the Local Board for permission to lease the area around one of three bo-trees in the Fort, and to use it as a Buddhist shrine. The Assistant Government Agent, H. Hay Cameron, had no objection and the land was rented for a nominal sum.[113] One Podi Singho established a shrine at the base of the tree. He was not an ordained monk, but as custodian of the shrine he was in a position similar to that of the local monks, and competed with them for the offerings of laymen. This arrangement continued without incident until the arrival of H. W. Brodhurst as Assistant Government Agent in 1891. Brodhurst did not share Cameron's sympathetic interest in Buddhism, and felt that the continued presence of a Buddhist shrine on Crown land constituted a challenge to his authority.

In order to commemorate the jubilee of Queen Victoria, Cameron had planted a bo-tree and an ironwood tree at the nearby village of Matugama in 1887. Brodhurst claimed that the two trees were interfering with each other, and had the bo-tree cut down as the 'less valuable' of the two trees. In the eyes of some Buddhists this action was a crime; in the Kandyan Kingdom wilful damage to a bo-tree was at least theoretically a capital offence. Local residents retaliated by destroying the ironwood tree.[114] This was an ominous start to Brodhurst's involvement with the bo-trees of the district.

In 1891 and 1892 petitions were sent to the government asking permission to repair the temple on the site of the Fort.[115] In fact there was no visible trace of any temple. Podi Singho was a signatory to these petitions, which claimed that a quarter acre of land was sacred. The government rejected the petitioners' requests. In 1894 a similar petition was presented, and this time Brodhurst, in order to 'nip the movement early', ordered the two bo-trees in the Fort which were not subject to Podi Singho's lease to be destroyed.[116] When the work began, O. M. Obeyesekere, a medical doctor and President of the recently formed Kalutara Buddhist Union, sent a telegram to Havelock, the Governor, complaining that sacred bo-trees were being felled. Havelock ordered the work to stop and had Edward Elliott, the Government Agent, conduct an inquiry.[117] Only part of one of the two trees was left standing.

Elliott supported Brodhurst's actions and Havelock agreed with him.[118] They perceived the issue as one of property, and maintained that the Crown had full legal control of its own trees. Havelock dismissed the Buddhist argument concerning the religious status of the trees by stating that since the Kalutara Fort had not been used for religious purposes during the British occupation, the bo-tree 'can have no sacred character or association'. Havelock, however, wanted to tread cautiously on Buddhist issues. Not long before he had received a severe reprimand from the Secretary of State for the Colonies for sanctioning the transfer to Anglicans of a piece of Crown land near Buddhist shrines at Anuradhapura.[119] So he referred the matter to London, asking permission to let Brodhurst destroy all the trees.

Officials at the Colonial Office were unconvinced. It was decided that Brodhurst had to be supported in the case of the first two trees, lest the government be seen as sanctioning claims to all bo-trees, but that the shrine around the third tree should remain.[120] The authorities in Sri Lanka were unhappy with this decision, and produced further evidence to convince London to change its mind.[121] Unfortunately for them, this evidence was patently weak, and the Secretary of State asked Ridgeway, by now Governor, for his views.[122]

Ridgeway instructed A. R. Dawson, the new Government Agent, to reach a compromise.[123] Dawson told Podi Singho that he had no intention of injuring the tree, but that the shrine had to be moved by 26 November 1896.[124] On 11 November the Kalutara Buddhist Union petitioned Dawson, asking that the tree be not cut down.[125] Dawson did not reassure them, because 'they knew the rumour was false'.[126] As a result of Dawson's failure to respond to the petition, the belief that the tree was in danger was confirmed among many Buddhists. On the morning of 26 November about one thousand persons gathered near the bo-tree, intent on its protection. The crowd was reinforced by villagers who arrived on the 11.45 train. The authorities had had no plans for action that day, for they did not have the legal right to evict Podi Singho. A few men were arrested by armed constables, but serious violence was avoided.[127] To Brodhurst's fury, the local headmen made no effort to stop the unlawful demonstration. One went home for breakfast when the skirmishes between the police and the crowd began, and another, who lived nearby, was busy finding out the price of grain for his weekly report.[128] The crowd dispersed gradually late in the afternoon, having successfully defied authority for one day. Several rioters were later convicted and fined or sentenced to short terms of imprisonment.[129]

The Kalutara bo-tree affair was another indication of the new willingness of Buddhists to assert religious claims. The rioters and their supporters were acting on the basis of Buddhist revivalist ideas, expressed by élites of laymen and monks. The bo-trees were sacred, and no secular law could change that fact. Buddhists justified the sacred status of the land by references to the Mahavamsa and other sacred texts.[130] Although officials rejected in principle the argument that the content of the Mahavamsa could affect the property rights of the Crown, H. C. P. Bell, the Archaeological Commissioner who was acting temporarily as Kalutara District Judge, was produced to dispute textual references.[131] The idea that bo-trees should be preserved was not new among Buddhists, but the willingness to campaign for a legal title to land, on account of its inherent sacredness, was a new development. At Kalutara, in the end, the government compromised. Podi Singho was secretly paid to leave the shrine and access to the bo-tree was restricted, but the tree itself was guaranteed protection.[132] The Kalutara riot, like that of Kotahena and the subsequent procession disputes, was the product of emerging Buddhist revivalist ideology which had widespread support.

Riots in the Twentieth Century

When Buddhists extended their claim of sacred space to Crown land, the response of the British was cautious. Brodhurst felt that

the way to handle the Buddhist claim at Kalutara was to destroy
the bo-tree. Ridgeway came to a more realistic conclusion. He
pledged to preserve the tree but had the shrine at its base
dismantled. When shortly thereafter Buddhists made a similar but
more extensive claim at the ancient city of Anuradhapura he
found it more difficult to reach a compromise, and in 1903 a
major riot ensued.

Anuradhapura had been a capital of the ancient Sinhalese
kings, and it maintained its role in Sinhalese society as a
pilgrimage centre long after its political importance had ceased.
By the nineteenth century the jungle had buried many of the
extant monuments, but the bo-tree and several *dagabas*, or relic
chambers, remained in continuous use. The tensions which led to
the riot of June 1903 were based on divergent interpretations of
the history of the city.

In the official view Anuradhapura was a formerly great city
which was sinking into the jungle until the British saved it by
making it the administrative centre of the newly-formed North-
Central Province in 1872.[133] The British took credit for bringing to
light new shrines through their excavations and for making
pilgrimages easier by improving transportation facilities. Buddhists, on the other hand, emphasized the continuity of the
ancient city as a pilgrimage centre.[134] They were not impressed by
the modern town which had grown up around the shrines, with its
churches, mosque, slaughterhouse and non-Buddhist majority.

Under a settlement of 1872 the Buddhist incumbents of the
shrines were awarded land immediately around eight important
sites, but the land in between was held to be Crown property.[135]
The first visible sign of discontent with this arrangement came in
1891 when the government transferred a piece of land between the
sacred bo-tree and the Ruvanveli Dagaba to the Anglican Bishop
of Colombo.[136] The Buddhist establishment in Colombo protested
against the possible erection of a church on the land, but received
no redress from Havelock.[137] They then appealed successfully to
the Colonial Office in London, which felt that although the
government had the legal authority to transfer the land, the construction of a church near Buddhist shrines used for pilgrimages
would surely lead to religious confrontation.[138] A compromise
was reached whereby the Anglicans accepted another site further
away from the sacred area. There were also scattered protests by
Anuradhapura Buddhists over archaeological excavations which
were thought to be damaging sacred buildings, but there was no
systematic local agitation until the turn of the century.[139]

In 1899 Walisinha Harischandra, a Low Countryman and a member of the Maha Bodhi Society, settled in Anuradhapura and began to promote his views on the proper status of the city. The Maha Bodhi Society had been established in India some years earlier to campaign for control of Buddhist shrines in India. Its leader was Anagarika Dharmapala, the Sinhalese lay preacher whose bombastic rhetoric gave much impetus to Buddhist revivalism in the early twentieth century.

Harischandra rejected the validity of colonial law in Anuradhapura, asserting that the city and its environs were sacred and should be controlled exclusively by Buddhists.[140] His claim was based on accounts in the Mahavamsa of the dedication of lands for religious purposes. He argued that the Archaeological Department and other government agencies were desecrating sacred land. Harischandra found a receptive audience among Sinhalese residents of Anuradhapura, many of whom were Low Countrymen. He also succeeded in winning cautious support from the temple incumbents.

Harischandra led and supported agitation against the local authorities on several fronts in the years 1899–1903. He campaigned against the efforts of the Government Agent, L. W. Booth, to evict Thai priests who were living in unexcavated ruins which were claimed to be buildings constructed by Sinhalese kings for the purpose of meditation.[141] A notice board stating 'Maha Bodhi Society' was put up on land which the government intended to use as the site for the Medical Officer's quarters. Harischandra wanted to build a Buddhist school there, and protested when work on the official residence went ahead.[142] When officials had a small open space in the centre of town enclosed and turned into a flower garden, there were protests because pilgrims had previously camped on the land.[143] There were also objections when two ancient ponds, which Bell, the Archaeological Commissioner, thought were of no interest, were filled in with dirt from other excavations.[144] These campaigns received support from the Low Country Buddhist élite, who agreed, in the words of W. A. de Silva, a veterinary surgeon, that 'a sacred site is sacred forever'.[145]

The immediate cause of heightened religious feeling in June 1903 was the use by the Public Works Department of blocks of stones from the ruins for the construction of a road.[146] On 15 May Bell accompanied the District Engineer to a site, and pointed out loose stones which he thought of no value. The next day Harischandra and several monks went to the Police Magistrate and obtained an order forbidding the Public Works Department

from using the stones, but when the Magistrate, shortly afterwards, was told that the removal had Bell's sanction, he rescinded
this order. Officials believed that the stones were 'rubbish' and
not worth preserving. For Buddhists the aesthetic value of the
stones was irrelevant. They were sacred and to use them for roads
was to insult the Buddhist religion. Word of the desecration
spread quickly to the Low Country.

The anti-government riot took place on 9 June, during the full-
moon pilgrimage.[147] It took the authorities by surprise; Booth was
away in Kandy and neither his assistant nor the Magistrate spoke
Sinhala. Shortly before noon the Christian *kachcheri mudaliyar*,
who was on horseback and probably drunk, knocked down an
elderly woman pilgrim. A row developed and stones were thrown.
Soon afterwards another group of persons attacked two sites
which had been claimed by the Maha Bodhi Society, the flower
garden and the Medical Officer's quarters. The garden was
destroyed and some timber was burnt at the Medical Officer's
house, which was still under construction. The crowd then turned
on the slaughterhouse and destroyed it before going on to the
Roman Catholic church, which was about five hundred metres
away. They burnt down the church and set fire to nearby
buildings, causing about ten thousand rupees worth of damage.
The nuns of the nearby convent fled into the jungle and the priest,
an elderly man, was later found unconscious.

Only a few hundred of the estimated ten thousand pilgrims
present in Anuradhapura took part in the riot. Many Low
Countrymen were said to be involved.[148] They left town immediately after the riot, and managed to avoid arrest. Sinhalese
residents of Anuradhapura also participated; most were of Low
Country origin. Government officials wanted very much to
implicate Harischandra, who was arrested and detained, but in the
end an all-Christian jury rejected the theory that the riot was
premeditated and acquitted him of all charges.[149] To the chagrin of
officials, the *ratemahatmaya* of a nearby district was implicated in
the burning of the Catholic church and was among the thirty-six
persons convicted by the Supreme Court.[150]

The rioters clearly shared the views of the local branch of the
Maha Bodhi Society. A participant in the destruction of the meat
market told the Magistrate that 'this is our property which has
been unjustly taken away'.[151] Harischandra had for several years
attacked the presence of the slaughterhouse in Anuradhapura.[152]
He also objected to Catholic, Protestant and Muslim religious
buildings. When singling out the Catholic church, perhaps some

of the crowd remembered that in 1896 the priest had used ancient balustrades to construct steps for his residence.[153] The Catholic church may also have been a target because many of the rioters came from Low Country districts where there was Catholic-Buddhist tension.

The Buddhist élite of Colombo condemned the violence, but continued to support the aims of the rioters. The *Sarasavi Sandarasa* raised funds to pay for the defence of those who were put on trial.[154] When the *Catholic Messenger* asserted that God had saved the nuns, another Buddhist newspaper, the *Lakminipahana*, sarcastically commented that it was remarkable that He had not also saved the old priest.[155] It asserted that if the Buddhists had been truly bent on violence, then God would not have been able to save the nuns. The *Lakminipahana* admitted that the majority of all peoples, even Buddhists, was coarse and uneducated, but it asked its readers to recall the Kotahena riot, when Catholics had frightened innocent rural monks, caused girls to fall into mud, broken people's heads open and killed a man and several head of cattle. The *Lakminipahana* attributed the relatively restrained conduct of the Buddhists to the fact that Buddhism was against killing, and contrasted this attitude with the Catholic belief that one could go to heaven for attacking non-believers.[156]

Before the riot Ridgeway had been conducting negotiations with the Kandyan member of the Legislative Council, S. N. W. Hulugalle, to increase the amount of land at Anuradhapura which was controlled by the incumbents of the shrines.[157] After the riot Hulugalle wrote to Ridgeway proposing that Buddhists pay compensation to the Catholics, in return for which the Catholics would move their mission further out of town.[158] This proposal contrasted starkly with the Buddhist memorial of 1894, which in rejecting the proposed location of the Anglican church, pointed out that the Catholic site was outside the sacred area.[159]

At the end of 1903 Ridgeway came to an agreement with a delegation of Buddhist revivalist leaders. The government ceded some land to the temples and the Buddhists promised to compensate the Catholics for their financial losses.[160] In 1905 the Bishop of Jaffna received 1,000 rupees and the agreement was implemented.[161] There was no more violence, but conflicts with the government over the definition of sacred space in Anuradhapura continued. In 1905, for instance, there were protests when Anglicans began constructing a church on the site which they had received in 1894.[162]

During the first decades of the twentieth century many assumptions of nineteenth-century colonial society came under attack, partly because of awareness of nationalist agitation in India. British officials in Sri Lanka gradually came to be less secure about their right to rule. Sri Lankans formed associations which, while remaining within the colonial order, implicitly challenged the dominance of the British. The willingness of the Buddhist establishment in Colombo to differ from the authorities over the issue of sacred land at Anuradhapura was one indication of increased self-confidence among the élite. Participation in the temperance movement of 1904 provided another outlet for those with social and political ambitions. This burst of activity began at Kogalla in Galle district and spread through the Southern and Western Provinces, and to a lesser extent into Kandyan districts.[163] Local temperance societies were formed in hundreds of villages, and in Colombo there was a branch in each ward. A president, secretary and treasurer were generally elected at mass meetings which established rules and set a weekly or monthly membership fee. Many societies hired peons to discourage members and sometimes non-members from entering taverns. Local notables, including small landowners, teachers, traders and notaries, were heavily involved in this campaign, but the English-speaking élite of Colombo, especially the Buddhists among them, soon came to support it, and some attempts were made to co-ordinate the local organizations. The movement petered out in less than a year, but when temperance agitation revived in 1912 it took on a more political character. The target was a change in government policy which it was thought would increase toddy consumption among the lower classes.[164] Although some Protestant clergymen supported these campaigns, temperance societies were dominated by Buddhists. It was often argued that drink was an evil introduced and encouraged by the Christian government.

Buddhist revivalist ideology was spread through temperance activities and the emigration of Low Country Sinhalese to Kandyan districts. One consequence of this geographical expansion was a decrease in the importance of Catholicism as a negative reference point. The colonial government became one target, though among the élite criticism was combined with avowals of loyalty. The focus also shifted towards the Moors, who unlike Catholics were scattered throughout the island. The Buddhist press periodically attacked the trading activities of Moors, especially Coast Moors, who were of recent Indian origin. Tensions also developed because increased religious and social consciousness among Moors themselves made it less likely that they would tolerate symbolic expressions of Buddhist supremacy. Though on a smaller scale than Catholics and Buddhists, Muslims founded schools, published newspapers and organized other activities in an effort to sharpen their social and cultural identity.[165] Their dress became more distinctive, and in some localities mosques were constructed or enlarged.

When the idea of processions as statements of social and cultural identity spread from Low Country to Kandyan districts, it was the Moors, and particularly the more aggressive, wealthy and self-confident Coast Moors, who resisted declarations of Buddhist hegemony. In the first decade of the twentieth century there were several disputes at the Kandyan town of Gampola. In 1912, when officials refused to allow Buddhists to play music in front of a mosque, the procession organizers cancelled the festival and took their complaint to court.[166] The District Judge ruled in favour of the Buddhists, who in this instance had a relatively strong legal case, but in early 1915 the decision was overturned on appeal. This controversy received a good deal of publicity everywhere in Sri Lanka, and provided fuel for the popular view among Buddhists that although they were numerically a majority they were treated like a disadvantaged minority.[167]

A disturbance in Kandy town set off the widespread anti-Moor riots of 1915.[168] Late at night on 28 May a group of Buddhist carollers clashed with a number of Moors who jeered at them from inside a mosque. The Buddhists, many of whom were spoiling for a fight, responded by damaging the mosque and nearby shops. In itself this incident, though unusual, was of limited significance. There had been other minor clashes between Buddhists and Muslims in the previous months. What was remarkable was the quick spread of rioting along roads and railway lines to most Sinhala-speaking areas. The disturbances were particularly intense in many large villages of the interior and in the Western Province, including Colombo. Official reports stated that seventeen mosques were destroyed and eighty-six damaged. Furthermore, 350 retail outlets were burnt and another 4,075 sacked. Most attacks were against property, not persons, but 39 Moors were killed and 189 injured.[169] The riots lasted nine days, and were the most serious since the Kandyan rebellion of 1817 – 18.

Much of the scholarly debate about the 1915 riots has centred around the relative importance which should be given to religious, ethnic and economic causes; another issue of dispute is the extent of premeditation. Early interpretations were influenced by the heavy-handed post-riots repression. Although the initial response of officials was largely ineffective, martial law was declared on 2 June and was not lifted until the end of August. After the riots were over many members of the national élite who were active in Buddhist and temperance causes were arrested because they were believed by some officials to have instigated or encouraged the disturbances. Moreover, there were serious abuses by patrols of British planters and merchants who were temporarily given special powers. This policy of repression marked the first open break between the British and the national élite. Many observers sympathetic to Sri Lankan national aspirations have consequently accepted the élite's claim that the riots were a spontaneous response to the unfair trading activities of Moors, and that once underway they were fanned by roughs and criminals who took advantage of the confusion for their own profit.

Material grievances against Moor traders were important in some localities. The sacking of shops was an extension of the nineteenth-century tradition of grain rioting; in many instances goods were strewn about, not stolen, showing that the attacks were symbolic protests rather than acts of greed. But although the violence in some places took on the external form of grain rioting, neither protest about the price of rice nor economic grievances in general explain the scale or nature of the 1915 disturbances. The price of rice was higher than normal, but it had peaked in February and then declined during the months immediately preceding the disturbances.[170] In contrast, nineteenth-century grain riots had always been a response to the initial shock of rising prices. In addition, only Moor shops were attacked; Tamil, Chettiar and Sinhalese merchants were left untouched. Moreover, other grain riots had been remarkable for their lack of extraneous serious violence, but in 1915 a significant number of Moors were murdered, dwellings were destroyed, and mosques were attacked and sometimes dynamited. Even in Colombo, where it has been argued that the rioting had few religious motives, five mosques were damaged, eleven Moors were murdered and members of the crowd justified their actions in religious terms.[171]

The 1915 riots reflected the spread of revivalist ideology, especially among Sinhalese urban and semi-urban workers in the interior of the island. They owed more to the tradition of the Buddhist-Catholic rioting of the late nineteenth century than to those of grain rioting or earlier Sinhalese-Moor clashes. The belief that Buddhism was under threat fuelled the rumours which were such a powerful force during the disturbances. The most common story was that armed Moors were advancing with the intention of destroying Buddhist temples, or that monks had been assaulted. There were also more specific rumours, such as that the Temple of the Tooth in Kandy had been attacked. In many places Buddhists first assembled to defend themselves. When no attack was forthcoming, the rioters instead fell upon the property and mosques of local Moors. In some instances fear was secondary, and the riots were seen as an opportunity to put Moors in their place. At Valgama, in Colombo district, Moors agreed to sign a pledge allowing Buddhists to beat drums when passing the mosque for the next one hundred years. This document had been presented to them by the local headman and monk; none the less, other Sinhalese soon attacked the Moor villagers.[172] The line between defence against rumoured Moor attacks and the desire to assert Sinhalese Buddhist supremacy was a thin one.

The issue of premeditation cannot be resolved without further research, but it is clear that many élite leaders arrested by the British had nothing to do with the rioting. Some of them had even attempted to quell the disturbances. But whether or not there was any planning, many local notables, including merchants, headmen and monks, condoned, encouraged and in some cases led the rioting.[173] Some low-caste localities supplied a disproportionate number of rioters, but the disturbances were too widespread to be characterized a low-caste affair. In Colombo skilled workers played a prominent role, but there is much evidence that their actions were supported by many members of the middle class. A police officer in Colombo who asked a man in European dress with a gold watch and chain to help him disperse the crowd received the reply: 'Why should I stop it? Am I not a Sinhalese man?'.[174] In parts of the Western Province rumours of Moor atrocities were spread by persons shouting from cars which travelled from village to village; their accounts were adapted so as to cause maximum alarm in each locality: it is certain that these men knew that their stories were false. Cars were also used to transport rioters from village to village along some Western Province roads.[175]

Unlike the Kotahena riot some thirty years earlier, the 1915 disturbances did not give further impetus to the Buddhist movement. In the wake of British repression aggressive revivalism fell out of fashion among élite leaders, and no attempt was made to resurrect the temperance movement. In the decades following 1915 the national élite turned its attention to constitutional issues. There were a few procession disputes in the 1920s and 1930s, but they did not pose a serious threat to public order. The authorities became more tolerant of processions passing religious buildings of other faiths, a policy which generally favoured the majority Buddhists.[176] In the years after 1915 there were also periodic caste affrays and factional battles, but these clashes were of only local interest.[177] More prominent was social unrest which was expressed through labour disputes.

In the late nineteenth century there were a few strikes by self-employed workers, such as washermen and carters. These stoppages were often protests against government regulations or changes in agreed levels of pay.[178] The carters' strike of 1906, which successfully forced the government to postpone enforcement of regulations which carters feared would be used by the police to extort money, demonstrated to the working class of Colombo that collective action could be effective.[179] Workers in Colombo began to express their grievances in more assertive ways.

In the years between 1912 and 1929 skilled labourers, especially printers, harbour workers and railway workshop employees, periodically took action to improve their working conditions and pay.[180] At first certain members of the Colombo élite acted as mediators between the workers and employers, but around 1920 A. E. Goonesinha, a lawyer who was also active in the temperance and Buddhist movements, took a more active leadership position. Strikes became legal in 1922, and the Ceylon Labour Union was formed that same year. In the prosperous 1920s some workers were able to exert pressure on their employers and obtain wage increases, though many strikes still ended with mass dismissals.

The only serious labour riot was an outgrowth of a strike by tram drivers and conductors in 1929.[181] Management kept the trams running by replacing the strikers, and after several days the Colombo labour movement called for a boycott by passengers. Crowds gathered along tram lines throughout Colombo, and many workers threw bottles and stones at the passing vehicles. The police presence was heavy, and many arrests were made for offences such as disorderly conduct, vagrancy and drunkenness. On 5 February, thirteen days after the beginning of the strike, Goonesinha himself was involved in a minor skirmish with the police. Rumours quickly spread that he had been seriously assaulted. Coincidentally, the strike was settled that afternoon. None the less, a large crowd gathered outside the police station where the two officers said to have assaulted Goonesinha were stationed. Stones and bottles were thrown at the police station, then several buildings and a fire engine were put to the torch.

Finally a group of armed policemen opened fire, killing five persons and injuring many others. Meanwhile, two carloads of men attacked the house of one of the police officers involved, causing nearly 2,000 rupees damage. The next day a crowd again gathered at the police station, but an appeal by Goonesinha convinced it to disperse.

The rumours of the assault on Goonesinha met with a powerful response not only because of his undoubted popularity but because there was long-standing resentment against the police among the poor of Colombo. The popular reaction to the death of John Kotalawala in 1907 is one indication of this distrust.[182] Kotalawala, a graphite mine proprietor, cart contractor and former police inspector, was a powerful figure. He did not scruple to use violence in his business dealings, but was popular in many quarters because he had assaulted Europeans who insulted him and was an aggressive supporter of Buddhist and temperance causes. He committed suicide in gaol a few hours after hearing damaging testimony during his trial on a murder charge, but many Colombo residents believed that he had been poisoned by the police. In the ensuing disturbances H. L. Dowbiggin, at that time Superintendent of Police for the Western Province, was attacked and his orderly's bicycle was destroyed. Dowbiggin's personal reputation suffered further during the 1915 riots, when he was widely believed to have acted with unnecessary violence. Labour disputes also inevitably undermined the popularity of the police among the urban poor because the police were placed in the position of enforcing laws which normally favoured employers.[183] Goonesinha had long advocated selective disobedience of the police, and the day before the 1929 riot a prominent supporter of Goonesinha, the monk Dhammatilaka, had invoked the gods to curse Dowbiggin.[184] He argued that no police were needed because Goonesinha could keep order. The monk's proposal to bring about this change was however hardly radical; he declared that Goonesinha's talents should be brought to the notice of the Governor.

In the aftermath of the 1929 riot several major employers decided to come to terms with Goonesinha and an agreement was signed which recognized the Ceylon Labour Union. But within a few months the onset of the world depression weakened the position of workers. Employers were easily able to replace strikers with the unemployed, including Malayalis from southern India who were willing to accept very low wages. Although Goonesinha was influenced by the moderate socialism of the British Labour

Party and in the 1920s attempted to form links with Tamil workers
in Colombo, his attitude towards the non-Sinhalese had always
been ambiguous. In 1930 he began a campaign against Indian
workers. There were several violent incidents, but these attempts
at intimidation failed, and the labour movement temporarily
disintegrated.[185] In 1931, with hardship on the increase, crowds
gathered outside Goonesinha's residence, asking for rice. Goonesinha, who was not a wealthy man, had to go to prominent
merchants to plead for rice to distribute.[186] In the following years
he lost influence to a small group of European-educated
intellectuals who introduced Marxist ideas to the Colombo
working class. Trade unionism began to develop roots in Colombo
and the Marxists also gained influence among Tamil workers on
some tea plantations.

In the early twentieth century two strands of unrest, one
religious and the other economic, were expressed in rioting, but
neither strand was able to take hold and change politics. After
1915 the Buddhist élite turned away from religion and paid more
attention to constitutionalist agitation for political power. They
did not however form an alliance with the Colombo workers who
were willing to use illegal ends to improve their standard of living;
this role was left to more marginal members of the élite whose
economic base was in the professions rather than business or land.
Religious passions lay dormant, to be revived after independence.
The failure of the nationalist movement in Sri Lanka to develop a
mass base may be largely attributed to the fact the élite leaders did
not identify with either religious or economic traditions of protest.
With the major exception of 1915, the last half-century of British
rule was no more turbulent than the previous hundred years.

The Social Context of Riots

Only a small proportion of the population participated in riots. It
is important to identify who these people were, and to establish
why it was they took to rioting. The proximate causes and social
settings of individual riots have already been discussed in some
detail. Each event was unique, and many different ideologies and
groups were involved. One approach in the search for consistent
patterns is to analyse disturbances in terms of existing social
hierarchies. Were riots conflicts between élite groups which used
dependents as fodder? Or did they upset and threaten patron-
client relationships?

In many riots where religious symbols were not used, one side was in a more favourable social and economic position than the other, though both sides often had élite links. The grain riots of 1866 provide an example. They pitted consumers of imported rice against the merchants and distributors who controlled the grain market. Although many well-off Sri Lankans shared the view of the rioters that grain merchants should not be allowed to profit excessively from the shortage of rice, they did not approve of the rioters' methods. The press sympathized with the 'half-starved and half-naked wretches' who attacked the grain shops, but there was no question that it also felt that the disorder had to be stopped. Some other economically-motivated riots, such as tax protests, also pitted two unequal sides against each other. Analysis of caste affrays provides more mixed results. Although one side often had a traditionally-higher status than the other, it was often the lack of economic disparity which led to disturbances. There were other non-religious riots where neither side was subordinate. The Colombo riot over Minakshi was based on a conflict between two discrete groups, both of which included persons of wealth and status. At the apex of one side were high status Moors of Colombo, on the other, leaders of the Karava community at Moratuva. The clash confirmed latent attitudes which were no threat to hierarchy, attitudes which were reinforced because some Colombo Moors and Moratuva Karavas were commercial rivals.

A more consistent pattern emerges when the social backgrounds of those involved in religious riots are examined. Religion was a unifying social variable which was capable of cutting across caste and class barriers. At Kotahena the rioters on the Catholic side were mostly Karavas, Salagamas and Tamil Paravas, many of them fishermen. These groups comprised most of the Catholic population in the Colombo area. The Buddhists appear to have been of most castes. They included Salagamas from the Southern Province who had come to Colombo especially for the celebrations.[187] Juan Naide, the fatal casualty, was probably a Navandanna. In the years after Kotahena leading Buddhists of all castes with a strong presence near the coastal strip were among those who organized processions which sometimes led to trouble.

The agitation over the Kalutara bo-tree also attracted a broad range of support. Podi Singho, the incumbent of the shrine, was probably a Karava.[188] Sixteen of the forty persons who were prosecuted for their role in the riot were residents of the largely

Salagama village of Vaskaduva.[189] The President of the Kalutara Buddhist Union, O. M. Obeyesekere, was a Goyigama. Brodhurst commented that the petitioners who first appeared before him were 'men of humble position'.[190] At a later meeting the Buddhists were represented by two proctor's clerks and two traders.[191] The Kalutara Buddhist Union had the sophistication to submit a petition written in eloquent English.[192] Of 281 names attached to another petition, 57 were signed in English, 179 in Sinhala, and 45 with an 'X'.[193]

It is striking that most riots in the mature colonial period took place in the Low Country, within a few kilometres of the coast. Religious riots were concentrated along the littoral from just north of Colombo south to Alutgama, the one region where there was a large Catholic minority. Clashes did not occur where Catholics were very few or where they predominated. Riots not inspired by religious passion also occurred near the south-western coast, but they were not limited to the areas with Catholic minorities. Many of the same social groups involved in religious riots also participated in other disturbances. One group frequently appearing in the records as rioters was the villages of Paliyagoda, and in particular the Vahumpuras of the hamlet of Vanavahala.

The Vahumpuras of Paliyagoda, a few kilometres north-east of Colombo, were of low social status, but had a reasonable economic position. They were not accepted as respectable by Goyigamas, Karavas, Salagamas and Duravas, who together formed a large majority of the population of the Low Country. As a result they were often on bad terms with their neighbours. They had a particularly strong rivalry with the Salagamas of Vattala and Modara which dated at least from the 1860s. Comparison of two important clashes between these two groups, in 1875 and in 1900, illustrates social changes which were taking place in the Low Country.

In September 1875 the Salagamas were enraged because a Vahumpura outbid a Salagama for the lease of a tavern in a predominantly Salagama locality.[194] After a festival at Vattala coarse words were exchanged, and an open fight ensued. The Salagamas got the worst of it, losing their combs, umbrellas and money. They decided to retaliate through the law, and charged some Vahumpuras with cattle stealing. When the police, accompanied by some Salagamas, arrived in Vanavahala on 19 September, violence broke out between the Salagamas and Vahumpuras. Police reinforcements were brought in from Colombo and many Vahumpuras were arrested.

On 25 February 1900 a Buddhist procession, including many people from Vanavahala, passed through Vattala, which was populated by Salagamas, Goyigamas and Karavas of the Roman Catholic faith.[195] The procession slowed down in front of a large cross at the junction of the main road and the lane leading to the Vattala church. According to the Catholics, two Vanavahala men attempted to get an elephant to uproot the cross. Whatever the truth of this allegation, a general fight developed during which two elephants in the procession damaged several houses and shops. The Vattala church bells summoned Catholics from across the river in Modara, and the Catholics then forced the Buddhists out of the village towards Vanavahala. One Buddhist died in the affray. Police arrived from Colombo and restored order with some difficulty. Although religious symbols were the subject of the riot, in the court cases which followed all the parties were either Salagama or Vahumpura.

In the 1870s a general sense of antipathy between the two castes, rooted in different conceptions of their relative status, was sufficient cause for frequent affrays. By the end of the century the fact that the Vahumpuras were Buddhist and the Salagamas Catholic took on a new importance. After the 1900 riot each side looked to their co-religionists for support. The *Sarasavi Sandarasa* took a pro-Vahumpura position, stating that the elephants had been subject to an unprovoked attack and that the Catholic priest had instigated it.[196] The Catholic newspapers pointed out that the priest was in Colombo at the time and reported the riot as an aggressive Buddhist assault.[197]

Vahumpuras had always been very resistant to conversion to Christianity, and those living near the coastal strip enthusiastically supported the Buddhist revival.[198] One of the two processions of Easter Monday 1883 originated in Paliyagoda. The Kalutara rioters dispersed on the afternoon of 26 November 1896 partly because Buddhists from Paliyagoda failed to arrive as expected on the 1.45 train.[199] In a Buddhist-Catholic clash at Maggona in 1889, the participants were Vahumpura on the Buddhist side and Karava on the Catholic side.[200] In 1903 Vanavahala villagers were said to have been in the forefront of the pilgrims who rioted at Anuradhapura, and in 1915 a number of them were present in Kandy when the rioting against Moors broke out.[201] Their presence had apparently been sought by the organizers of the carol party in case of trouble with the Moors. Buddhism offered Vahumpuras a respectable way to challenge high-caste Christians, and to join high-caste Buddhists in a common cause.

Other castes also made use of the Buddhist revival in this way. Where Salagamas were Buddhist, as in the Southern Province, they were enthusiastic in supporting their religion.

The social roots of many non-religious riots were similar to many religiously-motivated disturbances. One of the pretenders to the Kandyan throne in 1848 was said to have been from Vanavahala.[202] Vahumpuras from Paliyagoda played a prominent role in the 1866 grain riots in Colombo.[203] In 1889 they fought Goyigamas and Duravas after fireworks being set off as part of a celebration scorched the clothes of a Vahumpura.[204] Other social groups were also involved in both types of protest. The fishermen of Modara opposed tax collectors as well as Buddhist processions. These events suggest that much social protest was channelled into religious revival, or that religious revival was a product of the same types of social change which caused social protest. Moreover, élites could apply religious labels to disturbances in which religion had played no part. When the predominantly Catholic fishermen of Modara resisted paying the municipal tax, the Buddhist *Sarasavi Sandarasa* recalled their participation in the Kotahena riot some years earlier, and declared that the government ought to enforce the collection of the levy.[205]

What were the forces which produced rioting in the south-western maritime regions but not elsewhere? The distinct social features of the coastal strip were the long-standing dominance of a market economy and the existence of several discrete caste and ethnic groups which did not have clear hierarchical relationships with each other. In this region upward economic mobility was not limited to persons with specific social backgrounds. In the second half of the nineteenth century there was no clear link between caste and class along the coastal littoral. There were neither ritual ties between nor marked differences in the general standard of living of Karavas, Goyigamas, Salagamas, Duravas and Vahumpuras, although there was much variation in the proportion of rich persons according to caste, with the Karavas greatly over-represented. But caste remained important for social relations, and the resulting inconsistencies among economic, political and social status could lead to disorder. After the mid-nineteenth century traditionally-lower-status groups used religion, which was in theory egalitarian, to improve their self-image and raise their social status. Where an upwardly-mobile but low status caste was Buddhist, it tended to assert itself aggressively against higher caste Christian rivals. Religious movements were more capable of attracting broad support than narrowly-based local caste rivalries.

That two groups fell out over the use of technological advances in fishing was of little concern to outsiders, whatever their caste. If religious symbols were employed, there was wider interest.

In 1915 there was widespread rioting in the interior of the Low Country and in many Kandyan districts as well as along the coastal strip. By this time temperance campaigns, newspapers and internal migration had spread Buddhist revivalist ideology to other parts of the island. These ideas were stronger in towns and villages which were closely connected to the market economy than in villages where the production of rice remained the primary economic activity. It was the Sinhalese urban and semi-urban poor, led or encouraged by local notables, who were mainly responsible for the attacks against Moors. These social groups were relatively new; the geographical expansion of the market economy in the late nineteenth and early twentieth centuries had in some ways extended the economic and social structure of the coastal strip to other parts of the island. Many communities, though remaining relatively small, were no longer rural in the traditional sense. Economic pressure brought on by inflation in the decade before 1915 was a source of frustration, but discontent was channelled away from economic conflict and into religious revival. The Moors proved convenient scapegoats for both economic and social frustrations.

A. P. Kannangara has suggested that the 1915 rioting reflected social disorganization and the breakdown of kin ties among the poor who lived in the small market towns and partially urbanized villages.[206] Although family structure in these communities no doubt differed from that of many more rural villages, there is little evidence of social breakdown. The market towns of the interior were still very small, and the impersonal forces of urbanization had not proceeded very far. In addition, some of the low-caste Low Country villages cited as examples by Kannangara had long been integrated into the market economy, and had not undergone major change in the years before 1915. The rioters did not in any case turn on persons whom at any period had been considered part of their own community. Moors had always been a distinct social group apart from Sinhala-speaking people. The riots were indeed the product of social change, but these changes were a breakdown only if one measures social organization by its resemblance to Sinhalese rural social structure, which in any case varied according to district. The new forms of social organization were not any less organized or complex than earlier ones, but they were different. They were a product of economic change. In many districts of the interior the market economy was becoming integrated more fully with local economies, a situation which had existed for a century or more along the coastal strip.

Conclusions

Modern historical writing on social conflict in mature colonial Sri Lanka has concentrated on two main arenas: the competition between élite Goyigamas and the élites of the maritime castes, especially the Karavas, and the religious debate between Buddhists and Protestant Christians. Both these disputes were carried out mainly through pamphlets and the press at the island-wide level. It has been shown in this chapter that neither of these conflicts led to violence. There were clashes based on caste and religious antipathy, but they followed different social boundaries from those of primary importance to élites. For most people caste was not a national or regional but a local social group. There was no general tension between Goyigamas and Karavas. When caste violence broke out it was limited to specific localities. Salagamas, Karavas and Vahumpuras were more likely to be involved than Goyigamas. Similarly, there were no clashes between Buddhists and Protestants; the first attacks which followed from the assertion of a Buddhist social identity were instead aimed at Catholics. Although this religious confrontation was not unconnected with local rivalries over other issues, religious identity had a meaning of its own, and was able to cross caste and class lines. The major issue between Buddhists and Catholics in the last two decades of the nineteenth century was the right of Buddhist processions to pass through Catholic communities and by Catholic churches. The processions were symbolic expressions of the belief that Lanka was a Buddhist land, a proposition which Catholics were unwilling to accept.

Nor was the movement for self-government, a major theme of the historiography of Sri Lanka in the first half of the twentieth century, supported by acts of collective violence. The Anuradhapura riot of 1903 illustrates the anti-colonial potential of Sinhalese-Buddhist cultural nationalism, but after the passions of the Buddhist revival swept out of control in 1915 élites shied away from attempts to mobilize mass support over such issues. It may be that they realized that such unpleasantness was unnecessary; the devolution of power in Sri Lanka was largely a consequence of events in India, not of agitation in the island itself. Under

Goonesinha's leadership the labour movement of the 1920s uneasily fused British ideas of trade unions with a Sinhalese-Buddhist social identity, but its social base remained narrow and labour agitation did not receive the support of most prominent English-educated politicians. In the 1930s the Marxists who replaced Goonesinha appealed to Colombo workers with a more systematic economic programme, but they did not use language or symbols which could appeal to the masses outside Colombo. Mainstream Sinhalese leaders did not of course abandon Sinhalese nationalism, but they acted with caution. As British power declined, some of the earlier goals of the Buddhist movement were fulfilled. In the 1940s legislation was passed which ensured that the colonial town of Anuradhapura would be moved away to a new site away from the ruins of the sacred city. At the Kalutara Fort too the secular buildings were replaced with Buddhist shrines after Sri Lanka attained independence.

From the perspective of the late twentieth century the most striking lacuna is the relative absence of tension between Sinhalese and Tamils.[207] At Anuradhapura at the turn of the century Tamils were the largest ethnic group resident in the town, but it was Christians and Muslims, not Hindus, who were the targets of Buddhist propaganda. In 1915 Tamil merchants were untouched. There was little religious competition partly because Buddhists regarded Hinduism as an indigenous religion which shared many attributes of Buddhism, and partly because the Hindu revival, though strong, was confined to areas where there were few Sinhalese. Moreover, there was little direct economic competition between Sinhalese and Tamils because most Sinhalese did not covet the low paid employment of most Tamils who lived in Sinhala-speaking areas, and because Tamil traders were less prominent than their Moor counterparts. It was not until the 1930s, when universal franchise was granted and power was exercised by politicians on the national level, that Sinhalese and Tamils began to perceive each other as opposing political and social entities.

Explicitly economic protests were relatively subdued. The grain riots of 1866 were an extensive but short-term response to an extraordinary situation. There were a few cases of tax resistance, but the government had little problem overcoming opposition. Innovations led to several clashes over fishing rights, but on balance the impact of social and economic change was positive, at least in the short term. In the twentieth century skilled workers in Colombo organized along trade union lines in order to improve their lot, but labour unrest remained patchy. The peasantry remained quiet during the last century of British rule.

Officials twice panicked and over-reacted to disturbances. The first occasion was 1848, when the extent and strength of the 'rebellion' was greatly overestimated. The military detachments sent from Kandy mistakenly believed that they would be faced with a large and organized rebel force. In 1915 the authorities again over-reacted, not primarily against the rioters themselves but against prominent members of the élite who had been active in the temperance and Buddhist movements. Some officials believed that these men were involved in a conspiracy, and that the riots were ultimately aimed against the British. These responses demonstrate that there was an underlying sense of insecurity among some colonial officials and British residents, who despite outward self-confidence were aware of their position as a small minority. None the less, remarkably little anti-British feeling was expressed through rioting during colonial rule.

The study of collective violence illustrates the complex relationship between popular ideology and social change. Buddhist social groups which benefited from economic change in the nineteenth century fashioned a new religious ideology which was based on ancient symbols. Although it ostensibly sought to restore the past, it was in fact forward-looking and aggressive. Social groups which were involved in non-religiously motivated social protest tended to latch on to religious revivalism and use it for their own ends. On the other hand, some élite leaders found the channelling of economic and other grievances into religious revival as a way to generate support for themselves. S. N. W. Hulugalle, the Kandyan representative on the Legislative Council who negotiated with Ridgeway on behalf of the Buddhist claims at Anuradhapura, was of uncertain religious faith; when a younger man he was known to be a Protestant. In 1915 the élite lost control of the passions which they had helped foster, and when the British held them responsible their own privileged position came under threat. In the following years they turned away from movements with a mass popular appeal, and instead directed their efforts towards obtaining constitutional concessions from the British.

NOTES TO CHAPTER 5

1   K. M. de Silva, *UCHC*, III, 202 – 4.
2   Ibid.; Jayawardena, 27, 50 – 1, 114 – 15; Wickremeratne, 'Religion', 149; A. P. Kannangara, 'The Riots of 1915 in Sri Lanka', 150 – 3; Jayasekera, 318.

For an account of the Kotahena riot see Sumathipala, 'The Kotahena Riots and Their Repercussions'.

3 C. R. de Silva, 204 – 16.
4 Ibid., 176 – 94.
5 Pippet, 151, 153 – 4, 157, 163.
6 K. M. de Silva, *Letters*, 7 – 10, 19; Henderson, *The History of the Rebellion in Ceylon during Lord Torrington's Government*, 2 – 8; Pippet, 176.
7 K. M. de Silva, *Letters*, 12; Henderson, 11 – 13, 50.
8 K. M. de Silva, *Letters*, 19 – 20; Henderson, 8 – 11, 50.
9 This account of the 1848 disturbances relies mainly on K. M. de Silva, *Letters*; Henderson; Pippet; Forbes, *Recent Disturbances and Military Executions in Ceylon*.
10 *Pradipaya*, 25 Oct 1866; *Times*, 23 Oct 1866, 27 Oct 1866, 30 Oct 1866; *Observer*, 22 Oct 1866, 23 Oct 1866; *Examiner*, 24 Oct 1866, 31 Oct 1866; Digby, *Forty Years*, 327 – 31; Dep, 6 – 7.
11 Pippet, 217.
12 *Times*, 23 Oct 1866, 9 Nov 1866; *Observer*, 22 Oct 1866; *Lakrivikirana*, 2 Nov 1866, 9 Nov 1866; *Pradipaya*, 25 Oct 1866.
13 *Examiner*, 27 Oct 1866; *Observer*, 22 Oct 1866, 29 Oct 1866; Templer to CS, 26 Oct 1866, SLNA6/2992; *Pradipaya*, 25 Oct 1866.
14 *Observer*, 1 Nov 1866; *Lakrivikirana*, 9 Nov 1866; *Times*, 26 Oct 1866.
15 *Observer*, 1 Nov 1866.
16 *Observer*, 29 Oct 1866; *Examiner*, 24 Oct 1866, 27 Oct 1866; *Lakrivikirana*, 26 Oct 1866; *Pradipaya*, 25 Oct 1866; *Times*, 26 Oct 1866; Morris to CS, 18 Oct 1866, 23 Oct 1866, SLNA6/2995; Morris to CS, 3 Mar 1868, SLNA6/3180.
17 *Examiner*, 3 Nov 1866; Liesching to Morris, 29 Oct 1866, SLNA6/2995.
18 *Examiner*, 27 Oct 1866.
19 *Times*, 19 Oct 1866, 2 Nov 1866.
20 *Pradipaya*, 25 Oct 1866; *Examiner*, 24 Oct 1866; Dep, 6 – 7; Digby, *Forty Years*, 331.
21 *Pradipaya*, 25 Oct 1866; *Lakrivikirana*, 26 Oct 1866; *Observer*, 23 Oct 1866; P. E. Pieris, (ed.) *Notes on some Sinhalese Families Part IV*, 14 – 15.
22 *Observer*, 25 Oct 1866; *Examiner*, 31 Oct 1866.
23 *Times*, 23 Oct 1866.
24 Digby, *Forty Years*, 328 – 32.
25 Morris to CS, 27 Oct 1866, SLNA6/2995.
26 Digby, *Forty Years*, 321 – 2.
27 *Lakrivikirana*, 23 Nov 1866.
28 CS to Templer, 25 Oct 1866, SLNA6/2992.
29 *Examiner*, 20 Oct 1866; *Pradipaya*, 25 Oct 1866; *Times*, 18 Oct 1866; *Observer*, 18 Oct 1866.
30 *Times*, 2 Nov 1866; *Observer*, 22 Oct 1866; *Pradipaya*, 25 Oct 1866; CS to Layard, 25 Oct 1866, SLNA7/1517.
31 Morris to CS, 26 Oct 1866, SLNA6/2995.
32 *Lakrivikirana*, 9 Nov 1866.
33 *Times*, 26 Oct 1866; *Observer*, 25 Oct 1866; *Pradipaya*, 25 Oct 1866; *Examiner*, 27 Oct 1866, 7 Nov 1866; *Lakrivikirana*, 26 Oct 1866.
34 *Times*, 9 Nov 1866, 16 Nov 1866, 20 Nov 1866; Scott to General Secretary Methodist Missionary Society, 8 Dec 1866, Methodist archives, Box 450.
35 K. M. de Silva, *A History*, 476, 539; Maitland to Windham, 28 Feb 1807, CO54/25; C. R. de Silva, 354 – 5.

36   Dep, 84, 316, 434; *Messenger*, 9 Dec 1873, 23 Feb 1904; *Independent*, 5 Apr 1904; Burrows, *AR Nuvara Eliya 1897*, C17.
37   Short, D, 9 Feb 1896, SLNA42/22; Cumberland to GANWP, 3 May 1898, SLNA59/45.
38   'prasiddha danvimayi', SLNA42/826.
39   Cumberland to GANWP, 28 Dec 1897 & 3 May 1898, SLNA59/45.
40   Ibid., 28 Dec 1897.
41   Ibid., 31 Dec 1897.
42   M PkC to Cumberland, 2 Jan 1898, SLNA42/830; *Independent*, 7 Jan 1898.
43   It has been argued that the Chilaw disturbances were primarily religious because the price increase was no greater in Chilaw than elsewhere, and because the riots did not spread from Catholic to Buddhist areas. Although I accept that earlier ethnic hostility provided the setting in which rioting over the price of grain broke out in Chilaw town, there is no evidence of religious passions being aroused. The rioting did not spread to the heavily Catholic area around Negombo, and the disturbances elsewhere in Chilaw district were decidedly economic in character. See A. P. Kannangara, 151.
44   For some examples see Dep, 253 – 5; G. Baumgartner, D, 9 Apr 1894, SLNA33/75; Campbell to CS, 4 & 6 Nov 1884, SLNA6/6817; Vaughan, D, 17 Nov 1904, SLNA30/25; *Bi-Monthly Examiner*, 15 Feb 1868, 4 Mar 1868; Pippet, 200; Ward to Labouchere, 14 Sept 1857, CO54/330(Conf); Campbell to CS, 25 Aug 1890, SLNA6/8858.
45   The main account of this riot, and its background, is Campbell to CS, 7 May 1870, SLNA6/3400. This letter is printed in Pippet, 272 – 84. There is a somewhat different version in *Lakrivikirana*, 30 Apr 1870.
46   Campbell to CS, 7 May 1870, SLNA6/3400.
47   *Times*, 17 June 1870.
48   *Bi-Monthly Examiner*, 25 June 1870.
49   *Times*, 29 Apr 1870.
50   *Bi-Monthly Examiner*, 14 May 1870; *Lakrivikirana*, 30 April 1870; Morgan, CS, 27 Aug 1870, E, CO54/457(205).
51   *Messenger*, 3 May 1870; *Lakrivikirana*, 30 Apr 1870; *Bi-Monthly Examiner*, 3 May 1870.
52   Cumberland to GANWP, 7 Jan 1897, SLNA42/826. The pig story may have been invented by Moors seeking government support.
53   M Chilaw to AGA Chilaw, 1 June 1891, SLNA42/320; *Observer*, 29 Sept 1866; Moysey, *AR Hambantota 1890*, E11; G. Baumgartner, *AR Puttalam 1895*, G18; *Bi-Monthly Examiner*, 8 Aug 1868; Lushington, *AR Puttalam 1887*, 193A.
54   Dep, 265; *Times*, 2 Nov 1875; Pennycuick, *AR Puttalam 1890*, G10; Brodhurst, *AR Puttalam 1901*, G16; Haughton, *AR Puttalam 1893*, G11 & *AR Negombo 1885*, 159A; Lushington, *AR Puttalam 1888*, 201 – 2A; Noyes, *AR Chilaw 1888*, 207A; G. Baumgartner, *AR Badulla 1897*, 18.
55   *Bi-Monthly Examiner*, 28 June 1868, 11 July 1868.
56   Elliott, *AR Galle 1892*, E7; Campbell to CS, 31 May 1887, SLNA6/7783; Campbell to CS, 21 Jan 1868, SLNA6/3180; *Bi-Monthly Examiner*, 15 Jan 1868; Campbell to CS, 20 Mar 1868, SLNA6/3211; Campbell to CS, 19 July 1883, SLNA6/6665; Morris to CS, 3 Mar 1868, SLNA6/3180; Short, D, 4 Apr 1898, SLNA26/156; Ferguson, *Ceylon in the "Jubilee Year"*, 368; *AR Kalutara 1900*, B49; *AR Colombo 1903*, B24.
57   *Messenger*, 19 & 26 Apr 1887, 28 Apr 1905; Elliott, *AR Galle 1895*, E8; Short, *AR Matara 1898*, E18 & D, 14 – 17 Apr 1898, SLNA26/156; *Native Opinion*, 6 May 1898; Le Mesurier, D, 28 Jan 1894, SLNA26/152; Dep,

184 – 7; 'Correspondence on Paliyagoda Riot', May & June 1889, SLNA33/2758; Dowbiggin, *AR P 1925*, B5; *AR P 1903*, B24.
58 Holland, PO, 9 May 1887, SLNA6/7783.
59 Campbell to CS, 31 May 1887, SLNA6/7783; Saunders to CS, 21 July 1887, SLNA6/7783.
60 Gordon, 18 Aug 1887, SLNA6/7783.
61 *Messenger*, 9 Feb 1883.
62 Hansard, PO, 13 Aug 1890, SLNA6/8858.
63 Le Mesurier, D, 16 July 1893, SLNA26/151.
64 Vaughan, D, 17 Nov 1904, SLNA30/25.
65 Land grabbing is discussed in more detail in Chapter Six.
66 Dep, 355; Fowler, D, 27 Sept 1902, SLNA33/25.
67 Fowler, D, 16 Jan 1904, 5 & 6 June 1904, SLNA33/27; Fowler, D, 1 Apr 1902, SLNA33/25; *Independent*, 8 June 1904.
68 *Times*, 24 Apr 1874, 1 June 1874, 7 Nov 1874; *Messenger*, 24 Apr 1874, 2 June 1874.
69 *Messenger*, 13 & 17 July 1888.
70 Ibid., 10 July 1888; *Sandarasa*, 13 July 1888; GAWP to CS, 17 July 1888, SLNA33/994.
71 Fowler, *AR Galle 1901*, E7; Ridgeway to Chamberlain, 14 Dec 1901, CO54/672(511).
72 Fowler, *AR Galle 1901*, E7.
73 *Times*, 11 Dec 1901; Grenier, 199.
74 Ridgeway to Chamberlain, 14 Dec 1901, CO54/672(511).
75 A police inspector claimed at the inquest that the crowd numbered 100, at the magistrate's inquiry that it numbered 500, and at the trial that it numbered 5,000. *Times*, 11 Dec 1901.
76 The main descriptions of the riot are: *Times*, 25 Sept 1901; Dep, 353 – 4; *Sandarasa*, 27 Sept 1901; Ridgeway to Chamberlain, 14 Dec 1901, CO54/672(511).
77 *Hue and Cry*, 8 Oct 1901.
78 Ibid.; *Government Gazette*, 15 Feb 1901.
79 *Times*, 18 Dec 1901.
80 *Messenger*, 18 Oct 1901.
81 *Times*, 11 & 13 Dec 1901.
82 *Pradipaya*, 10 Oct 1901; Dep, 354; *SP 16 1916*.
83 Brodhurst, *AR Galle 1902*, E5; Arnolis de Silva, petition, 30 Oct 1901, SLNA6/13328; Fowler, *AR Galle 1901*, E7.
84 The trial testimony was reported in the *Times*, 11 – 18 Dec 1901. Other accounts include Grenier, 199 and Ridgeway to Chamberlain, 2 Jan 1902, CO54/675(1).
85 *Lakminipahana*, 28 Sept 1901; *Sandarasa*, 1 Oct 1901.
86 *Pradipaya*, 10 Oct 1901.
87 The riot and the preceding events are described in *SP 4 1883*.
88 Sumangala Hikkaduve, 20 Apr 1883, SLNA33/991; Bonjean to Campbell, 9 Oct 1883, SLNA6/6666; *Messenger*, 3 Apr 1888.
89 M. Don John, 27 Apr 1883, SLNA33/991.
90 David, PO, 2 Apr 1883, SLNA33/991; *Messenger*, 20 July 1883; *SP 4 1883*, 6.
91 Gooneratne, PO, 21 Apr 1883, SLNA33/991; Also see *SP 4 1883*, 3.
92 Miscellaneous correspondence in SLNA33/991; Balangero, 23 Apr 1883, SLNA33/991; *Overland Observer*, 3 Apr 1883; *SP 4 1883*.
93 Pagnani, 23 Apr 1883, SLNA33/991; *Messenger*, 28 Mar 1883.

94 J. de Silva & M. Don John, 27 Apr 1883, SLNA33/991.
95 23 Apr 1883, SLNA33/991.
96 Balangero, 23 Apr 1883, SLNA33/991.
97 Boudens, *Catholic Missionaries*, 131 – 9.
98 Pagnani, 23 Apr 1883, SLNA33/991.
99 *Messenger*, 28 & 30 Mar 1883, 3 Apr 1883, 1 May 1883.
100 Bonjean to Simeoni, 5 June 1883, Propaganda Fide archives, SC Ind Or, XXIV; Bonjean to Fabre, 17 June 1883, Oblate archives, Bonjean file.
101 Boudens, *Catholic Missionaries*, 139 – 54; Bonjean to Campbell, 19 Oct 1883, SLNA6/6666; Bonjean to Simeoni, 1 Nov 1883, Propaganda Fide archives, SC Ind Or, XXIV; Bonjean to Simeoni, 26 Mar 1884, Propaganda Fide archives, SC Ind Or, XXV.
102 Ferdinands to Longden, 5 Apr 1883, E1, CO54/547(306).
103 Campbell to CS, 8 Aug 1883, E1, CO54/548(66); Fleming to CS, 15 Aug 1883, E2, CO54/548(66).
104 Gordon to Derby, 29 Aug 1884, CO54/554(330).
105 K. M. de Silva, *UCHC*, III, 202 – 4; Olcott, *Old Diary Leaves*, III, 112 – 18.
106 Dep, 212, 264, 287; *Messenger*, 9 Nov 1883, 28 May 1889, 2 & 30 July 1889, 3 Sept 1889; *Sandarasa*, 28 May 1889, 4 June 1889; Le Feuvre, PO, 23 Mar 1885, SLNA6/7261; Crawford, D, 27 – 30 May 1889, SLNA35/7; Fowler, D, 2 May 1902, SLNA33/25; Saunders, *AR Colombo 1889*, B12; *AR P 1889*, B8; Bonjean to Simeoni, 1 Nov 1883, Propaganda Fide archives, SC Ind Or, XXIV; Campbell to CS, 8 Aug 1883, SLNA6/6665.
107 *AR Colombo 1889*, B12.
108 M Alutkuru Korale South to GAWP, 25 Apr 1890, SLNA33/995.
109 *Messenger*, 28 May 1889.
110 Bonjean to Farbos, 1 Mar 1888, Oblate archives, Bonjean file; Bonjean, 8 Nov 1887, Propaganda Fide archives, NS 1896, rubrica 128.
111 Ridgeway to Chambers, 31 Jan 1902, CO54/675(42); Dep, 350; 'Land at Tissamaharama Containing Certain Buddhist Relics', 1904, SLNA6/13599; Wickremeratne, 'The Rulers', 229 – 31.
112 Elliott to CS, 28 Aug 1894 & 20 Sept 1894, Es 2 & 4, CO54/617(363).
113 Elliott to CS, 13 Aug 1894, E1, CO54/617(363); Dawson to CS, 1 Dec 1896, SLNA59/100.
114 Dawson to CS, 1 Dec 1896, SLNA59/100.
115 Petitions of 19 May 1892 & [1891], SLNA59/100.
116 Elliott to CS, 20 Sept 1894, E4, CO54/617(363).
117 Havelock to Ripon, 6 Oct 1894, CO54/617(363).
118 Ibid.
119 Ripon to Havelock, 4 May 1894, SLNA59/1001.
120 Ripon to Havelock, 7 Nov 1894, CO54/617.
121 Havelock to Chamberlain, 9 Sept 1895, CO54/625(352).
122 Chamberlain to Ridgeway, 4 Sept 1896, CO54/625.
123 Ridgeway to Chamberlain, 22 May 1897, CO54/637(169).
124 Dawson to CS, 27 Nov 1896, SLNA59/100.
125 Kalutara Buddhist Union, petition, 11 Nov 1896, SLNA59/100.
126 Dawson to CS, 15 Dec 1896, SLNA59/100.
127 Thorpe, PO, to Dawson, 26 Nov 1896, SLNA59/100; Brodhurst to Dawson, 27 Nov 1896, SLNA59/100; Dep, 347 – 9; *Lakrivikirana*, 27 Nov 1896.
128 Brodhurst to Dawson, 30 Nov 1896, SLNA59/100.
129 *Lakrivikirana*, 16 Jan 1897.
130 Elliott to CS, 20 Sept 1894, E4, CO54/617(363); Petitions of 19 May 1892 & 11 Nov 1896, SLNA59/100.

131 Elliott to CS, 20 Sept 1894, E4, CO54/617(363).
132 Ellis to CS, 24 Sept 1897, SLNA59/100; Ellis, undated note, [1897], SLNA59/100.
133 Bell, 'Memorandum Regarding the Ruins at Anuradhapura', 27 June 1903, SLNA59/1001; Ridgeway, *Administration*, 82; Booth to CS, 26 Oct 1901, SLNA59/1001.
134 'Minutes of Public Meeting, Colombo', 13 July 1902, SLNA59/639; Dharmapala to Ridgeway, 14 Sept 1903, *Standard*, 7 Apr 1904; *Sandarasa*, 6 Nov 1903; Harischandra, *The Sacred City of Anuradhapura*, 61 – 9.
135 Bell to Booth, 14 Oct 1901, SLNA59/639; Wickremeratne, *The Genesis*, 87 – 9.
136 Havelock to Ripon, 12 Mar 1894, CO54/614(84).
137 Ibid.; 'Memorial of Buddhist Inhabitants', [1893 or 1894], SLNA59/1140.
138 Fairfield & Meade, 12 Apr 1894, CO54/614; Copleston to Havelock, 21 July 1894, CO54/616(276); Havelock to Ripon, 20 Apr 1894, CO54/614(Tel).
139 *Buddhist*, 30 May 1895; Ievers, 6 June 1902, SLNA59/639.
140 Booth, D, 19 Aug 1900, SLNA41/266; Booth, extract from D, Oct 1901, SLNA59/639; Booth to CS, 26 Oct 1901, SLNA59/639; Sri Sumana Medhankara Nayaka, petition, 7 July 1900, SLNA59/639; Anuradhapura Buddhist Defence Committee, petition, 10 Mar 1902, SLNA59/639.
141 Bell to Booth, 14 Oct 1901, SLNA59/639; Booth to CS, 26 Oct 1901, SLNA59/639.
142 Booth to CS, 24 May 1902, SLNA59/639; Silver, overseer, [May or June 1902], SLNA59/639.
143 Booth, D, 14, 15 & 18 July 1900, SLNA41/266.
144 Harischandra to CS, 12 Jan 1902, SLNA59/639; Anuradhapura Buddhist Defence Committee, petition, 10 Mar 1902, SLNA59/639.
145 W. A. de Silva, *Standard*, 15 July 1902; Memorial to the Secretary of State for the Colonies, 13 Sept 1902, SLNA59/639; Hulugalle, *CH 1901 – 2*, 8; Hulugalle to Lt Gov, 18 May 1902, SLNA59/639.
146 Booth to Ridgeway, 11 June 1903, SLNA59/1001; Hulugalle to Ridgeway, 26 June 1903, SLNA59/1001; *Sandarasa*, 10 Nov 1903.
147 Detailed material for the riot is found in SLNA59/1001. Also see Booth, *AR Anuradhapura 1903*, H16.
148 Ackland, engineer, 10 June 1903, SLNA59/1001; Booth, *AR Anuradhapura 1903*, H16.
149 Harischandra, *The Sacred City*, 89 – 91; Im Thurn to Lyttelton, 25 Nov 1903, CO54/684(509).
150 Harischandra, *The Sacred City*, 88; *Messenger*, 30 Oct 1903.
151 Brayne, [June 1903], SLNA59/1001.
152 Booth, [1903], E1, CO54/684(Conf).
153 Ridgeway to Lyttelton, 17 Nov 1903, CO54/684(Conf).
154 *Sandarasa*, 18 Dec 1903.
155 *Lakminipahana*, 27 June 1903.
156 A decade earlier, after a series of procession disputes, a letter to the *Sandarasa* also attributed Catholic violence to the character of their God. The correspondent mentioned His drowning people in the flood and the trust which He put in Moses, a murderer. *Sandarasa*, 4 June 1889.
157 Ridgeway, *Administration*, 82 – 3.
158 Hulugalle to Ridgeway, 26 June 1903, SLNA59/1001.
159 'Memorial of Buddhist Inhabitants', [1894], SLNA59/1140.
160 Ridgeway to Lyttelton, 17 Nov 1903, CO54/684(Conf).
161 Boudens, 'The Two Oblate Dioceses in Ceylon from 1898 to 1903', 52; *Messenger*, 28 Apr 1903, 2 & 9 May 1903, 23 June 1903.

162 See correspondence in SLNA59/1140.
163 This account of the 1904 temperance campaign is based on a survey of English-language newspapers and diaries of revenue officials from April to December 1904.
164 A. P. Kannangara, 137 – 9; K. M. de Silva, *A History*, 374 – 8.
165 Samaraweera, 'The Muslim Revivalist Movement, 1880 – 1915'; Ali, 'The 1915 Racial Riots in Ceylon (Sri Lanka)', 4 – 11.
166 A. P. Kannangara, 132 – 4; Blackton, 'The Action Phase of the 1915 Riots', 237 – 8.
167 This view of course had much justification. There were no Buddhists on the Legislative Council in 1915.
168 This discussion of the 1915 riots rests mainly on the extensive scholarly literature: Jayasekera, 247 – 424; A. P. Kannangara; Ali; Jayawardena, 163 – 88; Roberts, 'Hobgoblins, Low-country Sinhalese Plotters, or Local Elite Chauvinists?'; Blackton; Fernando, 'The Post Riots Campaign for Justice'. I have also consulted *SP 15 1916* & *SP 16 1916*.
169 These are the figures which are given by Blackton, based on the reports sent to London.
170 A. P. Kannangara, 149.
171 Jayawardena has argued that 'the rioting in Colombo had hardly any religious motives.' Although she furnishes convincing evidence that skilled workers who at other times were involved in labour protests were heavily involved in the 1915 riots, it does not necessarily follow that these men were motivated by economic grievances against the Moors. There are numerous references to the religious justifications of the Colombo rioters in *SP 16 1916*. Jayawardena, 172 – 7.
172 *SP 16 1916*, 31.
173 Roberts, 'Hobgoblins', 111 – 23.
174 *SP 16 1916*, 19.
175 There were 2,000 cars on the island at this time.
176 Dowbiggin, *AR P 1927*, B24 – 5; Dowbiggin, *AR P 1933*, A31; Harrison-Jones, *AR Galle 1936*, C8; Dowbiggin, *AR P 1930*, A22.
177 Dowbiggin, *AR P 1927*, B24; Dowbiggin, *AR P 1920*, B5; Ryan, 293 – 5, 298 – 300; Dowbiggin, *AR P 1924*, B26; Dowbiggin, *AR P 1930*, A22; Dowbiggin, *AR P 1934*, A27.
178 Jayawardena, 91 – 109; Dep, 364 – 5; *Bi-Monthly Examiner*, 29 May 1869.
179 Jayawardena, 122 – 32; Dep, 430 – 5.
180 Jayawardena, 151 – 62, 214 – 24, 241 – 52, 281 – 97.
181 Detailed information on this riot is found in CO54/896/1. Also see Jayawardena, 291 – 7.
182 De Witt & Weeresinghe, *The Atygalle Murder Case*; Dep, 437 – 41; Jayawardena, 125 – 7. For an account of some of Kotalawala's exploits while a police officer, see Perera, *suduhatanaya saha kotalavala inspaktartuma gana vananavak*; Dep, *passim*. During the rioting at Kandy in 1915 a police inspector attempting to remove a rioter was thwarted by a crowd which shouted to the prisoner: 'Don't go with that fellow. He is the man who arrested Kotalawala.' *SP 16 1916*, 93.
183 Dowbiggin, *AR P 1929*, A28; Jayawardena, 294 – 5.
184 Police reports in CO54/896/1.
185 Jayawardena, 310 – 31; Dowbiggin, *AR P 1930*, A22 – 3.
186 Jayawardena, 314.
187 *Messenger*, 27 Apr 1883.

188 Podi Singho was educated as a carpenter, a traditional occupation of Karavas. Podi Singho, 26 Oct 1896, SLNA59/100.
189 Dawson to CS, 31 Dec 1896, SLNA59/100.
190 Brodhurst to GAWP, 22 Aug 1894, E2, CO54/617(363).
191 Elliott, 'Minutes of Meeting at Kalutara', 12 Sept 1894, SLNA59/100.
192 Kalutara Buddhist Union, petition, 11 Nov 1896, SLNA59/100.
193 Don Cornelis Perera & 280 others, petition, [1892], SLNA59/100.
194 *Times*, 21, 22 & 28 Sept 1875; *Pradipaya*, 10 Sept 1895.
195 *Native Opinion*, 2 & 16 Mar 1900; *Messenger*, 2 Mar 1900; *Pradipaya*, 5 Mar 1900; Dep, 351 – 2.
196 *Pradipaya*, 5 Mar 1900.
197 Ibid.; *Messenger*, 2 Mar 1900, 4 Sept 1900.
198 Roberts, *Caste Conflict*, 175. Among those listed in the *Hue and Cry* all 209 Vahumpuras whose religion was known were Buddhist. In contrast, 121 of 375 Karavas were Christian, as were 50 of 267 Salagamas, 19 of 165 Duravas, 114 of 1,934 Goyigamas and 13 of 378 members of other Sinhalese castes.
199 Brodhurst to Dawson, 27 Nov 1896, SLNA59/100.
200 Crawford, D, 27 & 29 May 1889, SLNA35/7.
201 A. P. Kannangara, 148; Hulugalle to Ridgeway, 26 June 1903, SLNA59/1001; *SP 16 1916.*
202 A. P. Kannangara, 153.
203 *Pradipaya*, 25 Oct 1866.
204 There is extensive correspondence and testimony about this riot in SLNA33/2758. For a similar riot involving other Low Country Vahumpuras, see the reports of Ellis, 4 May 1897, and Peter de Saram, 23 Apr 1897, SLNA59/78.
205 *Sandarasa*, 13 July 1888.
206 A. P. Kannangara.
207 For minor clashes between Sinhalese and Tamils in the mature colonial period see Meyer, 'The Plantation System', 41 – 4; Dep, 197; Le Mesurier, *AR Nuvara Eliya 1889*, C35 – 6.

CHAPTER 6

THE SOCIAL CONTEXT OF CRIME

The past three chapters, while organized around the relationship between specific crimes and social change, have also considered the social characteristics of those involved in crime. Though the social profile of those responsible for each of these crimes varied, none were primarily the work of disadvantaged groups. Cattle stealing was organized by Goyigama notables. Homicide was committed by a broad cross-section of society. Serious riot, with the exception of the 1915 disturbances, was largely confined to the south-western littoral, the area with the highest standard of living. Though the poor were involved in all three crimes they were not proportionately more involved than wealthier persons.

The main aim of this chapter is to consider further the relationship between social position and crime. It is often assumed that the poor and economically-depressed ethnic minorities commit a disproportionate amount of crime. Alternatively it is argued that these groups appear to have high crime rates because the state discriminates against them. Colonial Sri Lanka exhibited a different pattern. Unusually, mainstream social groups dominated official crime statistics.

Perceptions by officials and the English-educated élite of who was responsible for crime were influenced by the widespread belief that crime was both extensive and increasing. The origin of this belief lay partially in comparison of the colony's crime statistics with those of Britain and India, but it took hold because it reinforced other assumptions held by these groups. For many officials the existence of much crime pointed to Sri Lankan inferiority and thus served as a justification for British rule. Elites too used the alleged criminality of the common people to distinguish themselves from the masses. The belief that crime was increasing also enabled some Buddhists to argue that social deterioration had taken place under colonial rule because education was divorced from the national faith. The proposed remedy was state support for Buddhist schools.

Officials were influenced by two main images of crime and criminals. The first blamed lawbreaking primarily on the urban and semi-urban poor. In particular, Sinhalese from the south-western coastal area who found employment in the plantation economy further inland were described by such terms as 'scum' and 'riff-raff'. These labourers were perceived much in the way of the Victorian 'criminal class' of Britain, the dissolute section of the urban working class.[1] It was alleged that they spent an inordinate amount of time drinking and gambling. According to this stereotype, in Sri Lanka the role of the 'respectable poor' of Britain was filled by the peasantry. A connection was drawn between urbanization and the growth of crime.

The other image derived much from the Anglo-Indian concept of 'criminal castes and tribes', which portrayed certain hereditary communities as possessing instinctive criminal tendencies.[2] It concentrated on flaws inherent in Sinhalese culture, and in effect turned the majority ethnic group of Sri Lanka into a large criminal class. Laziness was seen as an important cause of crime.[3] It was felt that food was too readily available and that as a consequence the Sinhalese had never developed regular work habits.[4] Lack of true religion was seen as another sign of inferiority. The Sinhalese were even labelled a 'criminal race', though some observers qualified this description by restricting it to violent crime.

These two strands of thought were often voiced by the same persons, but there was a contradiction between them. If the Sinhalese were inherently criminal because of their cultural backwardness, one would have expected that peasants, who had been least subject to European cultural influences, would have been the most criminal social group. However, according to the British-derived idea of a criminal class, it was the Low Country Sinhalese labourers who were the most criminal; indeed they were in many cases considered responsible for corrupting the innocent peasantry. Those of them who left their home villages to participate in the Kandyan market economy were showing initiative which did not fit well with the explanation of laziness as the cause of crime.

The first section of this chapter discusses the main forms of crime which came to the attention of the authorities, and considers the social background of the types of people who committed them. It is shown that crime was carried out by persons with a wide variety of social characteristics. The second section analyses the social profile of the prison population and of personslisted in the *Hue and Cry*. Several variables are considered, including ethnicity, religion, literacy, age, sex and caste. None of these variables in themselves describe a person's social position, but all were related to wealth, and all are amenable to ranking, especially at the lower end. Although with the exception of sex one would expect the administrative process to be biased against persons with a low social and economic status, these 'low' categories did not account for a disproportionate share of persons treated as criminal by the authorities; in some instances the disadvantaged were less numerous than one would expect from their proportion of the general population. Analysis of the relationship between crime and economic fluctuations, which in Sri Lanka was relatively weak, lends further support to the argument that crime was not primarily a response to hardship. The third section examines the relative involvement of various social groups in crimes against property and crimes against the person. Immigrant workers, whether Sinhalese, Tamil or Moor, committed relatively more property crimes, while residents of certain Low Country villages, many of which were mainly populated by castes other than the Goyigama, tended to commit relatively more violent crimes.

Major Forms of Crime

Although the three crimes studied in detail are examples of crimes against property, the person and the state, they are not typical of these broader categories. Crime was carried out in a great variety of ways for many different reasons. The aim of this section is to review briefly other major forms of crime prevalent in colonial Sri Lanka. It is argued that all social groups, including the well off, shared responsibility for criminality.

Much crime was related to non-traditional commercial and political rivalries. Upwardly-mobile groups within the capitalist economy sometimes used illegal means to further their ends. Cart contractors, who undertook to transport rice to plantations and take coffee or tea back to the coast or railhead, built up networks of supporters. A series of incidents involving Salagamas from the Western Province illustrates the type of illegal conflict which could develop.

Early in 1879 there were clashes in the Kandyan town of Navalapitiya between two factions of carters, one led by Louis Mendis, a Salagama from Ragama, near Colombo, and the other by Amaris Mendis, his brother.[5] A police constable was killed while trying to make an arrest after an affray. Amaris Mendis was allied with Miguel Perera, a wealthy honorary *mudaliyar* who lived in Ragama. On 6 October 1879 Perera was murdered, probably by some retainers whom he had mistreated. It was revealed that he had kept labourers in stocks at night to prevent them from deserting during the coconut-picking season. Four men were arrested for the murder, but the case was spoilt when two of Perera's sons tortured witnesses in order to force them into giving evidence implicating Louis Mendis. Perera's sons were imprisoned, and the faction suffered another setback in 1880 when twelve of its members were convicted of gang robbery and sentenced to twenty-five years imprisonment. These robberies had begun early in 1879, and were carried out partly to embarrass Peter de Saram, a Goyigama *mudaliyar* who later became a magistrate. Perera had twice been turned down for this position of *mudaliyar*, and he had hoped to achieve the dismissal of de Saram by showing him incapable of keeping order in his division. The robberies were also profitable; the criminals had informants in Colombo who gave them information about persons returning home with cash obtained from the sale of copra.

Fighting between the two groups continued for several years. In 1883, after another false murder charge was brought against Louis Mendis, seven members of the Perera faction were convicted of conspiracy.[6] Mendis went on to have a colourful career. He was widely believed to have organized many of the Roman Catholics who attacked the Buddhist procession at Kotahena in March 1883.[7] In 1889 he was employed by the Chettiar merchants of Colombo to ensure the safe passage of goods from the wharf to Chetty Street. When a bag of rice disappeared, neither Mendis nor another faction, which was employed to protect goods in Chetty Street itself, was willing to accept responsiblity. There was a threat of violence between the two groups, and the carters, many of whom supported Mendis, stopped working in order to demonstrate their support for him, bringing business to a standstill.[8] Finally, in 1891, Mendis was convicted of aiding and abetting rioting, and was sentenced to five years imprisonment.[9] The charges arose from an attempt forcibly to occupy disputed land at Katugampola in Kurunagala district. Mendis died in 1912 at the age of seventy-two. His obituary in the Ceylon *Times* described him as 'a fine type of Sinhalese gentleman of the older school'.[10]

Land grabbing was most common between 1880 and 1920. It was a result of the desire by the national élite and local notables to purchase or otherwise acquire land suitable for cash crops. Earlier in the nineteenth century British planters had had no official opposition to their own acquisition of extensive tracts of forest land. In fact, the government had been eager to sell them Crown land at a relatively low price. But by the end of the nineteenth century some officials were becoming concerned about the ecological effects of the disappearance of forests. There were also fears that the wholesale alienation of land would lead to social disruption among the peasantry. In some districts officials attempted to preserve forests from commercial development and slow down the sale of land to outsiders.

The most common form of land grabbing was to buy a dubious title from villagers, and then send men to the property to claim it by force.[11] It was then up to anyone else who claimed the property, or to the previous incumbent, to prove ownership in the slow-moving courts. Land grabbers retained skilful lawyers to ensure that the legal process was both uncertain and costly. Often the men who seized the property, as well as those behind the land grabbing, were from another district. Sinhalese from the Western Province were brought into other districts, especially Kurunagala and Chilaw, to claim land suitable for coconut cultivation. In 1905 S. M. Burrows, the Government Agent at Kurunagala, wrote in his diary that 'a typical case of riot came up. . . . One of the parties is a highly respectable person, a Dias Bandaranayaka, the other side are immigrants from the Negombo district. Both claim on probably fictitious titles. . . . They will not go to law because of the doubtfulness of their titles, and the many delays. It is also cheaper to break one another's heads.'[12]

Some land grabbers had island-wide status. Bertram Hill, when Assistant Government Agent at Chilaw, complained that riots, unlawful assemblies, murders and assaults continuously resulted from land disputes between the Coreas and Jayawardenas, both élite Goyigama families.[13] These men sometimes appealed over the heads of local officials. The Jayawardenas once sent a telegram to the Colonial Secretary stating: 'The noted advocate Corea with 100 men rioting on my estate, beg protection.' Hill believed that the parties failed to take civil disputes to court because they did not want to risk losing.

When the government was the opponent, more subtle means were often employed. E. M. de C. Short, when Assistant Government Agent at Matara, described a hypothetical case in his diary.[14] A piece of forest belonging to the Crown was selected, and a deed for it forged. The land grabber then employed a poor man to ask for a permit to carry out *chena* cultivation. Permission was granted because the headmen were bribed to report that the land was suitable and that the applicant was poor and deserving. After a couple of years the poor man would plant a cash crop such as citronella on the land. The headmen were again bribed not to report the truth to the *kachcheri*. After two or three years, when the land was clearly no longer forest, the land grabber produced the forged deed and made his claim, and the poor man turned the land over to him. It was then up to the government to prove its title in court.

The prevalence of bribery and corruption among the police, petty headmen and other minor government officials has been discussed in earlier chapters. There were periodic dismissals on grounds of corruption, but extortion was rarely punished judicially. The extent to which favouritism by headmen was popularly regarded as criminal is problematic, especially when the official acted on the basis of a personal or social obligation rather than a cash payment. *Mudaliyars* and *ratemahatmayas* were also sometimes involved in crime, especially the obstruction of justice. They could be put in a difficult position because the expectations of their networks of kin and supporters often ran counter to those of their official superiors. Chief headmen exercised less independent power in the Low Country than in Kandyan districts, where various degrees of organized extortion were not uncommon. In 1880 a petition accused a long-serving *ratemahatmaya* in Badulla district, Bibile A. Banda, of systematically committing serious crime.[15] Investigation showed that the notary, marriage registrar, temple-land incumbents and middle-level headmen in Banda's division were all related to him. For years he had run the remote area as his private fief; villagers were required to work on his land and construct irrigation works for his benefit. Those who refused were sometimes flogged. When Moor villagers once resisted carrying out Banda's orders, their growing crop was ruined by 200 men. He also collected over 2,000 rupees to help pay for a statue of a former governor to be erected in front of the Colombo Museum, but he remitted only fifty rupees of this sum for its proper purpose. Banda was no doubt an extreme example of criminality among high-level headmen; in the Low Country such blatant exploitation was not possible. On the other hand most chief headmen regularly received valuable gifts, and this practice was tacitly accepted by the British.[16]

A crime which required some education was counterfeiting. It was carried out at a modest rate throughout the colonial period.[17] In the late nineteenth century an average of about forty cases were instituted annually before the courts. Monks and members of the

Navandanna caste were often suspected of involvement in this crime. Navandannas were traditionally metal-workers, while monks apparently gained practice from drawing images of the Buddha.[18] Usually currency forgeries were not very skilful, but the tattered condition of most notes in circulation aided criminals.

Dutch and Kandyan land deeds were also forged. It is likely that this crime increased towards the end of the nineteenth century, a consequence of the increasing shortage of arable land in some districts. Often the land in question was regarded by the government as Crown land, and was suitable for cash crops. In the late 1890s the authorities went to great lengths to convict two brothers who had forged many Dutch deeds for land in Matara district. This effort was successful after extensive examinations of Dutch records in Colombo.[19]

About eight per cent of those listed in the *Hue and Cry* were charged with criminal breach of trust or fraud. A high proportion of the perpetrators fled when this crime was discovered. Often an employee or contractor simply absconded with goods or money entrusted to his care; in many of these cases the criminal was poor, a domestic servant or labourer. There were also occasions when commercial businesses and government were defrauded by ongoing schemes carried out by their employees. Traders and especially white-collar workers committed a high proportion of these crimes.

Theft and burglary were usually committed by the poor; in the case of burglary more wealthy persons were often the victims. The English-language press sometimes adopted a strident tone when discussing burglary, and in Colombo there were periodic scares about the crime.[20] Early in 1900, for example, there was alarm over a number of such crimes in which a gun was carried. Many residents armed themselves as a result. L. F. Knollys, the Inspector-General of Police, stated that they fired at noises at all hours of the night and endangered police patrols. The scare was aroused by a total of eight burglaries, all carried out by one man.[21] There were also some burglaries in the villages. Thieves burrowed through mud walls in the back rooms of houses where people rarely slept because of the heat.[22] Rural burglaries were often carried out by residents of villages ten or fifteen kilometres distant, but there was normally a local informant. It is likely that housebreaking was relatively rare early in the colonial period, but it became more common as the number of prosperous households increased. Although the value of stolen goods was usually small, occasionally jewellery or large amounts of cash were taken. In

1887, for instance, jewellery valued at 15,000 rupees was stolen from the Nuvara Eliya hotel room of a British visitor.[23]

In Colombo and other urban and semi-urban areas there were persons who made their living through various forms of theft or by receiving stolen goods. The increase of this form of crime no doubt paralleled urbanization and the spread of the market economy. Carters and harbour workers regularly stole rice and other goods at the Colombo wharf and in transit to retail establishments.[24] In the twentieth century the police discovered that many thieves defined their occupations narrowly.[25] Some pilfered specific items, such as trinkets and silverware, or clothes. Others used the same tactics over and over again. In 1921 a woman who accepted employment as a cook disappeared with jewellery a few hours later. An inspector remembered a similar case from 1913, and with the aid of police records she was traced and found with the items in her possession. She had had six previous convictions for such offences.[26]

Domestic servants accounted for nearly ten per cent of persons listed in the *Hue and Cry*; most were charged with thefts from their masters. They were more likely to flee than other criminals. Not only were their chances of avoiding conviction if tried not good, but they were subject to summary beatings from some masters when suspected of theft. Largely because this crime directly affected politically-vocal social groups, the government took special measures against it.[27] Under the Servants Registration Ordinance, which was implemented in Colombo in 1871 and later extended to some other towns, all servants with a salary of at least five rupees a month were required to register with the police and possess a 'pocket book' in which details of their past and present employment were entered. When a servant changed employment, employers were required to record their opinion of his or her character. Despite some misgivings as to its fairness, this system was retained well into the twentieth century.

Except for cattle stealing, most rural property crime involved the theft of garden crops. One-tenth of all homicides were the direct result of such pilfering. Cultivators often felt it necessary for a family member to sit up all night guarding growing crops. Coconut stealing was endemic particularly near the coast north of Negombo, where it led to much violence.[28] It was very difficult to get convictions in such cases; when thieves were caught red-handed property owners often attempted to administer physical punishment on the spot. It is likely that a large proportion of theft cases brought before the courts involved growing garden produce.

Much of this theft must have marginally redistributed wealth towards poorer villagers, but when the produce was sold traders also benefited, and smallholders were especially vulnerable to this crime when it was organized or carried out by a group.

There were also thefts of plantation produce. Coffee stealing was common when coffee was the dominant plantation crop. Both Sinhalese villagers and Tamil labourers stole coffee. They sold it to Low Country Sinhalese and Moor shopkeepers who added it to their legitimately-purchased stocks of 'native coffee' which were destined for export.[29] Since the crime was only in the planters' interest to detect, the authorities found it difficult to gain convictions. The British were more concerned than in the case of garden produce and in 1874 passed draconian legislation which required persons with coffee in their possession to prove that it was not stolen. There were however few convictions under this ordinance, which was found to be impractical to enforce.[30] Much coffee was stolen in transit to Colombo. Carters and boatmen substituted inferior quality for the best beans and soaked other beans in water to maintain the weight of their loads and thus conceal thefts.[31] Towards the end of the coffee era special police were established to enforce a registration scheme along the roads and waterways on which coffee was transported.[32] Coffee stealing died with the leaf disease, although cinchona and cocoa stealing succeeded it in some areas.[33] Tea, coffee's main replacement, required too much labour to steal profitably. Stolen tea was also much easier to detect because unlike coffee, tea was grown only on large estates. In the twentieth century the establishment of rubber plantations opened new opportunities for thieves. When the price of rubber was high it was stolen and disposed of to dealers much as coffee had been fifty years earlier.[34] In the 1920s the growth of tea smallholdings and the new practice of picking tea before it was ripe also made tea stealing more difficult to detect and thus profitable, though the extent of this crime was never great.[35]

A serious crime usually carried out by poorer villagers was gang robbery, sometimes involving substantial violence. As was pointed out in the chapter on homicide, deaths resulting from robberies, though not common, occurred at a steady rate. There was an upsurge in this type of crime in the central highlands and around Colombo at the beginning of the coffee-leaf disease depression.[36] A remote village in Badulla district was abandoned, some roads were unsafe for travellers, and a few estate stores were robbed. The culprits were in the main Kandyan Sinhalese, though in some instances they were led by Sinhalese from the Low Country. This increase in crime was the result of deprivation and desperation. Many Sinhalese in the central highlands kept small coffee gardens and used the proceeds from the sale of coffee to finance grain-tax payments. When the income from coffee was brought abruptly to an end, there was no money with which to pay taxes. It is not surprising that some villagers sought relief through crime.

In normal times gang robbery was more common in Kurunagala district and the Southern Province than elsewhere, and the targets were isolated houses where money and valuables were reputed to be kept.[37] In Kandyan districts, where monks controlled large amounts of land, Buddhist temples and monasteries were sometimes attacked.[38] Occasionally headmen were targets. In 1885 a *ratemahatmaya* in Kurunagala district was murdered and his house looted; his clerk and other Low Countrymen proved to be the culprits.[39] Local residents generally provided information about potential victims in return for a share of the proceeds; the robbers themselves usually lived some distance from the site of the crime, often as far as fifty kilometres. Sometimes information was provided primarily to further a dispute by impoverishing or humiliating the victim. This pattern of gang robbery changed little over the last century of colonial rule, though better communications enabled robbers to move more quickly as time went by. In the twentieth century motor vehicles were often used. Usually gangs were not caste-homogeneous, though Vahumpuras from around Elpitiya were often thought to be responsible for robberies committed in the Southern Province. After around 1880 gang robbery resulted in more convictions than many other crimes because officials personally investigated it rather than leaving the prosecution to victims. Convictions were possible when stolen property could be traced. Long-term trends in the incidence of this crime are uncertain, but it was never common. By the 1920s and 1930s there were only around twenty cases annually; this may have also been the level in normal years in the nineteenth century.

There were few bandit gangs which stayed together for weeks at a time or which were permanently on the run. Men involved in robberies generally dispersed to their home villages after committing a crime. One exception was the gang collected by the well-known bandit Deekirikewage Sardiel in 1863.[40] Sardiel's rather ordinary criminal career took an unexpected turn in July 1862 when he stabbed and killed a police informer while being arrested. He twice escaped from custody and in December returned to

Kagalla, his natal district, and formed a gang which preyed on traffic along the Colombo-to-Kandy road. In July 1863 a special police station was established in his area of operations, but Sardiel managed to foil all efforts to capture him. In January 1864 the reward for information leading to his arrest was increased to one hundred pounds. Two months later Sardiel shot dead two men who attempted to apprehend him, an action which resulted in even more extensive efforts by the authorities to bring him to justice. He was finally captured on 21 March on the basis of information supplied by an informer, but not before one of his colleagues had shot a policeman dead. On 4 April he was convicted of murder and a month later was hanged before an enormous crowd. His notoriety in part stemmed from a reputation for robbing the rich and giving to the poor. In 1869 the *Lakrivikirana* carried an article about Robin Hood which was entitled 'An English Sardiel'.[41]

Gambling and the illicit sale of arrack were crimes associated with the lower classes, though many organizers must have been quite wealthy. These crimes particularly offended some members of the Sinhalese Buddhist élite, many of whom believed that alcoholic drink was unknown in Kandyan districts before British rule.[42] Although this latter belief was incorrect, there is no doubt that intemperance increased in Kandyan districts during the nineteenth century. In the 1920s new restrictions on the sale of alcohol increased the profitability of the illicit production and sale of arrack.[43] Illegal drinking and gambling seem to have been more prevalent near the coast than elsewhere. Gambling increased during holidays and was common at marriages. There were regular gambling 'dens' which could accommodate fifty or a hundred men.[44] Some officials drew a direct link between gambling and other crime, arguing not only that many quarrels arose among gamblers but that the losers had to steal and rob in order to make up their losses.[45] After around 1865 the police periodically raided gambling dens. These excursions were often met with violence, and the police not infrequently got the worst of the clashes.[46]

Legislation concerning drinking and gambling favoured the wealthy classes and particularly British residents. Horse races, with legal gambling, were major social events in Colombo and Nuvara Eliya. Although many Sri Lankans and European sailors were taken into custody for offences relating to drunkenness, British planters were generally immune from the law in this regard. After a sports meet at Badulla in 1875 some planters set fire to the roof on the belfry of a church. When the police intervened they were severely assaulted. Eight planters were later convicted, but were let off with fines.[47] Several years later, after a similar incident, another convicted man's fine was paid by the planters present in the courtroom, 'and the defendant [was] carried out on their shoulders with cheers.'[48]

Assault was a charge often instituted before the courts. Many of these cases were very minor, but there was a good deal of casual violence. There were many unreported cases in which clearly lower-status persons suffered at the hands of their superiors. In a majority of assaults the parties were well acquainted; my enumeration of assault charges filed in Chilaw Police Court over a four-month period revealed that in four out of five cases both the complainant and the accused lived in the same village.[49] It is possible that a charge of assault was a common response to verbal abuse.

Criminality and Social Position

Even in the early years of British rule officials noted that well-off persons were often involved in crime. In 1807 Governor Maitland wrote that gangs of thieves had links with *mudaliyars*.[50] The Sitting Magistrate at Colombo observed in 1830 that the vagrancy law was of little use for convicting habitual criminals because 'some of the worst characters are persons of property'.[51] In 1844 it was discovered that only one-half of the prisoners held at Colombo were illiterate.[52] The impression gained from the discussion of important forms of crime, that mainstream social groups were heavily involved in committing them, is confirmed by an examination of the social characteristics of two sets of persons treated as criminal by the authorities: convicted prisoners, and defendants listed in the *Hue and Cry* between 1896 and 1905.

About one-quarter of the persons in the *Hue and Cry* were described as cultivators, and about one-half as labourers. The census data on occupation is unreliable but probably close to one-half of the adult male population were mainly cultivators and a majority of the rest were mainly labourers. Many persons were cultivators some years, and for part of a year, but also did casual labour. In the *Hue and Cry* about five per cent of those listed were described as 'loafers' or by a similar derogatory term. These men were mostly casual labourers.

Although the *Hue and Cry* seems to suggest that labourers were more criminal than cultivators, the listings were biased towards crimes committed in the market sector of the economy. A casual labourer was more likely to flee after stealing from his employer than was a peasant who had taken coconuts from a fellow villager's garden. The labourer was more likely to be suspected of the crime, and when he worked away from home he had few social ties to hold him at his workplace. He was also more likely to be convicted if accused, especially if the article he had stolen was distinctive. In any case, no conclusions concerning social hierarchies may be drawn by comparing the proportions of cultivators and labourers involved in crime, since these categories cannot be ranked by status or wealth.

The common belief that the Sinhalese were more criminal than other ethnic groups was partially supported by official statistics. The Sinhalese generally accounted for a higher proportion of prisoners than one would expect from their proportion of the population. The proportion of Tamil prisoners was in most years less than that of Tamils in general, while the Moor proportion of prisoners was similar to their proportion of the population. Towards the end of colonial rule there was an increase in Moor representation, probably because of increased prosecution of economic offences related to their trading activities.

There is no reason to believe that the judicial system worked against the Sinhalese; on the contrary they were more familiar with legal culture and procedure than were Indian Tamils, and thus better able to defend themselves.[53] Tamils were more often victimized by labour laws.[54] Breach of contract was a penal offence if committed by the employee, but non-penal if the culprit was the employer. Before 1885 Tamils also suffered from the presence of unofficial, part-time justices of the peace in plantation areas. The unofficial justices were invariably British planters, and they tended routinely to issue warrants for plantation workers accused of offences such as leaving their job without giving proper notice. In 1884 an official report stated that many workers arrested upon warrants as deserters 'had not in fact served on the estate from which they were alleged to have deserted.'[55]

On the other hand, many minor judicial matters involving plantation workers were not brought to the attention of the authorities, but were dealt with on the estates, by the plantation manager or foreman.[56] This practice may have led to under-representation of Tamils in the prison statistics. In some localities Moors too took minor disputes to alternative adjudicators, community leaders who held hearings in mosques.[57] Equivalent petty crimes might well have been taken to court by Sinhalese villagers.

However, the conviction rate for these minor crimes was low, and the punishment often a small fine, so the differential impact on prison statistics was not great, especially when one takes into account that Moors and Tamils generally lived closer to a court than the Sinhalese, and that the Sinhalese themselves had similar, albeit weaker, informal adjudication procedures which they could use.

Another feature of the ethnic distribution of prisoners was the high proportion of Europeans. They were nearly all working class, mostly sailors off ships which called at Galle and Colombo.[58] Some members of the European community were embarrassed by the presence of these men, who were mostly imprisoned for offences related to drunkenness. In the late 1890s Ponnambalam Ramanathan, the Solicitor-General, published figures in his annual report which showed that Europeans were the most criminal ethnic group. There were protests from some newspapers and members of the Legislative Council.[59] They asked that a distinction be made between resident Europeans and the others. The government replied that to be consistent the same distinction would have to be made for Moors and Tamils, and that such an undertaking would be both difficult and expensive.[60] Ramanathan modified the format of his report so as to omit the percentage of European prisoners as a proportion of the general European population, but he continued to state the absolute number in gaol.[61]

Other evidence of the relationship between ethnicity and crime may be drawn from the *Hue and Cry*. The proportion of Tamils was only eleven per cent, substantially less than their sixteen per cent proportion of the general population of Sinhala Sri Lanka. Since the *Hue and Cry* was biased towards the inclusion of persons involved in the market economy, this low proportion, viewed in conjunction with the prison statistics, suggests at the very least that Indian Tamils, the largest minority ethnic group, were not disproportionately involved in crime, despite their low economic and social position.

The religion of convicted prisoners and of those listed in the *Hue and Cry* is also available. The proportions belonging to the various creeds followed the lines one would expect in view of their ethnic and geographical characteristics. Religion does not seem to have acted as an independent factor. Christians accounted for a slightly higher proportion of persons thought to be criminal than of the population at large because the Low Country was over-represented in the prisoner and *Hue and Cry* populations.

Among the Sinhalese, caste provides one way of judging the status of an individual. The *Hue and Cry* mentioned the caste of most persons for whom warrants were issued. Persons of low caste were not listed disproportionately often (Table 6.1). Goyigamas accounted for a higher proportion than their overall size would warrant. The three upwardly-mobile maritime castes were also over-represented, the Karava somewhat less than the Salagama and Durava (Table 6.2). Only the low castes were under-represented. The Vahumpura, who had a reputation as scoundrels, accounted for six per cent of the persons in the *Hue and Cry*. This is the same figure as a recent estimate of their general strength.[62]

Table 6.1. General Caste Rank of Sinhalese Listed in the Hue and Cry

	Hue and Cry	General Population
	(%)	(%)
Goyigama	58	55
Karava, Salagama, Durava	24	20
Low Castes	18	25

(N = 3,442, MC = 282)

Note: The proportions for the general population are estimates. There has been no caste census in modern times.

One very small caste with a justified criminal reputation was the Demala Gattara. They inhabited a few inland villages in Kalutara district and the Southern Province. Not only were they implicated in crimes such as cattle stealing and highway robbery, but they had a high level of violence among themselves.[63] They often clashed with neighbouring Goyigama villagers. The Demala Gattara did not accept the position of a low caste, and although they were not considered polluting, they were despised by other groups. Two other very small castes, both of which were widely thought to be unclean, were also considered criminals. Rodis were traditionally beggars, but it was widely believed that they lived by theft.[64] Gahala Beravas, who were found only in a few Kandyan villages, were thought by H. L. Dowbiggin, the Inspector-General of Police, to possess a 'criminal instinct'.[65]

Table 6.2. Caste of Sinhalese Listed in the Hue and Cry

	N	(%)		N	(%)
Badahala	30	0.9	Navandanna	78	2.3
Batgam	42	1.2	Oli	12	0.3
Berava	21	0.6	Pali	2	0.1
Demala Gattara	16	0.5	Panikki	3	0.1
Durava	171	5.0	Panna Durayi	72	2.1
Goyigama	1,997	58.0	Rodi	14	0.4
Hena	70	2.0	Salagama	274	8.0
Hinna	15	0.4	Vahumpura	213	6.2
Hunu	22	0.6	Velli Durayi	2	0.1
Karava	388	11.3			
(N = 3,442, MC = 282)					

Very few women were treated as criminal. In the late nineteenth century they made up less than one per cent of those listed in the *Hue and Cry* and of the gaol population. Many of these were domestic servants who had stolen articles from their masters or mistresses. In the early nineteenth century women accounted for a slightly larger proportion of prisoners. The decline during the nineteenth century was probably a result of the judicial system extending its sway over rural areas where there were proportionately fewer domestic servants.

Crimes were committed mainly by adults; juvenile delinquency was not a major problem (Table 6.3). The persons by far most likely to commit crimes were men in their twenties and thirties. Surprisingly, in view of studies carried out with reference to other countries, persons in their thirties were nearly as likely to be listed in the *Hue and Cry* as those in their twenties. Males over the age of fifteen, who accounted for around one-third of the population, were responsible for almost all crime.

Some contemporary observers were surprised when late nineteenth-century censuses showed that the rate of literacy among convicted prisoners was considerably higher than that of the general male population.[66] They failed to take into account that a large proportion of children were classified as illiterate, thus artificially depressing the general rate of literacy. But the educational level of prisoners was none the less remarkable. In 1901, for instance, forty-seven per cent of male prisoners were

Table 6.3. Age of Persons Listed in the Hue and Cry *per 10,000 Members of Age Group*

10 – 19	8.4
20 – 29	34.9
30 – 39	32.8
40 – 49	16.1
50 –	5.2
(N = 4,373, MC = 132)	

literate, slightly more than the overall adult male rate. Geographical and ethnic factors were partially responsible for the high rate of literacy among prisoners, but even within such categories the literacy rate of prisoners was not substantially less than for the group in general. Among Low Country Sinhalese men forty-eight per cent of prisoners were literate, as opposed to fifty per cent in general. The four per cent of male prisoners who could read and write English equalled the proportion of English literates among all men. The literacy of prisoners is surprising given the common assumption that judicial systems work against the poor and illiterate.

The geographical distribution of crime may be measured through judicial statistics and the *Hue and Cry* listings. More court cases were instituted in the Low Country than in Kandyan districts, where the rate of criminal litigation was higher in the central highlands than in the Intermediate region. The low rate of criminal litigation in the Intermediate area was no doubt largely or entirely a result of the paucity of court sites. Serious crime, as measured by superior court cases, was more common in the North-Western Province, including Kurunagala district, and in the Low Country. The *Hue and Cry* showed high rates for most Low Country districts, including Galle, Colombo, Chilaw and Kalutara. Overall, according to the various sets of statistics crime was more prevalent in the Low Country and in Kurunagala district than elsewhere. This generalization is by and large supported by the detailed analyses of cattle stealing, homicide and riot presented earlier in this book.

The areas with high rates of recorded crime varied greatly in degree of prosperity. They included the coastal districts of the Western and North-Western Provinces, the most wealthy part of Sri Lanka. On the other hand Kurunagala district, notorious for both crimes of violence and cattle stealing, had a low standard of living. Other social indicators, such as education, urbanization, and the penetration of the market economy, do not bear any consistent relationship to the overall level of crime in a district. The patterns of certain individual crimes may be clearly related to such social variables, but crime in general may not.

Table 6.4. Region of Birth by the Region where the Crime was Committed, from the Hue and Cry

	Committed Low Country (%)	Committed Intermediate (%)	Committed Interior (%)
Born N & E Provinces	1	1	3
Born India	4	5	22
Born Low Country	91	36	26
Born Intermediate	2	53	4
Born Interior	2	4	46
	N = 2,632	N = 632	N = 951
(N = 4,215, MC = 290)			

It was a common view of British officials that Low Country labourers and traders who emigrated to Kandyan districts were prone to criminality.[67] The *Hue and Cry* listings support this opinion (Table 6.4). More persons emigrated to Kandyan areas from India than from the Low Country, but more Low Countrymen than Indians fled from warrants issued in Kandyan districts. In part the preponderance of Low Countrymen may be explained by the existence of a sanctuary outside the region, yet not a long distance away. It was natural for Low Countrymen to return to their home villages, or other places in the Low Country where they had kin, when they were wanted for a crime. It was much more difficult for Indian Tamils to flee to southern India, and native Kandyans might not have had relatives outside of their home districts where they committed crimes. None the less, Low Countrymen working in Kandyan districts were involved in the market economy and had ample opportunities to commit property crimes. It is clear that many took advantage of this situation. The extent to which the frequency of these crimes compared with certain rural crimes, such as the theft of agricultural produce, cannot be determined with any confidence.

Since the *Hue and Cry* mentioned the birthplace of most persons listed, it is possible to assess the extent to which a district imported or exported crime. For this purpose the proportion of the *Hue and Cry* population born in each district divided by the proportion committing crimes in the same district has been calculated. For instance, 6.4 per cent of the *Hue and Cry* population were born in Matara district, but only 3.7 per cent were wanted for crimes committed in the same district. The resultant ratio is 6.4/3.7, or 1.7. In other words, for each ten persons in the *Hue and Cry* who were wanted for offences committed in Matara district, there were seventeen persons who had been born in Matara district. The overall ratio is 0.9, not 1.0, because ten per cent of wanted persons were born outside Sinhala Sri Lanka.

Table 6.5. *Percentage of the Persons in the* Hue and Cry *born in each District as a Proportion of the Percentage of Persons in the* Hue and Cry *accused of an Offence in the same District*

Matara	1.7	Kandy	0.6
Kalutara Totamunes	1.6	Matale	0.5
Colombo (rural)	1.4	Kurunagala	0.5
Galle	1.2	Badulla	0.5
Kalutara (interior)	1.1	Colombo (city)	0.5
Hambantota	0.8	Puttalam	0.4
Kagalla	0.7	Nuvara Eliya	0.4
Ratnapura	0.7	Anuradhapura	0.2
Chilaw	0.6		

Many persons born in the more densely-populated parts of the Low Country, with the exception of Chilaw, committed crimes in other districts (Table 6.5). These men were mostly labourers who emigrated, often temporarily, to take advantage of employment opportunities in the cash economy. Chilaw itself attracted emigrants from the Western Province because of its cash-crop-based prosperity. The Totamunes, the coastal strip of Kalutara district, exported crime to a greater degree than the interior of Kalutara. This difference suggests that emigrants came proportionately more from such areas than from localities further inland. The very high rate at which Matara exported crime reflected a high rate of emigration which may have in turn reflected the uneven distribution of land ownership in that district. The rank order shown in Table 6.5 by and large reflected patterns of emigration in general. One exception is Anuradhapura district where emigrants accounted for a very high proportion of wanted persons. Both a low crime rate and weak penetration by the state probably accounted for the small number of indigenous inhabitants of this large but impoverished and sparsely-populated district who fled when a warrant was issued for their arrest.

The *Hue and Cry* and prison statistics indicate that the poor and marginal were not disproportionately involved in crime in normal times. What happened during periods of economic depression? In India many forms of crime, including gang robbery, homicide, burglary and theft, were strongly related to adverse economic conditions; such activity has often been termed famine crime.[68] In Sri Lanka the relationship between crime and periods of hardship was more ambiguous.

In the late nineteenth century there was no consistent relationship between economic fluctuations and the number of prosecutions for theft or assault. Even during the coffee-leaf disease depression there was no increase in the number of criminal cases. Similarly, there was no consistent trend in the crime rate during the boom of 1898 – 9, though in the Low Country thefts declined. On the other hand, it has been shown earlier in this book that the incidence of homicide, gang robbery and to a lesser extent cattle stealing bore a positive relationship with economic down turns in the late nineteenth century. It is possible that rates of assault and theft responded to economic change differently than these three crimes. Studies of homicide in other countries have often shown that its incidence is unrelated to that of other offences. The number of gang robberies was at no time large, and the increase around 1879 was the work of a relatively small number of men. In addition, the fall in cattle stealing in 1898 – 9 was not a direct response to prosperity but instead reflected the relative decline of subsistence agriculture in the areas where cattle theft was organized. Persons who had previously stolen cattle may have instead aided land grabbers, stolen produce for sale to traders, or contributed to the rowdy atmosphere for which many graphite mines were known. Nevertheless, it is possible that the judicial statistics masked real crime trends, and that theft and assault did increase when economic conditions declined. People may have instituted fewer court cases at times of hardship because they were less able to afford the cost.

Crime statistics from the twentieth century show a somewhat stronger relationship between economic fluctuations and crime. These figures were compiled by the police, and excluded both minor assaults and simple thefts where the value of the goods stolen was less than fifteen rupees. Cases believed to be false were also eliminated. Crime against property fell sharply in the years after 1921, a period when economic conditions improved quickly, but it increased after 1925, when the terms of trade turned against Sri Lanka (Table 6.6.). Property crime continued to rise after the onset of the world depression, but much of this increase may be accounted for by the revival of cattle theft. Officials also believed that petty thefts of plantation produce increased during the depression.[69] Since economic conditions deteriorated much more sharply after 1929 than 1925, the recorded increases in property crime do not exactly coincide with deteriorating economic conditions. It is probable that the increased police presence in the countryside in the 1920s and 1930s gradually inflated all crime figures during these years, and that administrative changes accounted for the general upward trend in crime, especially violent crime. If this was so, the decline in property crime in the early 1920s, a prosperous period, must have reflected a real decrease.

Overall, one can conclude that although there was a negative relationship between many forms of crime and economic conditions, it was not as strong as one might expect in a country where many persons lived in poverty. Crime statistics did not respond to

Table 6.6. Serious Offences Against the Person and Against Property, 1919–35

	Person	Property		Person	Property
1919	2,045	6,506	1928	2,881	5,866
1920	2,107	6,055	1929	2,978	6,055
1921	2,122	5,494	1930	3,235	6,389
1922	2,212	4,805	1931	3,407	6,638
1923	2,020	4,444	1932	3,564	6,817
1924	2,433	4,469	1933	3,738	6,952
1925	2,668	4,947	1934	3,562	6,659
1926	2,755	5,914	1935	3,252	6,871
1927	2,798	5,760			

Source: *Administration Reports.*

economic change in the same manner as they did in India. It is unlikely that this difference was accounted for by administrative procedures in recording statistics, though further research is needed before this question can be resolved.

All social groups, including the respectable, were involved in crime. When the economy faltered, criminals did not suffer disproportionately. There were no sudden increases in crime. One is left with the impression that in normal times persons of education, status and wealth benefited more from criminal activities than did the poor. The clearest case of a redistribution of wealth was the systematic stealing from coffee plantations, which was in the interests of estate workers, villagers, carters and traders. Only the mostly British plantation owners and managers lost out. But much crime was organized by the respectable and well off. The gains of the poor were limited in value, and were often at the expense of other poor persons.

Crimes against Property and Crimes against the Person

Thus far in this chapter it has been shown that the social base of criminal activity was broad. In this section an attempt is made to explore further the relationship between crime and social position by analysing the types of criminal actions committed by persons with various social characteristics. Dividing offences into crimes against property and crimes against the person is a common device when interpreting criminal trends.[70] Research on modern Europe has shown that there was in some countries a gradual trend towards an increase in the number of recorded crimes against property as a proportion of those against the person. These findings have prompted some scholars to speculate that a shift from violence to theft is characteristic of the 'modernization' of crime. Given the expansion of the market economy in colonial Sri Lanka, these theories would predict a gradual decrease in the violence of criminality as a consequence of the growth of urban, semi-urban and plantations settings. Examination of the official statistics does not reveal such a trend; there was little change in the relationship between the number of offences against the person and against property. On the other hand, the *Hue and Cry* shows that members of some social groups were much more likely to be accused of a violent offence than were others.

Violence ratios have been calculated from the *Hue and Cry* listings. Theft with violence, robbery, assault and homicide have been defined as violent crimes. Theft, burglary, cattle stealing, criminal breach of trust, forgery, counterfeiting and fraud have been defined as crimes against property. Of the 4,505 persons listed, 3,986 were wanted for one of these crimes; the other 519 persons were wanted for miscellaneous offences such as gambling, tax evasion and disorderly behaviour. Overall, the violence ratio was 0.43. In other words forty-three per cent of the 3,986 accused persons were wanted for violent crimes. There were significant differences according to ethnicity, religion, occupation, caste and region (Table 6.7). Since these characteristics were inter-related, some of these differences were caused by intervening variables. Most variations may be accounted for by two tendencies. The more important was the proclivity of persons employed away from their homes to commit property crime. In addition, certain localities in the Low Country, many of them inhabited by Salagamas or other non-Goyigamas, had traditions of violence.

Table 6.7. Violence Ratios for Selected Social Characteristics

		N			N
Ethnicity			*Caste*		
Sinhalese	0.46	3,292	Goyigama	0.45	1,780
Tamil	0.24	457	Karava	0.47	340
Moor	0.37	182	Salagama	0.61	238
Religion			Vahumpura	0.49	188
Buddhist	0.46	2,834	Durava	0.55	152
Christian	0.40	402	Other Castes	0.45	355
Hindu	0.26	312	*Region Committed*		
Muslim	0.39	200	Rural Low Country	0.52	1,926
Occupation			Interior	0.30	952
Labourer	0.44	1,773	Intermediate	0.47	617
Cultivator	0.52	884	Colombo City	0.26	490
Servant	0.10	350	Total	0.43	3,986
Trader	0.46	289			

The lowest violence ratio, 0.10, was among domestic servants. The ethnicity and geographical location of servants did not significantly affect this ratio. Outwardly servants were subservient, but some absconded with their masters' possessions. They rarely assaulted their employers, partly because they knew that violence would in turn be directed against them in a more severe form. Indeed, casual violence against servants was common, though rarely noticed by the courts. Variations among other occupational groups were not large.

The violence ratio of the Sinhalese was nearly double that of Tamils (Table 6.7). About half the crimes attributed to Tamils were thefts, and a further fourteen per cent were cases of criminal breach of trust. These crimes were often committed against the plantation and related industries. Tamils were rarely accused of using violence while committing a property offence. Only 22 Tamils were accused of such crimes, as opposed to 538 Sinhalese.

The two groups with very low violence ratios, domestic servants and Tamils, were near the bottom of the social heap. This suggests that there may have been a relationship between low social and economic status and a propensity towards non-violent criminal activity. These low ratios are also consistent with the hypothesis that the expansion of the market economy led to relatively more property crime.

Analysis of regional differences does not support either of these hypotheses. The ratio was low in the Interior region and the city of Colombo and high in the Rural Low Country and the Inter-mediate area (Table 6.7). If poverty had been associated with a high proportion of property crime, both Kandyan regions would have had low ratios. In addition, residents of the city of Colombo were not worse off than people elsewhere in the Low Country. The theory that there was a higher proportion of property crime in areas where the market economy had taken hold also fails to explain adequately regional differences. The heavily populated coastal strip, where a large proportion of the Low Country population lived, had long been governed by market relations. A more plausible explanation, in view of the ethnic differentials discussed above, is that the regional contrasts were caused by the large number of Tamils in the Interior region and Colombo city. This theory is however proven wrong when the ratios of Sinhalese alone are broken down by region; these figures show variations similar to the overall regional ratios.[71]

Another social group which stood out with a low violence ratio was emigrants from the Rural Low Country to Kandyan districts and the city of Colombo. Low Countrymen tended to change their criminal behaviour when they left their native region (Table 6.8). The proportion of property crime which they committed was related to the distance travelled. As Low Countrymen moved to

Table 6.8. Violence Ratios, by Region of Birth and Place Committed

		N
Born Rural Low Country, Committed Rural Low Country	0.54	1,758
Born Rural Low Country, Committed Intermediate	0.46	192
Born Rural Low Country, Committed Interior	0.31	178
Born Rural Low Country, Committed Columbo City	0.19	181
Born Colombo City, Committed Colombo City	0.45	153
Sinhalese, Born Interior	0.35	380
Born Intermediate, Committed Intermediate	0.50	306

the Intermediate area, the Interior region, and finally the city of Colombo, their violence ratio decreased. Their likely employment in each of these three areas was more and more socially removed from their natal background.

Emigrants from the Rural Low Country had a lower violence ratio than life-long residents of their adopted regions, even though the Rural Low Country itself had the highest violence ratio (Table 6.8). Other emigrants also had low violence ratios. Although most Indian Tamils at this time were socially divorced from the wider Sri Lankan Society, and may be seen as emigrants regardless of their place of birth, those born in India, who presumably had less strong links with Sri Lanka, had a lower ratio (0.22) than Tamils born in Sinhala Sri Lanka (0.35). Similarly, Coast Moors, who were by definition emigrants, had a lower ratio (0.22) than Ceylon Moors (0.43). The ethnic backgrounds of emigrants was of little importance. The contrast between the behaviour of emigrants and life-long residents was most marked in the city of Colombo. About two-thirds of those accused of committing crimes in the capital had been born elsewhere; their violence ratio was 0.19. In contrast, natives of Colombo had a ratio of 0.45.

The high proportion of property crime on the part of emigrants does not confirm the hypothesis that it was depressed and marginal groups which tended to commit property crime. Most emigrants were not particularly well off, but the Sinhalese and the Moors among them were not marginal either. Their natal villages in the Low Country suffered fron underemployment, but they also had, by Sri Lankan standards, a relatively high standard of living. It was often the more enterprising who took advantage of the employment opportunities in Kandyan districts and the city of

Colombo. Many were traders, others were skilled workers such as carpenters and masons. Most retained kin ties with the Low Country. For many emigration was temporary and their families stayed behind in their home villages.

Table 6.9. Violence Ratios, by Occupation and Region

Committed	Non-Cultivators	N	Cultivators	N
Rural Low Country	0.52	1,193	0.54	527
Intermediate	0.43	375	0.54	209
Interior	0.26	712	0.47	144

A possible explanation for the high proportion of property crime among servants, Tamils and emigrants is that occupation was the decisive variable. A very high proportion of all three groups worked for a wage, while probably about half the work force were primarily cultivators with a stake in agricultural land. Cultivators had a higher violence ratio than labourers (Table 6.7). If domestic servants, traders, fishermen and other persons who made their living in the market economy are combined with labourers, the difference increases. However, when one breaks down the rates of cultivators and non-cultivators geographically, the difference disappears in the Rural Low Country (Table 6.9). In this region, where nearly one-half of those listed in the *Hue and Cry* committed crimes, there was no difference between the behaviour of cultivators and non-cultivators. It was only in those areas where a large proportion of persons involved in the market economy were not indigenous that the behaviour of cultivators differed from the rest of the population. In Kandyan districts and the city of Colombo a high proportion of these persons were either Indian Tamils or Low Country Sinhalese. In the Intermediate area there were fewer plantations than in the Interior region and local villages provided a larger proportion of plantation workers. In the Rural Low Country most people, regardless of occupation, were indigenous to the region where they lived. Along the coastal strip there were few immigrant labourers, and the market economy was fully integrated into the local economy and culture. A high proportion of property crime was associated with emigrant workers within the market economy, not with the presence of the market economy itself.

The distinctly higher proportion of property crime among non-indigenous workers accounted for variations in the violence ratio along divisions of ethnicity, occupation and region, but the discrepancies among the Sinhalese castes cannot be explained in this manner. The violence ratio of Goyigamas was significantly lower than that of Salagamas and to a lesser extent Duravas (Table 6.7). The high ratios of Salagamas and Duravas, and the slightly higher than average Karava ratio, are unexpected because it is often assumed that a disproportionate number of Low Country Sinhalese emigrants to Kandyan districts, who had a low ratio, were members of the three maritime castes. In fact, although a large proportion of Sinhalese emigrants listed in the *Hue and Cry* belonged to one of the maritime castes, a large majority of the members of these castes listed in the *Hue and Cry* were not emigrants; they were charged with crimes committed in the Rural Low Country. In order to eliminate the special case of the emigrants from the analysis of caste and criminal behaviour, violence ratios by caste for crimes committed in the Rural Low Country were calculated (Table 6.10). It is clear that the low Goyigama and high Salagama and other maritime caste ratios stemmed from differences in the types of crimes committed in the Rural Low Country. The Goyigama ratio was also lower than that of Vahumpuras and other castes who lived in this region. These differences cannot be accounted for by occupation, for within the Rural Low Country there was little difference between ratios of cultivators, labourers and traders. It was only in the Rural Low Country that caste acted as a significant independent variable in determining criminal behaviour; among Kandyans the Goyigama ratio of 0.42 was little different from the 0.41 ratio of members of other Sinhalese castes.

Table 6.10. Violence Ratios in the Rural Low Country, by Caste

		N
Goyigama	0.49	1,002
Karava	0.57	211
Salagama	0.67	177
Vahumpura	0.54	116
Durava	0.59	97
Other Castes	0.60	140

Christians had a lower violence ratio than Buddhists (Table 6.7). Since sharply different proportions of the various castes were of the Christian faith, one might hypothesize that religion accounted for differences in criminal behaviour among castes in the Low Country. Two castes, the Karava and the Goyigama, had a sufficient number of Christians listed in the *Hue and Cry* to calculate significant violence ratios for Christian members of these castes. The results are contradictory. Among Goyigamas Christians had a lower ratio, but among Karavas the Buddhist ratio was lower. Although the absolute number of Salagama Christians was small, this caste, which had the highest violence ratio, was second only to the Karava in its proportion of adherents to Christianity. Religious identity does not explain the caste differentials. Christians had a lower than average ratio because a relatively high proportion of them were Low Countrymen who emigrated to other districts in order to find employment.

There were also geographical differences in violence ratios within the Rural Low Country. Persons who committed crimes in the Southern Province had a higher ratio, 0.56, than inhabitants of the Western Province. This difference was independent of caste variations. The Goyigama ratio within the Rural Western Province (0.45) was considerably lower than that within the Southern Province (0.57). Non-Goyigamas also had higher ratios in the Southern Province. Salagamas had the highest violence ratio within both the Southern and Rural Western Provinces. The high ratio of the Southern Province does not explain caste variations, but neither do caste variations explain geographical differences within the Rural Low Country. Geography and caste in the Rural Low Country were interrelated because many villages were caste-homogeneous.

Neither geographical nor caste variations in the Rural Low Country can be accounted for by other variables; they were instead the product of local traditions of violence. Certain localities near the coast had bad reputations for crime, particularly violent crime and general lawlessness. The nature of this violence was somewhat different from that discussed in the chapter on homicide. It was more controlled, and often committed in conjunction with a property offence. Victims were pushed, jostled and robbed, but rarely stabbed or seriously injured.

Some localities known for this sort of crime were caste-homogeneous villages. The bad reputation of Vahumpuras for criminality stemmed from a few Low Country villages, including

Vanavahala near Colombo, Magalkande in Kalutara district, and
several settlements near Elpitiya in the Southern Province.[72] Caste
solidarity undoubtedly played a role both in the actual criminality
and in the spreading of the criminal reputation of these villages.
When in 1869 a resident of a village near Magalkande wrote to the
Lakrivikirana complaining that Vahumpura villagers were stealing
cattle and committing robberies, the editor added a note which both
illustrated and propagated the reputation of Magalkande villagers as
bold characters.[73] He recounted a story in which Magalkande men
secretly went to a nearby village, killed a cow, and placed it in a
palanquin. They then made their way home, announcing that they
were carrying a smallpox victim. Most persons kept away, but one
man inquired why the smallpox victim had a tail. He was assaulted
and the Magalkande men quickly made their way home. The editor,
partly in jest, warned his correspondent to be careful.

These Vahumpura villages accounted for only a very small
proportion of crime in the Low Country. Other villages, including
several mainly populated by Salagamas, also had reputations for
lawlessness.[74] E. B. Alexander, the Superintendent of Police for the
Southern Province, wrote in 1906 that 'there is a foreign strain in the
Salagamas, and they have been bred in antagonism to their
surroundings. They provide the most dangerous criminals in this
district. They are very secretive, and the headmen are inclined to
form rings and to jealously shelter their own family interests.'[75] It is
possible that the enforced segregation of Salagamas in pre-British
times created a sense of alienation between them and other castes,
and that this was later reflected both in endemic caste conflict and in a
tendency towards violent crime.

There were also several large villages, usually market centres
situated a few kilometres inland, which were known for crime and
violence. Persons travelling to and from the markets were sometimes
robbed; the perpetrators of these crimes were not identified with any
one caste. Beliatta in Hambantota district, Minuvangoda near
Negombo, Madampe in Chilaw district and Horana near Panadura
were places often cited by newspaper correspondents and officials as
generating a disproportionate amount of crime.[76] In the twentieth
century these places continued to have bad reputations, and other
localities at road junctions also grew and became centres of this sort
of crime, often as a result of the growth in motor transport.

The main theme of this chapter has been that mainstream social
groups were heavily involved in crime. Crime was not disproportionately committed by the poor. Adult Sinhalese males of high
caste who lived in the wealthier districts committed their full share

of crime. Certain crimes were associated with specific social groups; in the case of crimes against property opportunity was often the most important variable. Some differences in the general types of crime committed by different social groups have also been uncovered. Analysis of violence ratios, based on the listings in the *Hue and Cry*, shows that migrant workers had a propensity towards property crime, while residents of the Southern Province and other Low Country Sinhalese who were not Goyigamas had a tendency towards violent crime. Because the overall criminality of these groups is not known, these findings do not mean that emigrants necessarily had a high rate of property crime, or that there was a high rate of violent crime in the Low Country. Any attempt to judge precisely the overall criminality of specific social groups runs into the methodological difficulties discussed in the introduction: the lack of complete information and the predetermination of the results by the criteria by which the crime rate is calculated.

NOTES TO CHAPTER 6

1   Jones, 8 – 9.
2   Cox, *Police and Crime in India.*
3   e.g. Copleston, *Buddhism, Primitive and Present in Magadha and in Ceylon,* 479 – 81; Robinson, *Addresses,* II, 93.
4   Nell, *AR CC Southern Circuit 1887,* 19C; Hill, D, 9 Mar 1904, SLNA42/1760.
5   Dep, 170, 184 – 90; Campbell, *AR P 1879,* 28 – 9B; *Native Opinion,* 9 Mar 1900; Hansard, PO, *AR P 1880,* 38B; Saunders to CS, 1 Sept 1879, SLNA6/5704.
6   *Messenger,* 19 & 23 Jan 1883; Dep, 190.
7   Dep, 210; Perera, 7 May 1883, SLNA33/991.
8   Dep, 286.
9   Ibid., 294 – 5.
10   *Times,* 2 July 1912, quoted in Dep, 480.
11   Burrows, *AR Kurunagala 1905,* F3; Hill, D, 21 July 1904, SLNA42/1760; Murray, *AR Kurunagala 1900,* G10; Elliott, *AR Galle 1886,* 65A; Saxton, *AR Matara 1899,* E40; Le Mesurier, D, 17 Feb 1894, SLNA26/152; R Katugampola, *AR Kurunagala 1904,* E10; Meyer, 'The Plantation System', 29 – 30.
12   D, 16 Feb 1905, SLNA38/13.
13   D, 9 Mar 1904, SLNA42/1760; Also see Dep, 196; Gibson, DJ Chilaw, 17 Mar 1888, SLNA6/5974.
14   D, 3 June 1898, SLNA26/156.
15   Dep, 193 – 4; Also see CS to Wace, 12 Dec 1902, E, CO54/683(Pr); Yalman, 79.
16   *Headmen's Commission.*

17   *Bi-Monthly Examiner*, 26 Jan 1869; Campbell, *AR P 1883*, 31C; Hay, *AR CC Western Circuit 1887*, 8C; Knollys, *AR P 1896*, B3; Hill, D, 2 Apr 1900, SLNA30/22; Torrington to Grey, 7 June 1849, CO54/259(76); *Examiner*, 2 July 1895; Dias, *AR CC Southern Circuit 1896*, A11.
18   Campbell, *AR P 1884*, 52C; Dep, 97, 189, 195, 281 – 2.
19   Lewis, DJ, *AR Matara 1899*, E43 & *AR Matara 1900*, E32; Lewis to CS, 7 Aug 1900, E, CO54/665(306).
20   *Messenger*, 28 Aug 1888, 4 Sept 1888; Dep, 269 – 70, 288 – 9, 400, 402; *Examiner*, 14 Mar 1891.
21   Knollys, in *AR Colombo 1900*, B1.
22   Cookson, *AR Matara 1904*, D40; Fisher, *AR CC NWP 1890*, A8; Saxton, *AR Matale 1891*, C14; Ridgeway, *Addresses*, IV, 375 – 6.
23   Dep, 258.
24   D. de Saram, PM, *AR P 1867*, 197; Letters in SLNA6/5785; Dep, 171 – 6.
25   Dowbiggin, *AR P 1921*, B11.
26   Ibid.
27   Ord 28 1871; Campbell to CS, 25 Sept 1874, E, CO54/494(45).
28   Lushington, *AR Puttalam 1886*, 56A & *AR Negombo 1890*, B12; Haughton, *AR Negombo 1885*, 161A; Davidson, *AR Chilaw 1889*, G20; Lewis, D, 13 – 18 Aug 1896, SLNA42/22.
29   Hartshorne, *AR Nuvara Eliya 1872*, 71; King, *AR DJ Badulla 1869*, 192; Gregory to Carnarvon, 20 Jan 1875, CO54/496(12); Dep, 100 – 2.
30   Ord 8 1874; Havelock to Ripon, 8 Mar 1894, CO54/614(75).
31   Dep, 50 – 1, 140 – 2.
32   Ibid., 140 – 3.
33   *SP 26 1895*; Saxton, D, 4 Feb 1893, SLNA34/26. P. Templer, *AR Kandy 1885*, 37A; G. Baumgartner, *AR Nuvara Eliya 1885*, 42A; Wace, *AR Kandy 1900*, C8 – 9; Alexander, *AR Matale 1901*, C33; Dep, 336 – 7.
34   Dowbiggin, *AR P 1916*, B6 & *AR P 1926*, B15.
35   Dowbiggin, *AR P 1924*, B11.
36   Longden to Hicks-Beach, 18 Oct 1879, CO54/521(409); King, *AR Badulla 1879*, 57 – 9; Ferdinands, *AR QA 1879*, 4B; Campbell, *AR P 1879*, 27B & *AR P 1880*, 28B; Tranchell, *AR P 1881*, 21C; Le Mesurier, *AR Nuvara Eliya 1881*, 65A; G. Baumgartner, *AR Nuvara Eliya 1882*, 72A & *AR Nuvara Eliya 1883*, 40A.
37   Dowbiggin, *AR P 1922*, B15; Ward to Labouchere, 5 Mar 1857, CO54/328(39); Aluwihare, *AR P 1947*, A28; Chief Justice to Dowbiggin, *AR P 1921*, B16 – 17; Dowbiggin, *AR P 1923*, B10 – 11; Dowbiggin, *AR P 1928*, B15; Gottelier, *AR P 1929*, A14; Bacon, *AR P 1944*, A19.
38   *AR P 1886*, 47C; *AR P 1884*, 61C; *AR P 1888*, 38C; Dep, 24, 258; Vaughan, *AR Anuradhapura 1907*, G2; Dowbiggin, *AR P 1922*, B15.
39   Dep, 255.
40   Pippet, 209 – 16. Another escaped criminal, Meepitiya Ranghamy, led a gang in the area between Kurunagala and Matale in 1885. Dep, 256.
41   *Lakrivikirana*, 18 June 1869.
42   Sinhala newspapers published numerous letters complaining about gambling and illegal drinking. Correspondents often linked these activities with other crimes. Also see Perera, *suduhatanaya*; Perera, *alutkade usaviya asala siduvuna maranaya gana duliyanu kathava saha juvan prerage nadutinduva*.
43   Meyer, 'Depression et malaria', 193; Dowbiggin, *AR P 1928*, B12 – 13.
44   Lawson to Robinson, 25 July 1870, SLNA6/3442; D. de Saram, *AR DJ Kurunagala 1871*, 319; Campbell, *AR P 1884*, 53C; *Bi-Monthly Examiner*, 21 Apr 1869.

45 Massie, *AR Matale 1872*, 62; Dawson, *AR Kagalla 1874*, 28; C. Liesching, *AR DJ Negombo 1874*, 51; Campbell, *AR P 1883*, 31C; Haughton, *AR Negombo 1886*, 142A; Byrde, *AR Negombo 1887*, 59A; P. Templer, *AR Kandy 1892*, C5; Crawford, *AR Kurunagala 1900*, G9; Ievers, *AR Galle 1893*, E6; Lushington, *AR Negombo 1890*, B12.

46 Lawson to Robinson, 25 July 1870, SLNA6/3442; Brodhurst, *AR Galle 1903*, E16; *Messenger*, 7 Nov 1873, 17 Aug 1875, 21 Aug 1903; *Times*, 23 Sept 1875; Dep, 45, 103, 198, 317, 358, 393, 398, 450 – 3; Dowbiggin, *AR P 1930*, A14.

47 Dep, 110 – 11.

48 Bremer, *Memoirs of a Ceylon Planter's Travels, 1851 to 1921*, 91.

49 Case Register, Oct 1871 – Jan 1872, SLNA39/172.

50 Maitland to Windham, 28 Feb 1807, CO54/25.

51 Barnett, 21 Dec 1830, CO416/18.

52 Stark, 94.

53 Samaraweera, 'Masters and Servants', 153.

54 Tambyah, *The Planters' Legal Manual*.

55 *SP 23 1884*, 9.

56 Samaraweera, 'Masters and Servants', 144 – 5.

57 Bowes, *AR Puttalam 1905*, F19, F23.

58 When the normal port of call shifted from Galle to Colombo in the 1880s, so did the place of imprisonment for most European prisoners.

59 Walker, *CH 1900 – 1*, 32; *Times*, 1 Oct 1901.

60 Layard, *CH 1901 – 2*, 18.

61 *AR SG 1898*, A7; *AR SG 1899*, A7; *AR SG 1900*, 1.

62 Roberts, *Caste Conflict*, 303.

63 Fowler, D, 3 Oct 1889 & 18 Nov 1889, SLNA35/7; Brodhurst, D, 8 June 1897 & 11 Dec 1897, SLNA35/11; Crawford, *AR Kalutara 1888*, 63A & D, 18 Mar 1889, SLNA35/7; Fox, D, 9 Aug 1900, SLNA35/14; Dowbiggin, *AR P 1928*, B19; Brayne, *AR Kalutara 1918*, A21. The criminal reputation of the Demala Gattara has extended into the post-independence period. See Wood, 49; Ryan, 136.

64 Ryan, 182 – 3; Parker, *Village Folk Tales of Ceylon*, I, 30.

65 Dowbiggin, *AR P 1927*, B17; Lewis, *AR Kandy 1906*, B8.

66 Campbell, *AR P 1883*, 27C; Lee, *Census of Ceylon 1891*, I, 50.

67 Alexander, *AR Matale 1902*, C11; Hartshorne, *AR Nuvara Eliya 1872*, 71; Le Mesurier, *AR Nuvara Eliya 1881*, 65A; G. Baumgartner, *AR Nuvara Eliya 1882*, 72A; Pennycuick, *AR DJ Badulla 1871*, 325; Fisher, *AR Badulla 1893*, I3; Ievers, *AR Anuradhapura 1886*, 15A; Burrows, *AR Kurunagala 1905*, F3; Dawson, *AR Kagalla 1874*, 28; Hill, *AR Kagalla 1900*, J12; Wace, *AR Ratnapura 1888*, 26A; Reid, *AR DJ Ratnapura 1872*, 573; King, *AR Kurunagala 1897*, G6.

68 See note 8, Introduction.

69 Meyer, 'Depression et malaria', 191.

70 Zehr, 120 – 2.

71 The violence ratios of the Sinhalese by region were: Rural Low Country, 0.53; Interior, 0.33; Intermediate, 0.48; Colombo city, 0.29.

72 Jayetileke, *AR DJ Kalutara 1872*, 561; *Bi-Monthly Examiner*, 28 June 1868; Campbell to CS, 27 July 1889, SLNA6/8527; M. Perera, petition, 13 Aug 1890, SLNA33/2758; Brodhurst, D, 19 Dec 1891, SLNA35/8; *Messenger*, 28 Mar 1883; Brayne, *AR Kalutara 1918*, A21; Dowbiggin, *AR P 1922*, B15.

73 *Lakrivikirana*, 30 Aug 1867.

74   Dowbiggin, *AR P 1928*, B19 & *AR P 1927*, B17; Godfrey, PO, *AR Galle 1907*, D5; Crawford, D, 14 Feb 1889 & 17 June 1889, SLNA35/7; Brayne, *AR Kalutara 1918*, A21.
75   Alexander, PO, *AR Galle 1906*, D11.
76   Lawson to Robinson, 25 July 1870, SLNA6/3442; Dep, 16, 43, 96, 196; Fox, D, 10 Sept 1900, SLNA35/14 & *AR Kalutara 1901*, B50; Layard, *AR Colombo 1875*, 112; Gibson, DJ, 17 Mar 1888, SLNA6/5974; Murray, *AR Hambantota, 1884*, 86A & *AR Hambantota 1888*, 161A; F. Campbell, *AR DJ Tangalla 1874*, 57; Horsburgh, *AR Hambantota 1898*, E12; Forrest, PO, *AR Hambantota 1906*, D48; Dowbiggin, *AR P 1914*, B9 & *AR P 1916*, B7 & *AR P 1918*, B9; *Messenger*, 7 Nov 1883.

CHAPTER 7

CONCLUSIONS

This study set out to examine several themes in the history of crime in colonial Sri Lanka, including the effectiveness of the administration of law and order, the relationship between the expansion of the market economy and crime, and the relative importance of unique cultural factors and broad forces of social change. The conclusion summarizes my main findings and attempts to draw some links between these major themes.

The administration of law and order generated little moral authority because colonial court procedure had few roots in local conceptions of justice. Cases were decided only upon evidence presented in accordance with strictly-defined regulations. According to indigenous values, these restrictions on the type of evidence to be considered were meaningless, and cases should have been decided on the basis of all known information, including the personal knowledge of the judge. From the Sri Lankan point of view British judicial procedure needlessly hampered justice. Sinhalese law was unwritten and popular conceptions of morality emphasized the specific situation in which the alleged offence had taken place and the social positions of the persons involved.

In the early nineteenth century British officials hoped that the superiority of the colonial system would become evident to Sri Lankans, and that popular attitudes would change. There was however little in the actual workings of the courts which propagated the moral assumptions which had led to their establishment. This failure was partly because the middle and lower levels of the colonial bureaucracy were staffed with persons who had little sympathy with the principle of rule by law which court procedure was meant to reflect. The mostly British civil servants were paid large salaries which guarded against corruption. Lower-level officials, who were usually Sri Lankans, were paid low salaries and often sought to augment them unofficially. Most headmen received no salary at all. They were expected by both their supporters and opponents to use their authority to further their own side in factional disputes. Many policemen also used their position to obtain personal material gain. Court interpreters and clerks were often similarly motivated. This situation saved the colonial government money and reinforced the British sense of moral superiority which served as a justification for colonial rule. It also ensured that the principle of rule by law which the judicial system was meant to enforce could not put down deep social roots.

The courts were not however ignored; there was a high level of both civil and criminal litigation. Instead of acting as a modernizing or Westernizing agent of ideological change, judicial institutions were adapted by litigants so that they functioned in a way more compatible with indigenous culture. The courts were treated as a legitimate but morally neutral and manipulable means of dispute settlement. The ritualistic approach to the demons and spirits of the lower end of the supernatural hierarchy of popular Buddhism provided a cultural precedent for this amoral power. There was no general opinion that lying in court was necessarily wrong. One did not in court make statements which were true or false but ones which were either effective or ineffective. Any moral judgement on court testimony was made on the basis of whether or not the defendant deserved punishment; the truthfulness of the particular charge or testimony was irrelevant.

In societies where an indigenous class or other social group has primary responsibility for the implementation of the administration of law and order, that class is likely to acknowledge the moral legitimacy of the legal system, whatever its success in propagating this moral legitimacy among other sectors of society. In Sri Lanka the British held most judicial positions, and the judicial procedure and criminal law were derived from Britain. The small number of Sri Lankan judges and magistrates, most of whom were far more comfortable speaking English than Sinhala or Tamil, did not alter the significance of this fact. Even in the twentieth century, when the number of Sri Lankan officials increased sharply, social differences between highly-Westernized judges and most litigants remained wide. Moreover, vested interests, including lawyers, petition-drawers, court officials and knowledgeable laymen, continued to act in ways which prevented significant change.

This failure of the administration of law and order to generate moral authority even among relatively better-off sectors of society was an important reason for high-status crime. In contrast to the findings on crime in many other countries, serious crime was largely the province of mainstream social groups.[1] Those on the margins of society did not appear in the official records as perpetrators of crime proportionately more often than their numbers warranted. It is generally believed that administrative systems, when producing data on criminals, discriminate against marginal groups. There is no reason to believe that this was not the case in Sri Lanka, where wealth and sophistication were advantageous for all dealings with officialdom. Persons of relatively high social and economic status were often thought to prosper from crimes for which they were rarely charged or convicted. Cattle stealing, the most important crime in many rural areas, was organized by Goyigama magnates who were very rarely touched by the law. Around the end of the nineteenth century wealthy Low Countrymen organized widespread land grabbing in order to gain title to land suitable for plantations.

There is no direct evidence as to the wealth of persons treated as criminal by the administration, but data are available for caste, ethnicity, sex, age and literacy. Although high economic and social status were not necessarily identical, each of these variables measures a different aspect of social position, and their values are amenable to ranking, particularly at the lower end. The more deprived social groups were not over-represented. The low-caste minority among the Sinhalese appeared proportionately less often in the *Hue and Cry* than did the high-caste majority. The Indian Tamils, an economically-depressed minority ethnic group, did not pose a serious crime problem for the authorities. Women accounted for less than one per cent of convicted prisoners, a much smaller proportion than in nineteenth-century Britain. Mature men in their thirties had a significantly higher rate of homicide than men in their twenties. Perhaps most remarkable of all, censuses consistently showed that the literacy rate of prisoners was close to that of men in general.

In parts of India specific social groups, many with traditionally high social status, were displaced by political and administrative changes accompanying British rule and consequently turned to crime in an attempt to maintain their social position.[2] There was in Sri Lanka no comparable social group which had been ousted from power by the advent of the British. In Sri Lanka crime was often one aspect of the commercial and in some cases political activities of powerful upwardly-mobile social groups, not a reaction to deprivation or a defensive attempt to maintain a declining economic and social position.

There is no evidence for either a general upward or downward trend in the incidence of crime in Sri Lanka under the British. The value of stolen property undoubtedly increased as a greater proportion of the island's wealth shifted from immovable property, such as land, to movable property which was easier to steal. But if one is concerned with the level of property crime as a proportion of goods and objects which could be stolen, the problem of measurement is more difficult. There is not enough evidence to compare the extent of theft in urban and semi-urban settings with that in rural areas. Thefts by domestic servants or casual labourers were more often reported than thefts from village gardens. The analysis of cattle stealing suggests that opportunity and profitability were important determinants of the level of crime against property. Many property crimes, including those which tended to remain unpunished, were rational actions aimed at improving the material lot of the offender. Short-term increases at times of depression may be seen as a response to the decreased value of other forms of labour, which resulted in an increase in the relative benefit of crime. Over the longer run crimes against property became more complex and sophisticated in parallel with changes in the wider society. This is scarcely an original conclusion, but it is different from stating that there was an increase in crime against property; whether or not there was an increase depends on whether one takes into account the relationship between the value of the economic gain and the value of the property which it was feasible to steal.[3]

Homicide figures provide a better statistical base for long-term changes in violent crime than is available for property offences. Homicide is not necessarily an accurate reflection of violence in general, but the consistency of the homicide rate is strong evidence that there was not a sharp change in patterns of unplanned violence. Neither does it seem that there was a radical change in the level of premeditated violence. In some villages near the south-western coast there was a higher than average rate of property crime accompanied by violence, but the local traditions of violence in many of these villages were not products of economic growth. They had existed since at least the beginning of British rule, and were perhaps a result of the uneasy position of the maritime castes, especially the Salagamas, who had never been fully integrated into the Sinhalese caste system. On the other hand, some market towns which were notorious for minor robberies were products of the expansion of the market economy. An examination of changes in the patterns of the three crimes which have been considered in detail serves to illustrate more precisely the relationship between crime and social change.

Organized cattle stealing functioned in much the same way as other commercial activities. It was dependent on market forces enabling it to be carried out at a profit. For most of the nineteenth century conditions were favourable, and the crime thrived. In the 1890s the expansion of coconut plantations in Kurunagala district, formerly the hotbed of the crime, changed land use patterns, upset the economic equilibrium upon which cattle stealing rested, and resulted in a decline in the crime in that district. On the other hand, in the interior of the Low Country, where the expansion of plantations came later and was more uneven, cattle stealing survived as an organized business for another fifteen years, when it succumbed to similar changes in the rural economy. Administrative attempts to stop the crime forced changes in the methods employed by thieves, but in the nineteenth century the overall effectiveness of these measures was marginal, and even in the twentieth century economic influences were more important. Cattle theft gradually declined to the point where it was no longer perceived by the authorities as a serious problem in the 1920s, although systematic stealing did not die out everywhere. This trend was reversed in 1930, with the onset of the world depression, which caused much hardship in Sri Lanka. The number of cases reported doubled; many thefts were for the sake of meat. When in 1936 the government lifted all voucher and branding regulations, the result was another doubling in the number of reported cases of cattle theft. The contraction of the market economy and the relaxation of administrative vigilance led to the revival of organized networks in the same districts where they had prevailed in the nineteenth century.

The relationship between riot and social change was more complex. Some riots were backward-looking protests against specific economic changes which were usually associated with the expansion of the market economy. The most significant of these were the agrarian unrest of 1848 and the grain riots of 1866. The former was essentially a protest against new taxes, while the latter was aimed against traders who were charging high prices because of poor Indian rice crops. Other local riots included protests against changes such as the levying of local taxes, technological innovations in fishing, the adoption by low castes of high-caste customs, and the loss of women to other communities. The parochial nature and weakness of these protests reflects the fact that the expansion of the market economy caused relatively little hardship in Sri Lanka. There was a thriving, indigenous capitalist class, and peasants who lost their rights in land were able to find employment elsewhere. In the early twentieth century Colombo workers, with the support of a small section of the élite, began to express economic grievances more systematically. Labour strife in the 1920s culminated in the anti-police riot of 1929, but strikes and other protests by Colombo labourers declined in the face of the unemployment of the depression of the 1930s.

The first religious riot took place in 1883 at Kotahena, and clashes between Buddhists and Roman Catholics were common for the next twenty years. These riots were directly linked with the Buddhist revival which began in the Low Country in the 1860s. The Buddhist ideology which helped underpin them was forward-looking and aggressive, and the riots show that revivalist ideas had deep social roots along the littoral.[4] Though rioters were often supported by the Buddhist establishment, Buddhist leaders were not always in control. These riots were not protests against but a product of economic change. The social groups which fuelled the riots were well-integrated in the market economy. Along the coast there was little relationship between traditional caste status and wealth, and Buddhism provided an ideology through which persons of traditionally lower social status, including many Vahumpuras in the Western Province and Salagamas in the Southern Province, could form alliances with persons of traditionally high status. In the process, non-Buddhists were newly defined as negative reference groups. The first riots were between Buddhists and Roman Catholics because the Catholic community was spatially and socially the closest non-Buddhist group in those areas where revivalist ideology first gained ground.[5] The later riots at Kalutara and Anuradhapura demonstrated the anti-colonial potential of Buddhist ideology. The widespread 1915 riots by Sinhalese against Moors were reminiscent of the grain riots of 1866 and the Buddhist-Catholic affrays of the 1880s, especially the latter. Economic frustrations were combined with powerful religious feelings, and the result was the most widespread disturbances since the Kandyan revolt of 1817 – 18. The geographical extent of the riots, which began in Kandy, showed that Buddhist revivalist ideology spread beyond the littoral in the early twentieth century. The British held the Buddhist élite responsible for these riots, and one result was a shift in the interests of the élite from religious to constitutional issues. When political power was devolved at the national level in the 1930s, tensions developed between Sinhalese and Tamils. The stakes were much higher than they had been in the Buddhist-Catholic clashes of the 1880s, and the ensuing violence of 1958, 1977 and the 1980s was incomparably fiercer.

In contrast to patterns of cattle stealing and riot, there was little change in the frequency or nature of homicide. Research carried out in the 1950s and 1960s shows not only that there was no general increase in the overall rate, but that other distinctive features of nineteenth-century homicide remained valid: the unusually high average age of offenders, the ethnic and sexual characteristics of offenders and victims, the geographical distribution, the weapons employed, and the rarity of premeditation. British officials and élite Sri Lankans thought that the rate of homicide was extraordinarily high, but this belief, the result of comparison with Victorian Britain and to a lesser extent with India, was not entirely correct. The homicide rates of the United States and parts of Europe were higher than that of Sri Lanka. Homicides were largely unplanned and irrational acts, the relatively high level of which stemmed from a high degree of sensitivity to personal status. This aspect of social relations was not greatly affected by economic, ecological or technological change. It was perhaps the result of a strongly hierarchical world view which was not convincingly justified by religion, and which was rendered ambiguous by the structure of the Sinhalese caste system, whereby the majority of persons belonged to the highest caste. Land disputes, quarrels over women and verbal abuse did not *cause* homicide; the vast majority of such incidents did not lead to a death. Instead they provided the settings in which normally repressed aggression, built up in a socially competitive society, exploded into violence.

In the nineteenth century the failure of the administration of law and order to generate much moral authority did not lead to general lawlessness. By adapting court procedure Sri Lankans manipulated the power of the state, but this manipulation of the courts was not always used for what were regarded as immoral ends. The social characteristics of convicted prisoners suggests that, for all their faults when evaluated on the criteria upon which they had been established, the courts may have administered justice reasonably well. In the late nineteenth and early twentieth centuries judicial reforms improved the efficiency of the courts, and the rate of litigation fell. None the less, the courts continued to be perceived as largely amoral institutions throughout the colonial period.

The primary aim of this book has been to place crime as accurately as possible in its social context. It has been shown that the courts did not in the eyes of the people represent 'justice', but that they were none the less able to function as an important dispute-solving mechanism. Sri Lankans adapted themselves to the administrative changes of colonialism and they were adapted

to economic change as well provided the colonial state did not fix
the rules so as to deny them the opportunity. It was from
economic growth, essential to the success of the colony, that new
and successful social groups emerged which were in the long run
better able to mobilize mass support than were the colonial rulers.
The study of crime shows the extent of the ideological gaps
between the rulers and the people, and the varying extent of the
impact of colonialism on different aspects of social life.

NOTES TO CHAPTER 7

1   There is some evidence that the social profile of convicted criminals was
     broad-based in parts of India, though not enough research has been done to
     come to any clear conclusions. Mukherjee, 'Crime and Criminals in
     Nineteenth Century Bengal (1861 – 1904)'; Trivedi. It has also been argued
     that the British middle class had at least an average crime rate at the end of the
     nineteenth century. Sindall, 'Middle-Class Crime in Nineteenth-Century
     England'. A similar argument is made for late twentieth-century Britain in
     Box, *Power, Crime and Mystification*.
2   Arnold, 'Dacoity and Rural Crime'; Trivedi.
3   A similar point is made in Rao, *Dynamics of Crime*, 11 – 13. In refuting the
     link between 'development' and the growth of certain forms of crime, he
     distinguishes between 'techniques of criminal operations' and 'sociological
     factors in criminality'.
4   Comparisons may be made with the religious mobilization which took place
     in many parts of India around this time. See e.g., Freitag, 'Sacred Symbol as
     Mobilizing Ideology'; Haynes, 'Changing Patterns of Dispute Settlement in
     Eastern Rajputana During the Late Nineteenth Century'; Yang, 'Sacred
     Symbol and Sacred Space in Rural India.'
5   For the shifts in Catholic identity and in late nineteenth and twentieth
     centuries, see Stirrat, 'The Riots and the Roman Catholic Church in
     Historical Perspective'.

ANALYSIS OF THE *HUE AND CRY* DATA

The *Hue and Cry* was a twice-weekly and trilingual bulletin published by the police. It contained detailed descriptions of persons who were not to be found after a warrant for their arrest had been issued by a magistrate. Two examples are given below:

LIYANAPEDIGE UKKUWA; charged with cattle stealing at Boyagoda on November 14, 1900; is a Sinhalese of the Paduwa caste; religion, Buddhist; occupation, cultivator and cooly; age, 35 years; height, 5 ft. 6 in.; make, thin; complexion, fair; nose, prominent; lower lip large; teeth, large and projecting; eyes, dark; hair, dark and tied in a knot; wears billy-goat beard; birthplace, Arandara, Kegalla; general residence, Arandara and Boyagoda; haunts plumbago pits in Three Korales; wife residing at Boyagoda; brothers, Rattarana and Hetuwa residing at Boyagoda; is well known to the Vidane Duraya of Arandara, Arachchi of Nadeniya, and the Arachchi of Bambaragama. The Police Magistrate of Kegalla has issued warrant No. 22,060 for his arrest. (*Hue and Cry*, 31 Dec 1900).

DON DAVITH ABEYANAYAKA *alias* DAVITH SINNO; charged with robbery and assault at Bentota on November 30, 1900; is a Sinhalese of the Goyigama caste; religion, Buddhist; occupation, cooly; age, 40 years; height, 5 ft.; make, stout; complexion, dark brown; nose, large; mouth, wide; one of the front teeth is broken; eyes, hazel; hair, curly, short and tied in a knot; wears slight beard; has spots on face; face, flat; head, large; birthplace and general residence, Bentota, Galle District; haunts Kalutara, Paiyagala, Ratnapura, Mapalagama, and Pasdun Korale; keeps a mistress named Mahagoda Vithanage Subaliya; brother, Abraham Abeyanayaka, teacher, Gintota Buddhist school; sisters, Abeyanayaka Nonnohamy and Alice Abeyanayaka; is well known to the Police Officer of Bentota, No. 1. The Police Magistrate of Balapitiya has issued warrant No. 21,149 for his arrest. (*Hue and Cry*, 4 Jan 1901).

Data for the following eleven variables were gathered for all 4,505 persons listed from 1896 through 1905. This information was processed by a computer program which provided frequency distributions and selected cross-tabulations.

1   Year crime was committed. (MC = 73)
2   Month crime was committed. (MC = 129)
3   Type of crime: (a) theft or burglary, (b) cattle stealing, (c) criminal breach of trust or fraud, (d) forgery or counterfeiting, (e) theft with violence or robbery, (f) assault short of causing death, (g) homicide, (h) other. (MC = 0)
4   Sex. (MC = 0)
5   Ethnic group. (MC = 2)
6   Caste, if Sinhalese. (MC = 282)
7   Religion. (MC = 248)
8   Occupation: (a) cultivator, (b) labourer, artisan or carter, (c) trader, (d) fisherman, (e) domestic servant, (f) white-collar worker, (g) gambler, loafer or criminal, (h) other. (MC = 485)
9   Age. (MC = 132)
10 Birthplace: by revenue district, with the following exceptions, (a) Colombo city differentiated from Colombo district, (b) Kalutara district divided into Panadura and Kalutara Totamunes, Rayigam Korale, Pasdun Korale East, and Pasdun Korale West, (c) if outside Sinhala Sri Lanka divided into other Sri Lanka, India, and other. (MC = 288)
11 Place crime committed: recorded as for birthplace. (MC = 1)

ANALYSIS OF THE SUMMARIES
OF HOMICIDE CASES

Brief descriptions of most homicide cases were printed in the *Administration Reports* for two blocks of years, from 1883 – 9 and 1900 – 4. Within each block the cases were presented in similar formats, but there were some variations in the way the information was compiled. The data for 1883 – 9 were compiled under the supervision of G. W. R. Campbell, the Inspector-General of Police. Each report included an account of the motive for the crime, as perceived by the police, and listed the name, ethnic group, occupation, and age of both the accused and the deceased. The reports printed for 1900 – 4 were not quite as consistent and detailed. During this period direct control of the police was not exercised by the Inspector-General but by government agents, so these accounts were compiled by different persons. In general the reports of the later period contained much information on the circumstances surrounding homicides, but did not include the data concerning the social background of those involved. Therefore, although for many purposes the two blocks of data have been combined and used as a sample for homicide during the mature colonial period, for questions involving ethnicity, occupation, and age a restricted sample of cases from the earlier block is used. There are 1,482 cases in the general sample, and 730 cases in the restricted sample.

Neither sample is statistically random, but there is no reason to believe that the years they cover are not representative for the general period of mature colonialism. The sample years contained no special disruptive economic or political circumstances. The provincial incidence of homicide was similar in the sample years to that of the period 1879 – 1905 (Table A.1.).

All 1,482 cases of homicide which occurred during the sample years were coded according to sixteen variables and processed by a computer program which provided frequency distributions and selected cross-tabulations. Only one value was assigned per variable per case of homicide. In a case with two or more accused persons, the social characteristics of the person who struck the fatal blow or who in some other way appeared to be the principal accused were recorded.

Table A.1. Annual Average Number of Homicides in Sample and Non-Sample Years.

	Restricted Sample	Full Sample	1879 – 1905
Central Province	25	23	23
North-Western Province	15	18	18
Southern Province	18	21	20
Western Province	50	55	52

Some of the material was inaccurate. Many persons did not know their age, and it is likely that many of the ages given were estimates based on appearances. Nevertheless, there is no reason to believe that there was any systematic bias when the police recorded age or other variables. Another problem, particularly relevant to the variable which recorded the proximate cause of the crime, lay in interpreting limited information. The lack of detailed accounts in the face of complex human motivations created many ambiguous cases. Probability, not certainty, governed the classification of many variables.

Data were gathered on the following variables:

1 Year. (MC = 0, N = 1,482)
2 Month. (MC = 721, N = 761)
3 Revenue district. A distinction was made between Colombo city and Colombo district. (MC = 25, N = 1,457)
4 Proximate cause: (a) by a thief surprised in the act, (b) against a thief surprised in the act, (c) part of a robbery, (d) against a thief after the fact, (e) by a thief after the fact, (f) dispute among rice-field shareholders, (g) dispute among garden shareholders, (h) dispute over land boundary, (i) unspecified land dispute, (j) dispute over debt, (k) dispute over other property, (l) for economic gain, (m) damage to property, (n) dispute over woman, (o) sudden quarrel, (p) unspecified feud, (q) infanticide, (r) insanity, (s) accident, (t) other. (MC = 299, N = 1,183)
5 Sex of accused. (MC = 136, N = 1,346)
6 Sex of victim. (MC = 148, N = 1,334)
7 Weapon: (a) sharp instrument, (b) blunt instrument, (c) firearm, (d) strangulation, (e) poison, (f) no weapon (blows), (g) other. (MC = 221, N = 1,261)
8 Ethnicity of accused. (MC = 63, N = 667)

 9 Ethnicity of victim. (MC = 44, N = 686)
10 Age of accused. (MC = 244, N = 486)
11 Age of victim. (MC = 101, N = 629)
12 Occupation of accused: (a) cultivator, (b) labourer, (c) artisan or service, (d) trader, (e) watcher, (f) white-collar worker, (g) domestic servant, (h) contractor/capitalist, (i) fisherman, (j) headman, (k) no apparent occupation, (l) foreman, (m) monk, (n) other. (MC = 240, N = 490)
13 Occupation of victim: as for occupation of accused above. (MC = 188, N = 542)
14 Were there kinship links known?: (a) spouse, (b) other relation, (c) no. (MC = 137, N = 1,345)
15 Number of persons involved in committing homicide. (MC = 182, N = 1,300)
16 Judicial outcome of case. (MC = 306, N = 1,176)

THE SINHALESE CASTES

Badahala	potters
Batgam (Padu)	perhaps palanquin bearers
Berava	tom-tom beaters
Demala Gattara	outcaste, occupation uncertain
Durava (Chandos)	toddy tappers of the coconut palm
Gahala Berava	outcastes
Goyigama (Vellala)	cultivators
Hannali	tailors
Hena (Rada, Dhoby)	washers
Hinna	washers to the Salagama
Hunu	chunam or lime burners
Karava	fishermen, carpenters
Kinnara	mat weavers
Navandanna (Achari)	artisans, often blacksmiths or metal-workers
Oli	dancers
Pali	washers to the low castes
Panikki	barbers
Panna Durayi	grass cutters
Rodi	beggars
Salagama (Chalia)	cinnamon peelers
Vahumpura (Hakero)	jaggery makers
Velli Durayi	keepers of the sacred bo-tree

Source: Ryan, *Caste in Modern Ceylon.*

REFERENCES

OFFICIAL DOCUMENTS, MANUSCRIPT

At the Public Record Ofice, Kew, London

CO54	Correspondence between the Governor of Ceylon and the Secretary of State for the Colonies.
CO58	Ordinances of Ceylon.
CO416	Records of the Commission of Eastern Enquiry.

At the Department of National Archives, Colombo

SLNA6	Correspondence to and from the Colonial Secretary.
SNLA7	Correspondence from the Colonial Secretary.
SLNA26	Records of the Matara *kachcheri.*
SLNA33	Records of the Colombo and Negombo *kachcheris.*
SLNA34	Records of the Matale *kachcheri.*
SLNA35	Records of the Kalutara *kachcheri.*
SLNA38	Records of the Kurunagala *kachcheri.*
SLNA39	Records of the Chilaw Police Court.
SLNA41	Records of the Anuradhapura *kachcheri.*
SLNA42	Records of the Puttalam and Chilaw *kachcheris.*
SLNA43	Records of the Galle *kachcheri.*
SLNA45	Records of the Ratnapura *kachcheri.*
SLNA59	Files on Special Subjects held by the Colonial Secretary.

At the Department of National Archives, Kandy

SLNA30	Records of the Kagalla *kachcheri.*

OFFICIAL DOCUMENTS, PRINTED

Addresses Delivered in the Legislative Council of Ceylon by the Governors of the Colony: Together with the Replies of Council, 4 vols. (1876 – 1905).
Administration Reports.
Blue Books.
Census of Ceylon.
Ceylon Civil List.
Ceylon Hansard.
Government Gazette.

Headmen's Commission: Notes of Evidence (1922).
Hue and Cry.
Sessional Papers of the Legislative Council.

OTHER DOCUMENTS, MANUSCRIPT

At the School of Oriental and African Studies, London

Archives of the Methodist Missionary Society, Correspondence from South Ceylon mission.

At the archives of the Oblates of Mary Immaculate, Rome

Personal Files of missionaries.

At the archives of the Sacred Congregation for the Propagation of the Faith, Rome

Correspondence from South Asia to Rome: Scritture riferite nei Congressi, Indie Orientali (1880 – 92) & NS, rubrica 128 (1893 – 1901).

BOOKS, ARTICLES, PAMPHLETS AND THESES

Ali, Ameer. 'The 1915 Racial Riots in Ceylon (Sri Lanka): A Reappraisal of its Causes', *South Asia*, n.s., IV, 1981, 1 – 20.

Archer, Dane & Gartner, Rosemary. *Violence and Crime in Cross-National Perspective* (New Haven 1984).

Arnold, David, 'Dacoity and Rural Crime in Madras, 1860 – 1940', *Journal of Peasant Studies*, VI, 1979, 140 – 67.

—— 'Looting, Grain Riots and Government Policy in South India 1918', *Past and Present*, 84, 1979, 111 – 45.

Bandarage, Asoka P. S. *Colonialism in Sri Lanka: The Political Economy of the Kandyan Highlands, 1833 – 1886* (Berlin 1983).

Bayly, C. A. *Rulers, Townsmen, and Bazaars: North Indian Society in the Age of British Expansion, 1770 – 1870* (Cambridge 1983).

Blackton, Charles S. 'The Action Phase of the 1915 Riots', *Journal of Asian Studies*, XXIX, 1970, 235 – 54.

Bloch, Herbert A. 'Research Report on Homicides, Attempted Homicides, and Crimes of Violence: Prepared for the Police Service of the Government of Ceylon', mimeo, (Colombo [1960]).

Boudens, Robrecht. *Catholic Missionaries in a British Colony: Successes and Failures in Ceylon 1796 – 1893* (Immensee 1979).

—— 'The Two Oblate Dioceses in Ceylon from 1893 to 1903', *Neue Zeitschrift für Missionswissenschaft*, XXXIX, 1983, 42 – 54.

Box, Steven. *Power, Crime, and Mystification* (London 1983).

Brantingham, Paul & Brantingham, Patricia. *Patterns in Crime* (New York 1984).

Bremer, Mounsteven. *Memoirs of a Ceylon Planter's Travels 1851 to 1921* (London 1930).

Cameron, Iain A. *Crime and Repression in the Auvergne and the Guyenne 1720 – 1790* (Cambridge 1981).

Capper, John. 'A Statistical Enquiry into the State of Crime in Ceylon', *Journal of the Royal Asiatic Society Ceylon Branch*, III, 1858 – 9, 293 – 307.
——— *Old Ceylon: Sketches of Ceylon Life in the Olden Time* (London 1878).
Carstairs, Robert. *Human Nature in Rural India* (Edinburgh & London 1895).
——— *The Little World of an Indian District Officer* (London 1912).
Chinniah, A. 'The Branding of Cattle', *Tropical Agriculturalist*, XX, 1900, 287 – 8 & 361 – 2.
Clarence, L. B. 'The Administration of Justice in Ceylon', *Law Quarterly Review*, II, 1886, 38 – 51.
Clinard, Marshall B. & Abbott, Daniel J. *Crime in Developing Countries: A Comparative Perspective* (New York 1973).
Cohn, Bernard. 'Anthropological Notes on Disputes and Law in India', *American Anthropologist*, LXVII, 1965, 82 – 122.
——— 'Some Notes on Law and Social Change in North India', Paul Bohannan, (ed.), *Law and Warfare: Studies in the Anthropology of Conflict* (New York 1967), 139 – 60.
Cooray, L. J. M. 'The Administration of Justice in Swabasha in Sri Lanka', *Sri Lanka Journal of the Social Sciences*, I, 1978, 95 – 117.
Copleston, Reginald S. *Buddhism, Primitive and Present in Magadha and in Ceylon* (London 1892).
Corner, Caroline. *Ceylon: The Paradise of Adam. The Record of Seven Years' Residence in the Island* (London 1908).
Cox, Sir Edmund C. *Police and Crime in India* (New Delhi 1976) [1910].
d'Alwis, James, 'Brand Marks on Cattle', *Journal of the Royal Asiatic Society Ceylon Branch*, V, 1874, 60 – 3.
——— *Memoirs and Desultory Writings*, A. C. Seneviratne, (ed.), (Colombo 1939) [1878].
Denham, E. B. *Ceylon at the Census of 1911, being the Review of the Results of the Census of 1911* (Colombo 1912).
Dep, A. C. *A History of the Ceylon Police (1866 – 1913)*, II, (Colombo 1969).
de Silva, Colvin R. *Ceylon Under the British Occupation 1795 – 1833: Its Political, Administrative and Economic Development*, 2 vols., (Colombo 1953, 1962) [1941, 1942].
de Silva, K. M. *A History of Sri Lanka* (London & Berkeley 1981).
——— (ed.) *Letters on Ceylon 1846 – 1850: The Administration of Viscount Torrington and the 'Rebellion' of 1848* (Kandy & Colombo 1965).
de Silva, W. A. *An English Translation of a Pamphlet on the Treatment of Cattle* (Colombo 1890).
——— 'Sinhalese Black Magic', *Ceylon National Review*, II, 1908, 201 – 7.
de Witt, A. L. & Weeresinghe, G. E. G., (ed.), *The Atygalle Murder Case* (Colombo 1908).
Digby, William. 'A Home Rule Experiment in Ceylon', *Fortnightly Review*, XVIII, 1875, 241 – 58.
——— *Forty Years of Official and Unofficial Life in an Oriental Crown Colony: Being the Life of Sir Richard Morgan, Kt.*, 2 vols. (Madras & London 1879).
d'Oyly, John. *A Sketch of the Constitution of the Kandyan Kingdom*, L. J. B. Turner, (ed.), (Dehiwala 1975) [1929].
Edwardes, S. M. *Crime in India: A Brief Review of the more Important Offences Included in the Annual Crime Returns with Chapters on Prostitution and Miscellaneous Matters* (London 1924).
Emsley, Clive. *Policing and its Context 1750 – 1870* (New York 1984) [1983].

Ferguson, John. *Ceylon in 1903: Describing the Progress of the Island since 1803* (Colombo 1903).

────── *Ceylon in the "Jubilee Year"* (London & Colombo 1887).

Fernando, P. T. M. 'The Ceylon Civil Service: A Study of Recruitment Policies, 1880–1920', *Modern Ceylon Studies*, I, 1970, 64–83.

────── 'The Legal Profession of Ceylon in the Early Twentieth Century: Official Attitudes to Ceylonese Aspirations', *Ceylon Historical Journal*, XIX, 1969–70, 1–15.

────── 'The Post Riots Campaign for Justice', *Journal of Asian Studies*, XXIX, 1970, 255–66.

Forbes, Jonathan. *Recent Disturbances and Military Executions in Ceylon* (Edinburgh & London 1850).

Freitag, Sandria B. 'Sacred Symbol as Mobilizing Ideology: The North Indian Search for a "Hindu" Community', *Comparative Studies in Society and History*, XXII, 1980, 597–625.

Gatrell, V. A. C. 'The Decline of Theft and Violence in Victorian and Edwardian England', V. A. C. Gatrell, Bruce Lenman & Geoffrey Parker, (eds.), *Crime and the Law: The Social History of Crime in Western Europe since 1500* (London 1980), 238–370.

'Going to Law in Ceylon', *All the Year Round*, XII, 1864, 80–4.

Gombrich, Richard. *Precept and Practice: Traditional Buddhism in the Rural Highlands of Ceylon* (Oxford 1971).

Gooneratne, Dandris de Silva. 'On Demonology and Witchcraft in Ceylon', *Journal of the Royal Asiatic Society Ceylon Branch*, IV, 1865–6, 1–117.

Grenier, Joseph. *Leaves From My Life* (Colombo 1923).

Griffiths, Percival. *To Guard My People: The History of the Indian Police* (London & Bombay 1971).

Gunawardana, R. A. L. H. 'The People of the Lion: The Sinhala Identity and Ideology in History and Historiography', *Sri Lanka Journal of the Humanities*, V, 1979, 1–36.

Gurr, Ted Robert. *Rogues, Rebels, and Reformers: A Political History of Urban Crime and Conflict* (Beverly Hills & London 1976).

Haikerwal, Bejoy S. *Economic and Social Aspects of Crime in India* (London 1934).

Harischandra, Walisinha. *The Sacred City of Anuradhapura* (Colombo 1908).

Hayley, Frederic. *A Treatise on the Laws and Customs of the Sinhalese Including the Portions Still Surviving Under the Name Kandyan Law* (Colombo 1923).

Haynes, Edward S. 'Changing Patterns of Dispute Settlement in Eastern Rajputana During the Late Nineteenth Century', *Journal of Asian History*, XIII, 1979, 152–87.

Henderson, J. M. *The History of the Rebellion in Ceylon during Lord Torrington's Government* (London 1868).

Hodge, Mark. 'Poetry and Magic in Southern Sri Lanka', *South Asia Research*, IV, 1984, 20–31.

Hula, Richard C. 'Calcutta: The Politics of Crime and Conflict, 1800 to the 1970s', Ted Robert Gurr, Peter Grabosky & Richard Hula, (eds.), *The Politics of Crime and Conflict: A Comparative History of Four Cities* (Beverly Hills & London 1977), 467–616.

Indraratna, A. D. V. de S. *The Ceylon Economy: From the Great Depression to the Great Boom. An Analysis of Cyclical Fluctuations and their Impact* (Colombo 1966).

Jayasekera, P. V. J. 'Social and Political Change in Ceylon, 1900–1919, with Special Reference to the Disturbances of 1915', PhD Thesis, U. of London, 1970.

Jayawardena, V. Kumari. *The Rise of the Labor Movement in Ceylon* (Durham, USA 1972).

Jayewardene, C. H. S. & Ranasinghe, H. *Criminal Homicide in the Southern Province* (Colombo 1963).

Jones, David J. V. *Crime, Protest, Community and Police in Nineteenth-Century Britain* (London 1982).

Kannangara, A. P. 'The Riots of 1915 in Sri Lanka: A Study in the Roots of Communal Violence', *Past and Present*, 102, 1984, 130–65.

Kannangara, P. D. *The History of the Ceylon Civil Service 1802 – 1833: A Study of Administrative Change in Ceylon* (Dehiwala 1966).

Kidder, Robert L. 'Courts and Conflict in an Indian City: A Study in Legal Impact', *Journal of Commonwealth Political Studies*, XI, 1973, 121 – 39.

Kitts, Eustace J. *Serious Crime in an Indian Province, Being a Record of the Graver Crimes Committed in the North-Western Provinces and Oudh During Eleven Years, 1876 to 1886* (Bombay 1889).

Knox, Robert. *An Historical Relation of Ceylon* (Dehiwala 1958) [1681].

Lane, Roger. 'Urban Homicide in the Nineteenth Century: Some Lessons for the Twentieth', James A. Inciardi & Charles Faupel, (eds.), *History and Crime: Implications for Criminal Justice Policy* (Beverly Hills 1980), 91 – 109.

Law Reform in Ceylon: Its History, Progress and Tendency (Colombo 1852).

Lee, Lionel F. *vyavastha sangrahava muladanin visin* [A legal compendium for the use of headmen] (Colombo 1874).

Lewis, Frederick. *Sixty-four Years in Ceylon: Reminiscences of Life and Adventure* (Colombo 1926).

Lewis, R. E. 'The Rural Economy of the Sinhalese, (More Particularly with Reference to the District of Sabaragamuwa), with some Account of their Superstitions', *Journal of the Royal Asiatic Society Ceylon Branch*, II, 1849, 31 – 52.

Ludovici, Leopold. *Rice Cultivation: Its Past History and Present Condition; with Suggestions for its Improvement* (Colombo 1867).

McDonald, Arthur. 'Death Penalty and Homicide', *American Journal of Sociology*, XVI, 1910, 88 – 116.

MacDougall, Robert D. & MacDougall, Bonnie G. *Sinhalese Domestic Life in Time and Space* (Ithaca 1977).

Malalgoda, Kitsiri. *Buddhism in Sinhalese Society 1750 – 1900: A Study of Religious Revival and Change* (Berkeley 1976).

Mendelsohn, Oliver. 'The Pathology of the Indian Legal System', *Modern Asian Studies*, XV, 1981, 823 – 63.

Mendis, G. C., (ed.), *The Colebrooke-Cameron Papers: Documents on British Colonial Policy in Ceylon 1796 – 1833*, 2 vols., (Oxford 1956).

Meyer, Éric. 'Bourgeoisie et société rurale à Sri Lanka (1880 – 1940)', *Purusartha*, VI, 1982, 223 – 50.

———— 'De la dette interne à la dette externe: observations sur les mutations du crédit à Sri Lanka à la période coloniale', *Purusartha*, IV, 1980, 207 – 25.

———— 'Depression et malaria à Sri Lanka: 1925 – 1939. L'Impact de la crise économique des années 1930 sur une société rurale dépendante', thesis presented for the 3rd stage of the doctorate, Paris, Ecole des Haute Etudes en Sciences Sociales, 1980.

———— 'L'impact social de la depression en milieu rural: le cas de Sri Lanka (Ceylan)', *Revue française d'histoire d'outre-mer*, LXIII, 1976, 668 – 86.

———— 'The Plantation System and Village Structure in British Ceylon: Involution or Evolution?', Peter Robb, (ed.), *Rural South Asia: Linkages, Change and Development* (London 1983), 23 – 56.

262   REFERENCES

Monkkonen, Eric H. *The Dangerous Class: Crime and Poverty in Columbus, Ohio, 1860–1885* (Cambridge USA 1975).
Mukherjee, Arun. 'Crime and Criminals in Nineteenth Century Bengal (1861–1904)', *Indian Economic and Social History Review*, XXI, 1984, 153–83.
Nadaraja, T. *The Legal System of Ceylon in its Historical Setting* (Leiden 1972).
Nayar, Baldev Raj. *Violence and Crime in India: A Quantitative Study* (Delhi 1975).
Obeyesekere, Gananath. *Land Tenure in Village Ceylon: A Sociological and Historical Study* (Cambridge 1967).
—— 'Personal Identity and Cultural Crisis: The Case of Anagārika Dharmapala of Sri Lanka', F. Reynolds & D. Capps (eds.), *The Biographical Process: Studies in the History and Psychology of Religion* (The Hague 1976), 221–52.
—— 'Sorcery, Premeditated Murder, and the Canalization of Aggression in Sri Lanka', *Ethnology*, XIV, 1975, 1–23.
—— 'The Buddhist Pantheon in Ceylon and its Extensions', Manning Nash, (ed.), *Anthropological Studies in Theravada Buddhist* (New Haven 1966), 1–26.
O'Brien, Patricia. 'Crime and Punishment as Historical Problem', *Journal of Social History*, XI, 1978, 508–20.
Olcott, Henry S. *Old Diary Leaves: The Only Authentic History of the Theosophical Society*, vols. II & III, (London & Madras 1900–4).
Parker, H. *Village Folk-Tales of Ceylon*, 3 vols., (London 1910).
Peebles, Patrick. 'Governor Arthur Gordon and the Administration of Sri Lanka, 1883–1890', Robert I. Crane, & N. Gerald Barrier, (eds.), *British Imperial Policy in India and Sri Lanka 1858–1912: A Reassessment* (New Delhi 1981), 84–106.
—— 'Land Use and Population Growth in Colonial Ceylon', *Contributions to Asian Studies*, IX, 1976, 64–79.
—— *Sri Lanka: A Handbook of Historical Statistics* (Boston 1982).
—— 'The Transformation of a Colonial Elite: The Mudaliyars of Nineteenth Century Ceylon', PhD thesis, U. of Chicago, 1973.
perakodoru hatane [About proctors] (Colombo 1869).
Pereira, J. C. W. *Out-door Proctor* ([Colombo 1883]).
Perera, K. R. *suduhatanaya saha kotalavala inspaktartuma gana vananavak* [A eulogy on J. Kotalawala, Inspector of Police, for suppressing gambling and other crimes] (Colombo 1893).
—— *alutkade usaviya asala siduvuna maranaya gana duliyanu kathava saha juvan prerage nadutinduva* [The story of Julia's death near the Alutkada court, and the trial of Juvan Perera] (Colombo 1895).
Pieris, Paulus E., (ed.) *Notes on some Sinhalese Families Part IV: Mid XIX Century from the Diaries of E. R. Gooneratne* (Colombo n.d.).
Pieris, Ralph. *Sinhalese Social Organization: The Kandyan Period* (Colombo 1956).
Pippet, G. K. *A History of the Ceylon Police 1795–1870*, I, (Colombo [1941]).
Pohath-Kehelpannala, T. B. 'Brandmarks on Kandyan Cattle', *Ceylon National Review*, I, 1907, 334–40.
Pollak, Otto. *The Criminality of Women* (New York 1961).
Radzinowicz, Sir Leon & King, Joan. *The Growth of Crime: The International Experience* (London 1977).
Rao, S. Venugopal. *Dynamics of Crime: Spatial and Socio-Economic Aspects of Crime in India* (New Delhi 1981).
Ridgeway, J. West. *Administration of the Affairs of Ceylon, 1896 to 1903* (Colombo 1903).

Robb, Peter (ed.). *Rural India: Land, Power and Society under British Rule* (London 1983).

Roberts, Michael Webb. *Caste Conflict and Elite Formation: The Rise of a Karāva Elite in Sri Lanka 1500 – 1931* (Cambridge 1982).

——— 'Elite Formations and Elites, 1832 – 1931', Michael Roberts, (ed.), *Collective Identities Nationalisms and Protest in Modern Sri Lanka* (Colombo 1979), 153 – 213.

——— 'Hobgoblins, Low-country Sinhalese Plotters, or Local Elite Chauvinists?: Directions and Patterns in the 1915 Communal Riots', *Sri Lanka Journal of Social Sciences*, IV, 1981, 83 – 126.

——— 'The Impact of the Waste Lands Legislation and the Growth of Plantations on the Techniques of Paddy Cultivation in British Ceylon: A Critique', *Modern Ceylon Studies*, I, 1970, 157 – 98.

Rudé, George. *The Crowd in History: A Study of Popular Disturbances in France and England 1730 – 1848* (New York 1964).

Rudolph, Lloyd I. & Rudolph, Susanne H. *The Modernity of Tradition: Political Development in India* (Chicago & London 1967).

Ryan, Bryce. *Caste in Modern Ceylon: The Sinhalese System in Transition* (New Brunswick USA 1953).

Samaraweera, Vijaya. 'British Justice and "Oriental Peasantry": The Working of the Colonial Legal System in Nineteenth Century Sri Lanka', Robert I. Crane & N. Gerald Barrier, (eds.), *British Imperial Policy in India and Sri Lanka 1858 – 1912: A Reassessment* (New Delhi 1981), 107 – 41.

——— 'Litigation and Legal Reform in Colonial Sri Lanka', *South Asia*, II, 1979, 78 – 90.

——— 'Litigation, Sir Henry Maine's Writings and the Ceylon Village Communities Ordinance of 1871', L. Prematilleke, K. Indrapala & J. van Lohuizen-De Leeuw, (eds.), *Senarat Paranavitana Commemoration Volume* (Leiden 1978), 191 – 203.

——— 'Masters and Servants in Sri Lankan Plantations: Labour Laws and Labour Control in an Emergent Export Economy', *Indian Economic and Social History Review*, XVIII, 1981, 123 – 58.

——— 'The Ceylon Charter of Justice of 1833: A Benthamite Blueprint for Judicial Reform', *Journal of Imperial and Commonwealth History*, II, 1974, 263 – 77.

——— 'The Judicial Administration of the Kandyan Provinces of Ceylon, 1815 – 1833', *Ceylon Journal of Historical and Social Studies*, I, 1971, 123 – 50.

——— 'The Muslim Revivalist Movement, 1880 – 1915', Michael Roberts, (ed.), *Collective Identities Nationalisms and Protest in Modern Sri Lanka* (Colombo 1979), 243 – 76.

——— 'The "Village Community" and Reform in Colonial Sri Lanka', *Ceylon Journal of Historical and Social Studies*, VIII, 1978, 68 – 75.

Selvadurai, A. J. 'Land, Personhood and Sorcery in a Sinhalese Village', *Journal of Asian and African Studies*, XI, 1976, 82 – 96.

Sharpe, J. A. *Crime in Seventeenth-Century England: A County Study* (Cambridge 1983).

Shenoy, B. R. *Ceylon Currency and Banking* (London 1941).

Shelley, Louise I. *Crime and Modernization: The Impact of Industrialization and Urbanization on Crime* (Carbondale & Edwardsville, USA 1981).

Sindall, Rod. 'Middle-Class Crime in Nineteenth-Century England', *Criminal Justice History: An International Annual*, IV, 1983, 23 – 40.

Skinner, Thomas. *Fifty Years in Ceylon: An Autobiography* (Dehiwala 1974) [1891].

Smythe, P. R. *A Ceylon Commentary* (London 1932).
Stark, Hon. Justice. 'On the State of Crime in Ceylon', *Journal of the Royal Asiatic Society Ceylon Branch*, I, 1845 & 1846, 64 – 81 & 91 – 8.
Stirrat, R. L. 'Caste Conundrums: Views of Caste in a Sinhalese Catholic Fishing Village', Dennis B. McGilvray, (ed.), *Caste Ideology and Interaction* (Cambridge 1982), 8 – 33.
────── 'The Riots and the Roman Catholic Church in Historical Perspective', James Manor, (ed.), *Sri Lanka in Change and Crisis*, (London 1984), 196 – 213.
Stone, Lawrence. 'Interpersonal Violence in English Society, 1300 – 1980', *Past and Present*, 101, 1983, 22 – 33.
Straus, Jacqueline H. & Straus, Murray A. 'Suicide, Homicide and Social Structure in Ceylon', *American Journal of Sociology*, LVIII, 1953, 461 – 9.
Straus, Murray A. 'Westernization, Insecurity, and Sinhalese Social Structure', *International Journal of Social Psychiatry*, XII, 1966, 130 – 8.
Sumathipala, K. H. M. 'The Kotahena Riots and Their Repercussions', *Ceylon Historical Journal*, XIX, 1969 – 70, 65 – 81.
Tambyah, T. Isaac. *The Planters' Legal Manual* (Colombo 1911).
Taylor, Ian, Walton, Paul & Young, Jock. *The New Criminology: For a Social Theory of Deviance* (London 1973).
Thomson, Henry B. *Institutes of the Laws of Ceylon*, 2 vols., (London 1866).
Tilly, Charles & Lodhi, Abdul Qaiyum. 'Urbanization, Crime, and Collective Violence in 19th Century France', *American Journal of Sociology*, LXXIX, 1973, 296 – 318.
Trivedi, Dinesh B. 'Law and Order in Oudh 1856 – 77', PhD thesis, U. of London, 1978.
University of Ceylon History of Ceylon, III, editor-in-chief: K. M. de Silva. Contributors include K. M. de Silva, Michael Roberts, Vijaya Samaraweera & L. A. Wickremeratne. (Colombo 1973).
van der Aa, J. B. *Ile de Ceylan: croquis, moeurs, et coutumes: lettres d'un missionaire* (Louvain 1899).
Vijayatunga, J. *Grass For My Feet: Vignettes of Village Life in Sri Lanka* (Colombo 1974) [1935].
Walsh, Cecil. *Crime in India* (London 1930).
────── *Indian Village Crimes* (London 1929).
Washbrook, David A. 'Law, State and Agrarian Society in Colonial India', *Modern Asian Studies*, XV, 1981, 649 – 721.
Wesumperuma, D. 'The Evictions Under the Paddy Tax, and their Impact on the Peasantry of Walapane, 1882 – 1885', *Ceylon Journal of Historical and Social Studies*, III, 1973, 28 – 53.
Wickremeratne, L. Ananda. *The Genesis of an Orientalist: Thomas William Rhys Davids and Buddhism in Sri Lanka* (Delhi 1984).
────── Religion, Nationalism and Social Change in Ceylon, 1865 – 1885', *Journal of the Royal Asiatic Society*, LVI, 1969, 123 – 50.
────── 'The Rulers and the Ruled in British Ceylon: A Study of the Functions of Petitions in Colonial Government', *Modern Ceylon Studies*, I, 1970, 213 – 32.
Wolfgang, Marvin E. *Patterns in Criminal Homicide* (New York 1966).
Wolfgang, Marvin E. & Ferracuti, Franco. *The Subculture of Violence: Towards an Integrated Theory in Criminology* (London 1967) [1966].
Wood, Arthur L. 'Crime and Aggression in Changing Ceylon: A Sociological Analysis of Homicide, Suicide, and Economic Crime', *Transactions of the American Philosophical Society*, LI, 1961.

Woolf, Leonard. *Growing: An Autobiography of the Years 1904 – 1911* (London 1961).
────── *The Village in the Jungle* (London 1913).
Wright, Gordon. *Between the Guillotine and Liberty: Two Centuries of the Crime Problem in France* (New York 1983).
Yalman, Nur. *Under the Bo Tree: Studies in Caste, Kinship, and Marriage in the Interior of Ceylon* (Berkeley 1967).
Yang, Anand A. 'Sacred Symbol and Sacred Space in Rural India: Community Mobilization in the "Anti-Cow Killing" Riot of 1893', *Comparative Studies in Society and History*, XXII, 1980, 576 – 96.
────── 'The Agrarian Origins of Crime: A Study of Riots in Saran District, India, 1886 – 1920', *Journal of Social History*, XIII, 1979, 289 – 306.
Zahn, Margaret A. 'Homicide in the Twentieth Century United States', James A. Inciardi & Charles Faupel, (eds.), *History and Crime: Implications for Criminal Justice Policy* (Beverly Hills 1980), 111 – 31.
Zehr, Howard. *Crime and the Development of Modern Society: Patterns of Criminality in Nineteenth Century Germany and France* (London 1976).

NEWSPAPERS AND JOURNALS PUBLISHED AT COLOMBO

In English

Bi-Monthly Examiner.
Buddhist.
Catholic Messenger.
Examiner.
Independent.
Native Opinion.
Observer.
Overland Observer.
Standard.
Times.

In Sinhala

Lakminipahana.
Lakrivikirana.
Nanartha Pradipaya.
Sarasavi Sandarasa.

INDEX

Note: Regions, provinces and districts are not listed individually. For entries about the spatial distribution of crime, see *geography of crime*